Gender, Citizenship and Newspapers

Palgrave Studies in the History of the Media

Series Editors: Professor Bill Bell (Cardiff University), Dr. Chandrika Kaul (Department of Modern History, University of St Andrews), Professor Kenneth Osgood (Department of History, Florida Atlantic University), Dr. Alexander S. Wilkinson (Centre for the History of the Media, University College Dublin)

Palgrave Studies in the History of the Media publishes original, high-quality research into the cultures of communication from the middle ages to the present day. The series explores the variety of subjects and disciplinary approaches that characterize this vibrant field of enquiry. The series will help shape current interpretations not only of the media, in all its forms, but also of the powerful relationship between the media and politics, society, and the economy.

Advisory Board: Professor Carlos Barrera (University of Navarra, Spain), Professor Peter Burke (Emmanuel College, Cambridge), Professor Denis Cryle (Central Queensland University, Australia), Professor David Culbert (Louisiana State University, Baton Rouge), Professor Nicholas Cull (Center on Public Diplomacy, University of Southern California), Professor Tom O'Malley (Centre for Media History, University of Wales, Aberystwyth), Professor Chester Pach (Ohio University)

Titles include:

Jane L. Chapman
GENDER, CITIZENSHIP AND NEWSPAPERS
Historical and Transnational Perspectives

Michael Krysko
AMERICAN RADIO IN CHINA
International Encounters with Technology and Communications, 1919–41

Christoph Hendrik Müller
WEST GERMANS AGAINST THE WEST
Anti-Americanism in Media and Public Opinion in the Federal Republic of Germany 1949–68

Forthcoming titles:

Joel Wiener
THE AMERICANIZATION OF THE BRITISH PRESS, 1830s–1914

James Mussell & Suzanne Paylor
NINETEENTH-CENTURY IN THE DIGITAL AGE
Politics, Pedagogy and Practice

Martin Conboy & John Steel
THE LANGUAGE OF NEWSPAPERS IN NINETEENTH-CENTURY ENGLAND
Commercializing the Popular

Palgrave Studies in the History of the Media
Series Standing Order ISBN 978–0–230–23153–5 hardcover
Series Standing Order ISBN 978–0–230–23154–2 paperback
(*outside North America only*)

You can receive future titles in this series as they are published by placing a standing order. Please contact your bookseller or, in case of difficulty, write to us at the address below with your name and address, the title of the series and one of the ISBNs quoted above.

Customer Services Department, Macmillan Distribution Ltd, Houndmills, Basingstoke, Hampshire RG21 6XS, England

Gender, Citizenship and Newspapers

Historical and Transnational Perspectives

Jane L. Chapman
Professor of Communications, Lincoln University, UK

palgrave
macmillan

First published 2013 by
PALGRAVE MACMILLAN

Palgrave Macmillan in the UK is an imprint of Macmillan Publishers Limited, registered in England, company number 785998, of Houndmills, Basingstoke, Hampshire RG21 6XS.

Palgrave Macmillan in the US is a division of St Martin's Press LLC, 175 Fifth Avenue, New York, NY 10010.

Palgrave Macmillan is the global academic imprint of the above companies and has companies and representatives throughout the world.

Palgrave® and Macmillan® are registered trademarks in the United States, the United Kingdom, Europe and other countries.

ISBN 978–0–230–23244–0

This book is printed on paper suitable for recycling and made from fully managed and sustained forest sources. Logging, pulping and manufacturing processes are expected to conform to the environmental regulations of the country of origin.

A catalogue record for this book is available from the British Library.

A catalog record for this book is available from the Library of Congress.

10   9   8   7   6   5   4   3   2   1
22   21   20   19   18   17   16   15   14   13

Printed and bound in Great Britain by
CPI Antony Rowe, Chippenham and Eastbourne

To two Kates
Kate Allison and Kate Lacey
each in their own way essential to this book

Contents

Detailed Chapter Summary

Part I Setting the Parameters

Chapter 1 – Introduction: Tracing Patterns, Linkages and Evidence Boundary crossing

Choice of trends and 'moments'; Scope and positioning; Defining cultural citizenship; Comparative transnational themes and methodologies; Conservative feminization; Theorizing mainstream press transnationally; Why colonial communications?; Processes of subaltern mediation.

Part II Pioneers and Emerging Commercial Tensions

Chapter 2 – France: Pioneering the Popular Newspaper Brand and the Female Market

The Roussean legacy and women's moral obligation; Newspaper contexts; *Le Petit Journal* blazes a trail in popularism; Lay-out and writing style; Content and readership; Readership, the serialized novel and fact-fiction cross over; 'Faits divers'; Consumerism; Methodology; Advertising; Business orientation; 'Puff' or advertorial journalism; Analyzing women as news sources; Conclusions – the emergence of gendered tabloid properties.

Chapter 3 – France and Britain: Cultural Citizenship and the Rise of Consumer Society

The influence of periodicals; Audience and the evolution of newspaper visual appearance; New Journalism; 'New woman' and other fashionable new terms; Press barons and trans-national gendered considerations; Comparisons between *Le Petit Journal* and *The Daily Mail*; Readers, stunts and advertisements; Evolution of emphasis and tone; *La Fronde* and the *Daily Mirror*; Female journalists; Blaming women; Press barons and transnational gendered considerations; The power of political consumerism; Conclusions.

Part III Labour Movement Roots and the Politics of Exclusion

Chapter 4 – French India: From Private to Public Sphere

Research methods for female protest and communications; Context and background; Class, gender and counter-hegemonic communications; Publicizing women activists; Press censorship escalates; The threat of 'banditism' to press communications; Conclusions.

Chapter 5 – Britain: Collective Organization, Public Communications and the Vote

The newspaper landscape for suffrage; Cross-fertilization between newspaper and periodical sectors; Early campaigns and their newspapers; Labour movement background; Solidarity and public communications; Labour issues as public discourse on citizenship; Suffrage, parliamentary politics and public opinion; The vote and newspaper commercialism; Early militancy; Peaceful tactics; Lobbying and emulating the mainstream press; Conclusions.

Part IV Cultural Citizenship and Direct Action

Chapter 6 – Britain: Apocalypse and Press as a Double-edged Sword

The anti campaign; *The Manchester Guardian*; Positive coverage for the vote; The changing barometer; Press fluctuations; Hardening of attitudes; Bias; The 'pilgrimage'; The frustration of notoriety; Watershed; Conclusions.

Chapter 7 – British India: Women and the Hegemonic Colonial Press

Why *The Pioneer*?; Editorial influence of F.W. Wilson; Advertising; Assessing the influence of women as contributors to news; Women and peaceful democratic self-emancipation; Women and direct action; Simon Commission; Women and strikes; Foreign cloth boycott and burning; Conclusions.

Part V   Traces and Outcomes

Chapter 8 – Conclusion: Comparing and Contrasting Transnationally

Ongoing tensions in newspaper gender awareness; Interpreting fragments; Transnational aspects of cultural citizenship; The demands of the performative in direct action; Tabloidization; The outcomes of cultural citizenship; Stereotypes, vanguards or followers?; Timing, significance and evolution of gendered traces; Interpretations of class, performance and collective action; Counter-hegemonic significations through repetitive challenges to stereotyping.

List of Tables and Figures

Tables

Figure

Preface

Tracing histories of the engagement between media and disempowered people – in this case women – is never going to be easy. There is no one central record, no archives of audience or systematic market research, as exist today. There are no folders or boxes (let alone digital items) marked 'women and newspapers' amongst relevant archive holders. The connections between gender, citizenship and newspapers from a transnational historical perspective are not obvious. Yet people who struggle for social and political inclusion have always needed to communicate as widely as possible, and to create public discourses by whatever means possible. As soon as the press is acknowledged as an agency for communication, the historical theme of women and mass circulation dailies becomes an obvious one. How to tackle it is less obvious, and this study does not take an easy route.

From its very inception, the research in the pages that follow attempted to fill gaps in scholarship, and this motivation mushroomed. It started with a relatively modest ambition, endorsed by a British Academy grant – to investigate the feminizing influence on the growth of mass circulation dailies in Britain and France in the late 19th century. We set about newspaper analysis in detail, and the findings are included later. The importance for this wider study is that the empirical data came first. The experiment was repeated, once more over a two year period, this time for an ESRC (Economic and Social Science Council) grant, featuring gender in the colonial world, entitled 'Women, Press and Protest in British and French India, 1928–48'. Again, the empirical enquiry came first, but the seeds of comparative method had already been sown, and needed to grow. The media related activities of British suffragettes provided the stimulus for further attempts to compare and contrast.

Of course, all of this primary record collection across continents and countries (we visited 13 different libraries and archives in India alone) was underpinned by theorizations on class, gender and counter hegemony, but the relevance of the concept of cultural citizenship only became obvious at the data analysis stage, when comparing and contrasting the experiences of women and their representation in newspapers. It emerged as a shared historical experience, part of the process of collective action, as a social and political impact relating to public communication.

Perhaps that is the way it should be – a practical outcome of public discourses relating to struggles to change disempowerment, rather than a preconceived theory. Yet some scholars may find that the empirical findings do not fit their theorizations. This is a high risk strategy, but also an attempt to face the music. The introduction addresses potential criticism: why compare colonial with non colonial, why choose mass circulation dailies in the case of Britain and France, why select different episodes and points in history?

Taking women as readers, news sources, and journalists, the point is also to explore some confluences of influence: between consumerism and citizenship, between demands for constitutional reforms and direct action protest, between ideology and economics, between continuity and change. These are not always straight binaries, but rather mosaics with uneven contributory pieces, varying according to country, context and periods of history. Amongst the fluidity there are constants, however – issues of class and performance as they impact upon gender, for instance.

Among the complexities the reader will also discern empathy. We need to restore a place in history to those who tried to communicate in the public sphere, but were frequently forgotten almost as quickly as their ephemeral newspaper pages were. In 1937–8, some 10,000 Tamils fled from Pondicherry across the border to escape gangs of bandits who were setting fire to their homes at night, but female collective action emerged, and was communicated in the public sphere. In British India many women were jailed for protest, as well as suffragettes in imperial Britain. Their bravery acts as a motivation to restore the media record of such acts, and of many others that are mentioned later.

Newspaper records are not always complimentary, and could be damaging to campaigns for different forms of citizenship, but they act as a reminder of the potency of gender discourses, and of the fact that many issues are still live today. This is not dead wood history, but a continuing relationship in the public sphere between action and interpretation. Above all, this study uncovers some of the neglected workings of female influence on counter hegemonic communications. There is more to be uncovered. If others are motivated to elaborate on, or to contradict, the analysis and interpretations presented here, then all of the attempts to find gendered needles in haystacks will have been worthwhile.

Acknowledgements

The period of gestation for this book has been a long one, dating back to 2007 when the British Academy first decided to fund one of my projects. Thus, it is difficult to express thanks for the long trajectory of support without adopting some well-worn terminology, such as 'without whom this work would not have been possible', but these words are literal in every sense. Without the support of Lincoln University, the School of Journalism and Dean of Faculty John Simons, I would never have submitted grant applications and without funding from the British Academy and the Economic and Social Science Research Council (ESRC), research assistants Kate Allison and Piers Clarke I would never have been able to visit archives in France and India. In addition, John Tulloch joined our ESRC team to contribute research on F.W. Wilson and Kate Lacey at Sussex University kindly contributed time and ideas during the early stages of the book project. At Lincoln University Ann Gray continues to provide vision and Rebecca Hewson-Heathorn organizational support, for which I am grateful.

At the time of writing, digital archives do not exist for most of my sources, so most of the primary work involved research on location, and thanks go to all the archivists in various parts of the world who helped my teams. This included visits to France's Bibliothèque Nationale, Archives Nationales, the Museum of Paris and the labour history archives at Roubaix. I spent considerable time at France's colonial archives in Aix-en-Provence. In India we visited the Nehru Library, the National Library and Archives in Delhi and Calcutta, the Regional Archives in Pondicherry and Allahabad, the State Archives in Lucknow, Chennai and Pondicherry, the French Institute in Pondicherry, and the offices of AITUC (All India Trade Union Congress), who kindly donated a large number of pamphlets, copies of theses and other material in Tamil. We visited *The Pioneer* headquarters and *The Indian Express* newspaper contributed articles. In the United Kingdom, I am grateful for the continuing support of the Cambridge University Library and the Centre of South Asian Studies in Cambridge, the British Library at St Pancras and Colindale. Archivists at the British Library's African and Indian section deserve much gratitude for kindly allowing us to consult uncatalogued (for reasons of conservation) versions of *The Pioneer*. Special thanks to Kate Allison for compiling the data sets (that are publically available due to the efforts of ESRC) and thanks also to Piers Clarke for compiling the website of visual evidence, http: www.pressandprotest.com

During all of this time, my continuing visiting fellowship at Wolfson College, Cambridge and the Centre of South Asian Studies, Cambridge has been invaluable, as has the support of Macquarie University, Sydney, where I am an Adjunct Professor. Members of the Macquarie Department of Modern History, the Centre for South Asian Studies, Cambridge, the History department at University College, Dublin, Women in French, and the French Media Research Group (ASCMF) all contributed feedback at presentations of the findings, which has been really helpful.

It was at Macquarie's art gallery that I helped to curate, with Rhonda Davis and Leonard Janiszewski, an exhibition of some of the research, entitled 'India, Past, Present and Abroad'. Their enthusiasm, along with that of Bridget Griffin Foley and her Media History Research Centre, has been constantly energizing.

I must underline the importance of support from Sandy Wilkinson at University College, Dublin for his unwavering faith in the project, along with the other series editors. At Palgrave Michael Strang, Jenny McCall and Clare Mence, along with production staff, have been constantly helpful and enthusiastic. The incisive comments of peer reviewers have contributed more than they will ever realize.

The essential support of the following journals and publishers has allowed re-publications of sections from articles and one of my earlier books, for which sincere thanks are due:

Journalism Today (2011)*: A Themed History* (Malden, MA: Blackwell-Wiley) – Chapter 3 reproduces sections on New Journalism and on Ida Tarbell.

'A Business Trajectory: Assessing Female Influence and Representation in *Le Petit Journal,* Europe's First Mass Circulation Daily' in *Parcours de femmes – Twenty Years of Women in French* (2011, Peter Lang, Oxford & Bern) pp. 41–57. Chapter 2 reproduces some parts of this article, on the theme of business.

'Female representation, readership and early tabloid properties' *Australian Journal of Communication,* 2011, 38, no. 2, 53–70. Chapter 2 reproduces some sections on tabloidization and quantitative tables relating to *Le Petit Journal.*

'The origins of a public voice for marginalized workers and anti-colonialism in French India, 1935–37', *Web Journal of French Media Studies* (WJFMS), 2010, no.8, ISSN 1460-6550 single author http://wjfms.ncl.ac.uk/splash.htm

Chapter 4 reproduces some sections on private versus public in French India.

'Women and the press in British India 1928–34: a window for protest?' *International Journal of Social Economics (IJSE)*, 2011, 38, no. 9 (July), 676–92, co-author Kate Allison. Some sections, including quantitative tables are reproduced in Chapter 7. www.emeraldinsight.com/journals. htm?articleid=1938131&ini=aob

Finally, thanks to my long suffering family and friends who have always had to endure my continuing obsession with research, writing and talking about it!

Jane Chapman, Cambridge, 2012

Part I
Setting the Parameters

1
Introduction
Tracing Patterns, Linkages and Evidence

Boundary Crossing

Contemporary sources between the 1860s and the 1930s point emphatically to the existence of wider debates not only about the changing role and attitudes towards women, but also concerning the nature, influence and role of the press. Gendered analysis of this adds to our understanding at a time when conflicting, multifaceted ideas and female images were emerging within the public sphere, but a connection needs to be made between press and social attitudes, between media development from a gendered standpoint and wider trends in society. How such trends or strands, as expressed and mediated in newspapers, contributed to the process of cultural formation forms part of our general appreciation of modernity.[1]

This is an integrated exploration of: women's representation in the press; their role as news sources and their professional activity; women as an influence on editorial matter; how women were perceived as a readership and/or as consumers by newspapers; and how through their actions in the public sphere they sought and received coverage.[2] These are the traces from the past of female influence in the relationship between newspapers and society that are analyzed through examples of print mass communications across continents, empires and periods. Arguably, historians do not know enough about the connections between women's emerging citizenship and the communication of that process by the public press and other communications distributed to the wider polity. Every example presented in this study focuses on the issues of press and democracy, press and change, and press as a vehicle for the articulation of female citizenship. This historicization addresses the extent to which newspaper mediation and women's attempts to

3

influence public opinion for political demands constituted a form of citizenship specific to the process of knowledge and information production.

This text focuses on the phenomenon of *cultural citizenship*, associated newspaper-related consumerism and the relationship between ideology and economics as evidenced through the communication of women's protest in the public sphere and the way it impinged upon newspaper commercial considerations. The approach is a comparative historicization of the concept of cultural citizenship, revealing aspects of its origins and development transnationally as these related to the agencies of gender and print communications. How female citizenship was framed and evolved through the prism of the public press is analyzed with examples taken from the 1860s through to the 1930s. The development of newspapers as mass communication systems in several different countries provides the framework for a series of detailed cameos of usage, representation and influence at selected formative and critical periods within media history. For Britain and France, this was the second half of the nineteenth century and the early twentieth century – the 'golden age' of newspapers. For India it was during the 1920s and 1930s.

The years between the1860s and the 1930s are examined thematically, with chapters on developmental aspects of cultural citizenship. The aim is to trace patterns, linkages and evidence of gender through and in newspapers that existed in places and in ways that are not immediately obvious.

Choice of trends and 'moments'

Moments

The task is addressed via a collection of selected aspects and moments transnationally that provides insight into the process of negotiation between women and some organs of communication, in varying contexts. This is a mosaic of complementary and conflicting influences that are explored in detail, each contributing to an evolution in the manifestations of female cultural citizenship, but in different ways at differing periods of modern history, according to the country studied. Any emerging patterns are uneven.

Van Zoonen, referring to media as part of feminism's material and cultural struggle, reminds us: 'Mass media are central sites in which these negotiations take place, evidently at the level of media texts, but also at the level of the other "moments" of the mass mediated production of meaning' (1994: 148). Selection of 'moments' in this study has been made around some dates and events that were important as *turning points*, although not necessarily successful ones. These include, during Europe's 'golden age' of the press: the launch of Europe's first mass circulation daily – *Le Petit Journal* – followed by the launch of Britain's first mass circulation daily – *The Daily Mail* – to cater for women by acknowledging them as a readership; the launch of two separate, and very different dailies – *La Fronde* and *The Daily Mirror* – run by and aimed at women; the adoption of direct action as a tactic by British suffragettes; and the peak years of militant violent agitation for the female franchise.

In a colonial context, the criteria for the study was also to look at local press, rather than those produced in metropolitan France or imperial London. Counter citizenship is traced through the launch and struggle for survival in the face of censorship of an indigenous paper in French Indian territory – *Swandanthiram* – that, at the time of writing, still exists. Most other contemporary journals were short lived. In British India, a local colonial daily – *The Pioneer* – has been selected because it supported women's emerging citizenship in a period of heated politics during the twilight of empire when constitutional negotiations and the economic effects of pro-independence protest were making headway. The moment selected coincides with a crucial change of editorship.[3]

Trends

These 'moments' have been selected because their significance goes beyond the event itself, allowing for wider contextual analysis. For example, Part II addresses the way in which pioneering popular dailies in Britain and France catered for women. A theme that emerges is a wider tension between the old and the new, between commercial considerations and political content. As people became defined not only by production but also by consumption, women were acknowledged as a market for newspaper consumerism. Although circulation doubled between 1896 and 1906 and then doubled again by 1914 (Williams, 1961: 203–4), by and large female oriented content was still decided upon by men on behalf of readers belonging to the opposite sex. Perceptions about the nature of this communication were challenged by some women, who had a different vision of both content and operation.

Part III identifies a parallel formative experience for women who participated in labour organizations in Britain and in French India, where they were able to acquire experience of collective activities in the public sphere that were rooted in class actions. The emergence of subaltern women from private to public sphere in French territory is significant in timing because it heralded the origins of an independence movement.

Part IV continues the study of female activists by addressing the effectiveness of women's interactions with the media in Britain and in British colonial India when it came to protests and other direct action tactics, as opposed to more peaceful lobbying and 'educational' activities. Many women took to the streets, using newspapers to disseminate specific messages to a wider polity, seeking publicity for social and political reasons, important also because of the organizational and leadership experience that they gained and for their impact on the development of the media.

In Part V, the conclusion, attempts to draw together some common transnational experiences, continuities over time and the identification of similar processes across class, cultures and time periods.

Scope and positioning

For the purposes of this study, a distinction should be noted on the one hand between 'feminist' publications, sometimes but not exclusively allied to progressive organizations or groups with a structured membership who aimed to achieve the emancipation of women in some way, and on the other hand what British suffrage supporters called the 'public press'. Scholars have studied the way in which campaigners used the former – that is, specialist publications – and also the general trend for the nineteenth century and earlier, focusing on individual pioneers, female journalists, feminist writings and/or social movements (see for example Mills, 1998; Onslow, 2000; Gleadle, 1995, 2002; DiCenzo, 2011).

There were also commercial publications, mainly dailies, which aimed to bring news and features to a wider 'public' audience (usually national) of women and men, but recognizing the female interest within that large audience[4] – mass dissemination is the focus here. Within this area of research there is still inadequate understanding by scholars about the ways in which people, usually organized into their own interest groups and specific communities, aimed to influence the 'public press'. At a time in history when opinion management was largely unprofessionalized, with 'PR' and corporate lobbying very much in their infancy, records of attempts to influence press coverage have to be sought elsewhere. We are mostly dependent on anecdotes from individual memoirs, internal administrative communications (such as reports from colonial officials to their ministers), the coverage itself, reader letters, 'op-ed' and other newspaper editorials commenting on the views of competitor journals and the discursive press environment more generally at the time.

Women's history and gender studies are now well established at the cutting edge of new approaches in many fields of study, yet there is still a need for more in-depth, cross-disciplinary understanding of the role that gender considerations played during the development of mass communications from the second half of the nineteenth century. Although working-class people and women constituted a new readership in the Western world from the second half of the nineteenth century onwards, press historians still know very little about the details of how the new market for popular daily newspapers became more female oriented. It is acknowledged that the popular press contributed to the expansion of public discourse, but the precise nature of representation of women in its pages is less clear. A process of 'feminization' of the British popular press has been identified during the 1880s and 1890s (Holland, 1998: 19) but the full details of how this development evolved have yet to emerge. This book adds some comparative, transnational pieces to the historical jigsaw, for it was not confined to Britain. While this study focuses on neglected areas of scholarship, it nonetheless builds on research in allied fields that has helped to prepare the ground by challenging generalizations concerning how far women were restricted to the domestic sphere (DiCenzo, 2011: 10).

The potential for newspapers to act as an efficacious tool for democratic expression in the discourses of the public sphere has been an ongoing theme throughout the history of communications (Chapman and Nuttall, 2011[5]). As Holland points out, 'Women's democratic participation, and the role of a newspaper in furthering democratic involvement, is also an issue. A democratic press must also appeal to women and, by the end of the nineteenth century, women were already demanding the space to express their public concerns. Democratisation *entails* feminisation' (1998: 18). Unfortunately attempts to examine this tend not to be transnational: Bingham's (2004) study of the popular press and gender, for example, deals uniquely with Britain between the wars; that of Rogers (2000) is also uniquely British. Sometimes studies concentrate on different time periods (for instance Holland deals with the 1970s onwards) or do not address the topic from the standpoint of institutional development of the press.

These research findings contribute to the ongoing task of feminist historians and their work.[6] This has raised awareness of gender difference in a variety of ways across a full range of aspects of life. The effort is being redefined constantly, for discussions on women are germane to literature, anthropology and sociology where for some time there has been interest in historicizing fields of study and opening up to interdisciplinarity, exemplified, for instance, by the work of Clifford Geertz (1983: 30) and Michael Schudson (1982: 97–112). Equally, 'New Cultural History' has been influenced by literary studies, resulting in close examinations of texts (Hunt, 1989: 22). Yet an acknowledgement that the relationship between gender and communications is primarily (although not exclusively) a cultural one, made by scholars such as van Zoonen (1994: 148) does not necessarily mean that research has connected historical aspects of gender and media. In fact, the attention given to topics relating to women, media and politics has not been proportionate to their societal relevance (Krijnen et al., 2011: 5).

Although media history tends towards boundary crossing, mainly between media studies and history (O'Malley, 2002: 170), it is still a relatively new field,[7] which may account for the shortage of gendered analysis of mainstream communications. Furthermore, interdisciplinarity has sometimes been neglected in gender studies (Krijnen et al., 2011).

However, the task is not merely to fill important gaps in knowledge: it is also, to borrow a now famous phrase from John Berger, to record a different way 'of seeing'. Joan Scott summarizes the challenge in her reappraisal of gender and history in the light of deconstructionist theory: 'Feminist history [then] becomes not the recounting of great deeds performed by women but the exposure of the often silent and hidden operations of gender that are nonetheless present and defining forces in the organization of most societies'(1999: 27). The way that other historians have come to accept the need for such an approach, and how this has transformed the field of study, has been elaborated by Laura Lee Downs (2010). While she draws on cultural and social analysis to explain the move from women's to gender history and the poststructuralist challenges to that history, the issue of media agency is left out in the cold.

Defining cultural citizenship

Over recent years there has been a considerable revival of interest in citizenship, a concept that can be broadly defined as encapsulating shared rights, responsibilities and symbolic aspects of membership within a polity. For John Corner, culture centres on 'the conditions and the forms in which meaning and value are structured and articulated within a society' (1991: 131). It is a shared experience involving symbolic forms, as defined by John B. Thompson: 'patterns of meaning embodied in symbolic forms, including actions, utterances and meaningful objects of various kinds, by virtue of which individuals communicate with one another and share their experiences, conceptions and beliefs' (1990: 132). Nick Stevenson elaborates on the significance of 'meaning': 'in the interpretation of an event it is the meanings that become attached to the "event" that are crucial for understanding its significance' (2003: 17). In fact, the 'public press' developed its own organizational methods to produce distinctive categories of representation, knowledge and power as a form of interpretation and influence by women: these are analyzed here as the symbolic media category of gendered cultural citizenship. In a present day context, Jan Pakulski (1997) argues that cultural citizenship can be seen as satisfying demands for full social inclusion. Cultural citizenship encapsulates activities conducted in the public sphere for political and/or social ends, in this case articulated through or by the media.

The concept is a relatively fluid one – it can involve difference as much as sameness (Stevenson, 2003) and is interpreted in a range of different ways by scholars, witnessed by its hybrid location at the intersection of diverse fields of study that include the sociology of culture and of art, cultural studies, social and political theory, international relations and multicultural studies. Therefore, it impinges upon social phenomena that are bigger than the constituent parts as evidenced in the pages that follow.[8] For Stevenson, 'cultural citizenship is overwhelmingly concerned with communication and power', and should be considered within 'the context of social transformation' (2003: 33).

In fact, cultural citizenship can be discerned both inside and outside formal structures of power, for questions of exclusion and inclusion are central. Media manifestations of cultural citizenship were not confined to formal rights such as the vote, although that is an important aspect. Research in this study addresses marginalization, stereotyping, lack of visibility, concurring with Renato Rosaldo who argues that cultural citizenship is about 'who needs to be visible, to be heard, and to belong' (1999: 260). In terms of this particular historicization, a number of different strands of developmental explanation are examined: business factors, labour movement roots, direct action protests, questions of entitlement, women participating in representational politics and 'educational' or peaceful persuasion for reforms, sometimes as journalists themselves. More generally, this involves an enquiry into how mediated cultural citizenship encapsulated ways in which, in their movement from private to public spheres, women wanted to be perceived by others. Cultural citizenship addresses attitudes such as 'the degree of self-esteem accorded to . . . [the citizen's] manner of self-realization within a society's inherited cultural horizon' (Honneth, 1995: 134).

The concept is also applied in this study as a normative phrase to describe the effect and the process of engagement in newspaper publicity by women. Cultural citizenship emerged as part of the act of press mediation – an ever changing phenomenon – and as a phrase that encapsulates a mobile process, as it became embedded within civil society and public consciousness. It has been assumed in the West, for instance, that the widening of audience and new products catering for the working class and women for the first time were necessarily positive developments, because of the democratizing tendency that the trend represented. Most French historians believe that popular newspapers encouraged isolated communities into a new, common identity as an integrated nation (Delporte, 1998; Kalifa, 1995). This argument is an extension of the Benedict Anderson (1991) thesis on 'imagined communities', supported by Jean-Yves Mollier when he refers to 'a silent cultural revolution' (Rioux and Sirinelli, 2002: 73, 114).

Generally, what can be called 'positive democratization theses' tend not to adopt a gendered perspective and underestimate process, tone, and effect of representation, so some qualification is required. At the same time as providing criticism, this study seeks more generally to avoid an overtly celebratory approach to gender enquiry. The examples presented started in mid-1860s France, with the first mass circulation daily in Europe to eventually reach sales of 1 million. *Le Petit Journal* was clearly a pioneering initiative in newspaper publishing, but it did not contest bourgeois societal values. The paper was ahead of its time in terms of targeting a new readership of women and peasants, but the recipe for this was a diet of snippets of information and crime stories, recognized by the proprietors as a sure seller. This male assessment of what sold newspapers was by no means new: there was a shared transnational interest, at least to some extent, in crime coverage. In terms of content analysis of the daily newspaper, it is possible to differentiate between subject matter involving women and aimed at female readers that involved some form of interest in citizenship (public sphere activities, charity and community work), as opposed to consumer oriented articles – but consumer issues can be highly politicized.

Cultural citizenship acts as the defining force that emerges in this study, but there is a precursor in the form of cultural consumerism in the Western world. For instance, by the Edwardian period in Britain, 10,000 people were employed in advertising as part of the 'Retail Revolution' (Searle, 2004: 111). The phrase cultural consumerism is defined here as consumerist values and content that are featured in media and public communications, developing a style and form specifically in such publications. The crossover between politics and consumerism provides a fertile ground for analysis of women's direct action in this field – a central thread manifested in colonial India as well as in Europe.

Comparative transnational themes and methodologies

One purpose is to identify both qualitatively and quantitatively which aspects of today's discourses on cultural citizenship can be traced historically within the parameters of the work. This study uses quantitative and qualitative content analysis and borrows analytical tools and concepts from a range of fields of scholarship in order to tease out the less obvious aspects of women's impact on newspapers as an underacknowledged operation of gender. Thus, the research cuts across existing fields of study and methodological barriers: economic and cultural history approaches are merged with media content analysis, while political theory and gender studies are also addressed. Quantitative methods are used for detailed appreciation of trends over longer time frames, enhanced by qualitative methods that facilitate our understanding of narratives connected to particular moments and aspects, as they relate to perceptions of gendered citizenship. Both are also required in order to understand the processes of influence on public opinion and the public sphere through a range of organs of communication.

What are the connections, if any, between the historical cameos of communications in India and other chapters? There are various aspects to examine. First, how cultural citizenship can develop in a variety of different ways and also change according to political circumstances. Second, how cultural citizenship emerged as a discourse of awakening and as a counter-hegemonic challenge. If the feminist mantra that the 'personal is the political' calls for the deconstruction of barriers between public and private, then a study of local newspapers in colonial India can contribute to that discourse by demonstrating that traditional ideas were under challenge. Third, how cultural citizenship was expressed as a political phenomenon through varying economic strategies in all countries concerned. Fourth, whether newspapers in every country led the perceived public opinion of their readerships or whether they followed it politically when questions of gendered citizenship suited their existing agendas, instincts, allegiances and other organizational definitions.

To address these issues, this work undertakes extensive sampling of daily newspapers such as *Le Petit Journal* (France), *The Daily Mail* (Britain), *La Fronde* (France), *The Daily Mirror* (Britain), *The Pioneer* (British India) and the weekly *Swandanthiram* (French India). In addition there are two chapters on Britain's suffrage movement where the scope of activist influence on Fleet Street and women's attitudes towards the mainstream media is tackled thematically by examining a broad range of examples from what campaigning female organizations called the 'public press'.

Three common, transnational trends are studied between the 1860s and the 1930s: the development of a form of conservative feminization by the mass media; formative experiences of lobbying and public persuasion in the labour movement; and from this root, the role of women as a significant force in communications involving direct action protests.

Conservative feminization

Newspaper business initiatives in Europe began to embrace women as a distinct market category of readership and of consumerism, catered for with advertising and features that enhanced consumer interest. Yet women's spending power became associated with ethics and politics, bringing women further into the public sphere. At the same time, female interest as readers was defined conservatively by male editors. The phrase 'conservative feminization' is used in Andrews and Talbot (2000) in relation to consumption and advertising for Britain's Ideal Home Exhibition, but here it is applied for the first time to editorial content. Historians often connect this phenomenon to post-1970s 'dumbing down' and in Britain, to Thatcherite deregulation of the media. In fact, the salient aspects of the approach were already present during the second half of the nineteenth century in France.

Labour movement roots

Women's public activities, as communicated in the press, found their organizational roots for persuasion in the labour movement. Outdoor activities involved the adoption of political symbols of protest, such as banners, brooms and visual iconography, adopted for ease of identification and in order to provide eye-catching publicity.

Direct action

Increasingly extrovert protest tactics enabled and enhanced regular interaction with the media. How were moments of political and economic resistance and rebellion mediated? Did newspapers, as vehicles for public articulation, lead or follow? Such questions are grounded in a range of ongoing theoretical discourses in historiography and media theory. Activists could not ignore newspapers: newspapers other than their own needed to be high-jacked in a performative way as tools for communication.

Theorizing mainstream press transnationally

Gender theorists are fully acquainted with the way that Judith Butler, through the examination of the politics of jurido-discursive power, constructs a feminism from which the gendered pronoun is no longer considered essential (1990, 1987, 1983). She claims that even the traditional binary of subject/object of feminism, whereby women must become the subject, is a hegemonic and artificial division. The notion of a subject, instead, is for her formed through repetition, through a 'practice of signification'. The process by which women acted counter-hegemonically to first achieve that repetition in and through newspapers is less familiar to scholars, but the binary of the public sphere as a site for largely male politics, and the 'private' domestic sphere being a female domain divorced from real labour, provides a backdrop against which to understand the 'hidden' nature of female contributions to strike protests, for instance.

Similarly, Michel Foucault's influence in posing questions about how the certain knowledge of 'natural' sexual difference was established, and about how and when 'regimes of truth' in this respect superseded each other, is well known (Scott, 1999: xi),[9] yet the chicken and egg aspects of media framing are rarely addressed. Political identity, social institutions and cultural symbols are all forms of knowledge production, and present-day[10] socially constructed identity is a widely accepted concept within media studies. Conflict, hierarchy and power emerge as underlying factors behind the linguistic process and are inherent to it. How hierarchies of difference are constituted, how exclusions and inclusions operate are also questions that extend much wider than this study, but they are gendered issues, 'a way of critically understanding how history operates as a site of the production of gender knowledge' (Scott, 1999: 10).

For most of the 'conflictual processes that produce meanings ', and the exclusions, (Scott, 1999: 7), there is a parallel process of communication to understand within the printed word. Thus we need to know how these were constructed, and what collective meanings they helped form. Lisbet van Zoonen suggests that for feminist media theory and research, the central question should be 'how is gender discourse negotiated in "moments" of the construction of media meanings – production, text and reception? (1994: 9).[11] Socially constructed gender and the recognition of agency also has sociological roots, for 'both communication and gender are discursive and social phenomenon at the same time, to be studied through an array of methods' (van Zoonen, 1994: 127).

An interdisciplinary methodology must strike a balance between historical empiricism and broader theorizations: specificity is necessary if broad generalizations are to be challenged, tested and fully understood. Symbolic interactionalism and the canonical work of Erving Goffman (1979) is particularly relevant to this study, for he believed that people are actively 'doing' gender, and according to some scholars, his theory allows the socially constructed agency of performance to be reclaimed from the theoretically totalizing effect that the concept of 'performativity' can have on subjective action (Bricknell, 2005: 24–43). Suffragette performance (Green, 1997) in relation to newspapers and changing perceptions of identity is discussed in Chapter 6.

If performance was a factor in British suffrage relations with what contemporaries called the 'public press', then is this equally the case in France, or India ? If so, how did this factor relate to others that are presented and analyzed here, such as class, direct action protest, conservative feminization and cultural consumerism? Previous research has identified the significance for the suffrage movement in Britain of visual iconology and performance (Tickner, 1987), but what impact did this have on the development of newspapers? The public press acted as an agency for both discursive and performative influences, with differing levels of importance at different times in different countries.

An investigation of the fluid and evolving relationship between discursive and performative aspects of the public press necessitates a return to two ongoing and distinct theoretical formations that must be traced historically: the discourse of separate spheres – public and private – and the discourse of gender difference. These intersect throughout this study. The specific confluence to be identified here by research is between direct action with organizational origins in class, and newspapers as an agency for public communications.

As feminist scholars have rightly identified, research that addresses the relationship between gender and power in language has of necessity to confront binary gender, and the discourses of separate spheres and of gender difference still come together today to naturalize workplace control and exclusion (Kearney, 2012: 405; Acker, 1990: 139–58). Notwithstanding, both the way that mainstream media produced various forms of knowledge, and the way that these were represented (and also excluded) in relation to women both clearly changed during the period in question in this study.

This line of enquiry requires us to engage with the notion of stereotyping. Women are researched as both the subject of stereotyping, and at times, agents to challenge it. The various processes by which this happened are examined in detail and comparatively, but always in the light of Michael Pickering's note of caution that 'If stereotyping is a major discursive device in the ideological construction of social groups and categories, we cannot assume that its significance and force as a concept is transparent and so able to be applied uninspected in analytical work on the politics of representation' (2001: 1). The point for this study is to understand its contributory role in the erratic and multifaceted evolution of gendered cultural citizenship in and through the printed word. The task is not an easy one, when one considers the dilemma within a dilemma that Pickering identifies: 'This is the dilemma which stereotyping faces: to resort to one-sided representations in the interests of order, security and dominance, or to allow for a more complex vision, a more open attitude, a more flexible way of thinking. Stereotyping functions precisely in order to forget this dilemma' (2001: 4). This is an insightful comment that reveals a paradoxical quality that can also be discerned in the mainstream press, particularly when it comes to the process of tabloidization, which is examined in Chapters 2 and 3.

Pickering's remark does not presuppose that historical stereotypes of women are simplistic, and this study discerns a number of contrary features emerging from empirical analyses. To identify contrary features is to thereby acknowledge the conflicting processes at work in our understanding of past relationships between gender and print publications. Pickering further proposes that stereotyping should be viewed as 'a process of symbolic confinement and risk, tied up with self-identity but always within a historical basis' (2001: 46). This definition is emphasized in Chapter 2 through an examination of the contribution of 'faits divers' (news snippets) interpreted as a newspaper development with a double-edged sword through its appeal to a new female readership, accompanied by representation of female centred content that because of its brevity and the economy of information, can be interpreted as presenting women in a number of stereotypical categories.

What of the risk referred to by Pickering? In late nineteenth-century France, new styles of presentation were accompanied by innovative commercially oriented business models that required shareholder support and large investment in printing technology; but the requirement for newspaper sales and advertising income dictated a certain social conservatism. Yet another paradox arose – business risk-takers as pioneers of early tabloids manifested political caution when it came to editorial content that displayed attitudes towards female departure from accepted social norms.

This has its theoretical roots in studies of Gramsci's hegemony (Joll, 1971: 12–13) and, more recently, counter-hegemony, relevant to the relations of power and disempowerment in connection with newspapers. 'The "normal" exercise of hegemony . . . is characterized by the combination of force and consensus that vary in their balance with each other, without force exceeding consensus too greatly. Thus, it tries to achieve that force should appear to be supported by the agreement of the majority, expressed by the so-called organs of public opinion – newspapers and associations' (Gramsci cited in Joll, 1977: 99). This canonical statement serves to inform much of the analysis in this study because of the relevance of his emphasis on the process by which proponents of dominant ideologies aim for general consent that generates forms of natural, almost invisible acceptance. In his book *The Indian Chaos* (1932), for instance, F.W. Wilson, editor of *The Pioneer*, describes the country as effectively being a police state.

Since Gramsci's time, scholars have argued that if there is hegemony, then there can also be counter-hegemony. The concept was first developed – in terms of definitions of modernity – by structuralist philosophers such as Louis Althusser (1969). Theodor Adorno (1970) subsequently critiqued by the post-structuralists Marshall Berman (1983) and Jacques Derrida (1992), and has been widely discussed by scholars. Thus although Althusser's and Gramsci's theories neglect gender issues, the ideological mechanisms that they dissect have inspired socialist feminists (van Zoonen, 1994: 23) and also journalism historians, for the resonance with minority communication (Downing 1984, 2001; Murdock, 2000; Cottle, 2000; Chapman 2007, 2011a).

Most scholars would agree that studying women is not necessarily the same as feminist research. This work reveals what socialist feminists have always argued – gender awareness is often inseparable from class. Certainly women cannot be studied in isolation, a problem that Erving Goffman (1974) appreciates when he argues that events and thinking can only meaningfully become 'experience' when they are integrated into an interpretative, cognitive framework. He uses theatre and drama as a metaphor for how the individual presents herself by analyzing the interactional order and social situations (1979). This idea resonates with the enquiries here into social movements – whether lobbyists, reformers, suffragettes, strikers, freedom fighters or consumer protesters. When these were featured in the mainstream press, changes took place on both sides – in laws, policies, and in symbolic representations of women as subjects. Political alliances and synergies for the process of reporting and carrying such information – that is the process of cultural production – also changed the papers themselves. Historical examples range from C.P. Scott's diary entries of conversations and meetings with Lloyd George on the issue of the vote for British women to evidence of the fortunes of *The Pioneer* in India, influenced by F.W. Wilson's support of the women's cause and his sympathy for constitutional change.

Why colonial communications?

There is a huge literature on gender and its relationship to war, nationalism and popular culture. Kathyrn Tidrik (2009), Catherine Hall (2000); Hall and McClelland 2010) and Laura Ann Stoler (Cooper and Stoler, 1997) have made major contributions to scholarship on the question of colonialism, gender and consumerism – but gender and the *mass media* is not within their scope. Furthermore, the failure of our English language media scholarship to deal with the French press and newspapers in colonial countries is a glaring omission. In fact, existing empire communications scholarship tends not to be comparative and has either concentrated on the high level political role of government/press relations, news and propaganda agencies, and the diffusion of news (Kaul, 1999, 2003, 2006; Milton, 1994; Potter, 2003), or on cultural representation and propaganda more generally (Ramamurphy, 2003; Chafur and Sackur, 2002; MacKenzie, 1984, 1986).

In general, French colonial historians have tended to concentrate on Africa and Indo-China (Blanchard and Lemaire, 2003; Ezra, 2000; Chafer and Sackur, 1999, 2002), although the latter authors acknowledge that anti-colonial feelings originated during the period of France's Popular Front government of 1936–1938. However, there is no discrete research on the press within French territories, although the rise of a Tamil press and the growth of a communist press more generally in India are both given some attention by scholars (Mazumdar, 1993; Murthy, 1966). Kate Marsh (2007) analyses representations in metropolitan France of French India, but only studies a small number of Paris-based newspapers, and she does not look at any local communications.

From the hegemonic side cultural imperialism was integral to the economic and political landscape of middle- and upper-class European women (Burton, 1994; Chaudhuri and Strobel, 1992; Cooper and Stoler 1997).[12] Thus, colonialism was widely accepted (Blanchard and Lemaire, 2003) and promoted in product advertising as an exotic form of consumption (Chafer and Sackur, 2002). However, the inclusion of India in this study alongside Western societies raises historical issues of gender status that were complicated by the colonial relationship and became intertwined with questions of alleged Western cultural and racial superiority. These need to be confronted. McClintock (1995: 4–5) makes the essential point that race, gender and class are not separate – they exist *in* and *through* each other. This relationship is elaborated in subsequent chapters.

The challenge of these questions is to confront the point that imperialism is not something that happened elsewhere – it is a basic aspect of Western industrial modernity. The project of ensuring that histories of imperialism treat 'both coloniser and colonised . . . as gendered subjects, and that attention is paid to the ways in which imperial involvements and interactions were shaped by gender as well as race and class' is also supported by Midgeley (1998: 14–15). She points out, that in doing so, we introduce a shift of emphasis through the centring of 'another history of agency and knowledge alive in the dead weight of the colonial past' (Prakash, 1994: 5).

Both gender and newspapers can act as agencies for forms of knowledge and histories, but any study of the impact of this presents the scholar with a number of problems, touched upon by Seymour-Ure when he contended that the British press 'by anticipating an event which would happen anyway, change its character' (1968, p. 288). In effect he raises issues of cause and effect, as we must do here. How extensively did events and actions prompt coverage? How far did women adapt or change their behaviour in the public arena, influenced by previous reporting and publicity, or by the desire to achieve a different sort of newspaper representation? The significance of Seymour-Ure's contention needs to be tested against different transnational examples and also needs to be considered in specific contexts that extend beyond one single event or country, pointing instead to a longer process of evolution in a relationship between women as social actors and newspapers as mediators of change. Thus, enquiries here extend beyond representation to consider the nature of mediation and how it was facilitated by women' actions in civil society.

In the Western world, the new economic dependence of newspapers on advertising as a source of revenue during the twentieth century prompted a furtherance of private and economic domestic values as well as women's participation in acts of citizenship based on consumption, but how did this factor play out in a colonial context, especially in terms of editorial content?

Scholarship has come to emphasize the role of agency and the importance of the 'active' as opposed to the more passive consumer, yet no studies have examined the mass circulation press as an agent for both positive and negative influence in this area.

In India, consumer protest in the form of Indian women's nationalist boycotts was the major plank within the civil disobedience movement. This is important not only for gendered media history but also for two further reasons: decolonization has provided a central arena for the development of critical models such as subaltern studies; and the press as agency between colonizer and colonized is insufficiently studied. According to Landry and MacLean, subaltern studies, 'are re-writing the history of colonial India from the perspective of peasant consciousness and insurgency – a history of subaltern agency' (1993: 129). Yet there has been a lack of detailed analysis of journalistic forms, no attempt to investigate how this relates to economic aspects of the empire press role and no comparative studies of newspapers across national boundaries specifically on these themes.

Clearly, patterns and structures of consumption (and therefore consumerism) were very different in India. The contradictions of imperialism constantly emerge in the colonial press: on a 1921 page from *The Times of India* (British Museum, 1921: BL 013894677) a huge drawing of a beautiful reclining European 'flapper' shows her flaunting a long cigarette holder. This is placed next to a lead article on Indian famine. Such examples bring the business of press analysis alive and restore its original human dimension by providing stark visual messages. A same-page juxtaposition from *The Times of India* 1936 (British Museum, 1936: BL 013894677) features a very large advertising image of a victorious female aviator who explains that she could not have broken the world record for solo flight over the Cape without drinking Ovaltine. A long report on a religious conference urging Indian women to renounce traditional Hindu practices such as 'sati' (immolation of widows) appears next to it, while on a previous page a detailed article discusses how Indian women should be educated.

Such colonial incongruities in the press from a gendered perspective should not be dismissed as modernist disjunctures inherent in the newspaper mode of production: they also demonstrate the range of potential female representation, as well as the profundity of class and ethnic difference that cultural consumerism manifested, and that cultural citizenship came to challenge. There has been some research on censored material and issues of press freedom (Barrier, 1974; Israel, 1994; Jones, 1983) but not of censorship and its effects on a local, ethnic press. What this scholarship established is that minority voices are cut out because of the choice of official sources, reflecting the outlook of the (colonial) organization. This point about framing has provided the main focus for post-colonial theory, focusing frequently on the decolonization of the Indian subcontinent by the British. In particular works by Edward Said (1978), Homi Bhabha (1983) and Spivak (1988) have stressed that subalterns are exclusively framed by colonial power. However, subaltern studies scholars have not looked at alternative communications historically.

In media expression, the selectivity of sources referred to above allows alternative media to use a different set of sources and voices (Murdock, 2000; Cottle 2000: 434–5). Hence the insider/outsider divide has prompted categorization of attempts to challenge existing ideological frameworks. These have been labelled as 'counter-hegemonic' and are referred to by John Downing as 'radical alternative media' (2001: x). However, the restrictions of mainstream (hegemonic) rule are usually reflected in the raw material that is selected by media communicators reporting on the system. This can be seen in the hegemonic press as well as 'alternative' press. Yet dissenting voices squeezed their way into the mainstream, despite political opposition and frequent exclusions.

As soon as the historian embarks upon any enquiry that involves newspapers, questions arise concerning how far counter hegemony in texts acts as a social mirror and how far it acts as a social agent for either change or continuity. This book takes several different eras in several countries – France, Britain and colonial India – to address the conundrum. Chapter 7 analyses examples and usage of women's dissent in the pages of an establishment daily – *The Pioneer*. In French Indian territories (Chapter 4) the formation of legal worker organizations for the first time and a new political party provided the context in which activist leaders used print publications in order to promote their formative anti-colonial ideas. Women were significant players, but unlike women in the majority British-controlled sector, they were not leaders. The chapters that follow address the expression of societal comments in both hegemonic and counter-hegemonic communications of economic and social protest that, despite censorship, provided a challenge for the media by extending the scope of newspapers' role within the evolution of gendered citizenship.

Processes of subaltern mediation

Earlier examples of female influence include Sister Nivedita and the 'zenana' evangelization of India (Weitbrecht, 2009); the first 'swadeshi' movement of 1903 to 1908, and the female pickets in Allahabad of cloth and liquor establishments, led by Kamala Nehru in 1921 (Bakshi, 2000).

Could these examples or the selling of khaddar (homespun cloth) fall into the category of what Nancy Fraser (Fraser and Barkty, 1991) calls in a French context a women's 'counter civil society'? Equally the influence of nationalist supporters such as Dr. Annie Besant (Cousins, 1947) and Sarojini Naidu (Navarane, 1997; Datta, 1997) should be noted. Chronologies for the development of what today is called 'media literacy' were different to those in parts of the Western world, but newspapers were also used differently. Frequently articles were read aloud to groups of people and used for collective discussion. In Europe this was the eighteenth century coffee-house model, for the press has a long tradition of association with the furtherance of democracy (Chapman and Nuttall, 2011), thus similar themes can be identified in differing contexts and points of development.

Female citizenship in India has been recognized by women's colonial studies with work by Taneja (2005), Kleinberg (1988), Midgeley (1998), Samson (2001), Sussman (2000), Wieringa (1995), Levine (2004) and Sangari and Vaid (1989). Indigenous women's organized protest had only just begun to express its potency, fired and focused by the anti-colonial 'freedom movement'. In the case of French India, it was expressed as an essentially working-class movement from private to public sphere. In British India, women already had the vote, whereas in Britain, after the final 1929 victory of women's suffrage, feminists faced a problem: 'The process of attempting to educate women for citizenship ultimately seemed to submerge any specific feminist ideas or demands for change under the weight of women's duty to understand how to carry out their local and national responsibilities in ways that would keep the existing social and political order functioning smoothly' (Caine, 1997: 200). This was not the case in India during the 1930s: here the responsibilities of leadership in a post-colonial phase provided a sequel to the struggles led by the Congress Party and their women during the 1930s. Similarly in 1947 10,000 women rallied in the French territory of Pondicherry: they were still preparing for the fight. It is not the stage of development but the beginnings of gender awareness, enhanced by, and represented in, public communications, that need to be acknowledged as part of the process of women's struggle for equality in the polity.

Women attracted journalistic attention to their social and political cause, some directly and others indirectly – for this was a period when notions of female citizenship were in the process of being redefined. The task now is to address the multifarious ways in which this was happening.

Part II
Pioneers and Emerging Commercial Tensions

2
France

Pioneering the Popular Newspaper Brand and the Female Market

This and the following chapter establish that there were three contributory trends towards cultural citizenship by and for women: recognition of women as readers and consumers, women as journalists, and women as sources of news content, through their actions in society – particularly in public affairs.

First, I examine the early orientation of newspapers towards female readership. It is clear, as this chapter shows, that business orientation, politics and cultural factors combined to contribute to the identification of a female readership by Europe's first mass circulation daily. This was substantiated by a convergence of four basic trends, analyzed here as a combined phenomenon of 'cultural consumerism', manifested in tension with other early features of cultural citizenship, the roots of which can be discerned through the example of France's *Le Petit Journal* in the second half of the nineteenth century. Contributory aspects consisted of:

- Content changes: the introduction of content that was devised in order to recognize women's needs as potential readers.
- Consumerism: the growth of a new phenomenon – the department store – with connections to newspapers and to the concept of promotion more generally.
- Business and technological development: the tendency for newspapers to become more business oriented, manifested by increased set-up and modernization costs due to technological advances in printing and production, and a more proactive role by banks in cross-ownership and investment.
- Women making the news: a trend for women and all things female – including the 'new woman' – to increasingly find their way into newspapers as content for discussion.

The founders of *Le Petit Journal* undertook an energetic and far reaching effort to tap a large new market consisting of people (not just women), often in inaccessible rural areas, who were not in the habit of reading daily newspapers, and had not previously been catered for. This extension of the availability of a newspaper that was also popularist meant that a new kind of appeal was developed – an appeal to both consumer interests and citizenship. This process gradually became a gendered one, as this chapter reveals.

The Roussean legacy and women's moral obligation

The nineteenth century was the period of great newspaper consolidation as a political and cultural force. French women blazed a trail in newspaper history during the 1830s and 1840s, with a brief explosion in feminist activity during the earlier part of the 1848 revolution when a proliferation of radical journals produced by and aimed at women appeared then collapsed (Adler, 1979; Walton, 2000; Ferenczi, 1993; Sullerot, 1966).[1] Yet within the field of newspaper development, between 1852 and 1870 France's Second Empire witnessed censorship, controls on newspaper distribution and sales, content, and on a woman's right to become an editor and publisher. The law of 11 May 1868 prohibiting the latter was based on the assumption that this function involved the exercise of a political right (even for the so-called 'non-political' press), which women did not have.

The timing of this particular law was significant: it coincided with the resurgence of a demand for women's suffrage in France that echoed debates in Britain, where only two years previously John Stewart Mill had unsuccessfully attempted to introduce an amendment to the Second Reform Bill to include women. In the United States, the conclusion of the Civil War and the subsequent campaign to enfranchise black men and all women had led to the State of Wyoming giving women the vote in 1869 – the same year that in England women ratepayers gained the municipal but not the parliamentary vote.

However, the extension of the male franchise was such a battle in many countries that any similar campaign for women was seen by some as a potentially weakening factor. In the case of France this factor was underpinned by historic factors such as the legacy of Roman law, the industrial revolution and the economic insecurity of men, the influence of the Code Napoleon, and social conservatism epitomized by the ideologies and institutions of Catholicism. Hause (1984) adds to the shopping list of French handicaps the characteristically turbulent history of Republicanism and of the Radical Party during the Third Republic.

Such aspects help to explain the weakness and small size later in the century of the organized women's movement in France by comparison to those of Britain and the United States. Indeed, Christine Bard refers to the century as a black period for France – 'La siècle noire des femmes' (2010). She points out that the adjective 'feminist' was not even used until 1882 (1995: 9). Michelle Perrot gives examples that concur when she identifies three trends during the nineteenth century: 'the comparative withdrawal of women from the public arena; the constitution of a private, female-dominated family sphere and a huge investment of masculine imagination and symbolism in the representation of women' (Reynolds, 1986: 55). However, this masculine imagination and symbolism concerning the representation of women was coloured by men's politics (not women's) and by men's perceptions of what sort of content sold newspapers (not women's). To understand the contemporary rationale for this male monopoly on public communications, we need to return once more to the late eighteenth and early nineteenth centuries.

The wider debate about rights within the public sphere proved to be one of the longest running in modern history, as French women finally obtained the vote in 1944–1945. 'Gynaecocracy' (Offen, 1994: 154), or the issue of women and political authority, dates back to at least the late sixteenth century when heirs through the female line were prohibited from taking the throne. By the late eighteenth and early nineteenth centuries, the position of women within society as mothers had expanded to reflect a sense of civic importance attached to maternity and wifehood. The inauguration of the republic was not favourable to women. In fact, Sian Reynolds argues that because civil rights were not extended to them, the Republic 'was constructed as much against women as without them' (1986: 104, 113).

Although the republican political beliefs that accompanied the American and the French Revolutions brought demands from women for the rights of citizenship and a new emphasis on the importance of education, the idea of 'republican motherhood' articulated in these two countries and to some extent in Britain, was essentially based on a family ethic. At the same time the scope of the 'public' world was strengthened by the establishment of more and more political and commercial groups and activities – from which women were excluded. Indeed, Jurgen Habermas (1989: 20) construes this as the period when the concept of the 'public sphere' became evident, with public opinion increasingly powerful as a significant force within politics and society.

Barbara Caine has pointed out that during this period, women – especially bourgeois women in Britain – were expected 'to raise the moral and religious tone of their family, household, and local community, and through that, of the wider economic and political world – a world to which they were denied any direct access' (1997: 16). During 1792 members of female republican clubs in Paris took oaths to 'persuade on all occasions my husband, my brothers, and my children to fulfil their duties towards the country' (Hunt, 1992: 123).[2] Although in practice, this kind of thinking was likely to involve some crossover into the public sphere – newspaper reading for instance – a strong philosophical justification for the separation of public and private spheres deriving from the writings of Rousseau was widely supported. He maintained that women's confinement to the separate domestic world was essential to the maintenance of social and political order. The ideas expressed particularly in his educational work *Emile* were hugely influential internationally, and as we shall see later, were frequently echoed in the pages of newspapers in the form of editorial comment in news columns.

The disparity between what 'polite' society expected of women on the one hand, and their legal rights on the other, has been described in a similar British context as a contradiction between fact and faith that is 'breathtaking' (Millett, 1977: 66). The Enlightenment's emphasis on natural rights and rationality would seem to support such rights for women, but at the same time the differences between the sexes were being reinforced and elaborated. Rousseau's ideas concerning women's 'nature' (1906) together with the highlighting of women's 'moral' potential were both ways of thinking that could be used by both conservatives and feminists. Such discourses regularly found their way into the pages of daily newspapers and were accompanied by a gradual redefinition of masculinity. Middle-class women tended to focus on the need for educational reform and on the pros and cons of domesticity. Patriarchal authority in the family was changing, but with mixed blessings: a more authoritarian role based on lineage and family interest was giving way to a closer-knit unit in which marriage was becoming accompanied by ties of affection, but this did not necessarily *reduce* patriarchal power – it simply changed its nature (Shorter, 1976: 62–75; Caine, 1997: 19).

Marriage and the family unit provided an elaborate code of chivalrous protection for upper-class and bourgeois women, whereby they were treated to expressions of concern but to no personal or political freedoms. Contemporary commentator Thorstein Veblen (1899) perceived the economic aspect of this when he referred to 'vicarious consumption': women purchasing with money earned by their spouses. He disdainfully described the leisured lady as having the function of displaying her husband's wealth by spending, thus becoming a status symbol as 'a means of conspicuously unproductive expenditure'. This theory effectively supports the inevitability of class-based cultural divisions and consequently arguments against cultural democratization, as Stevenson points out: 'Thorstein Veblen's notion of a leisure class suggests that the high/low culture division is likely to persist in an industrial society where subordinate groups derive their livelihood from manual labour' (2001: 16).

Of course a young middle-class girl could be frightened into social and sexual conformity by the risk of the alternatives such as employment as a governess, factory work, service or prostitution. Conversely the factory girl dreamt of self-betterment through the sexual patronage of the male – a recurrent fantasy in the literature of the period. 'The psycho-political tactic here is a pretence that the indolence and luxury of the upper-class woman's role . . . was the happy lot of all women' (Millett, 1977: 73). By her 'vicarious consumption' she had been transformed into a species of commodity (Veblen, 1899: 70–1, 231–2) – this was the way that the bourgeois class displayed its wealth – and it reflected an approach that newspaper advertisers and content writers were to capitalize on. In many ways, their influence pulled in several directions, both for and against cultural democratization, as analyzed later.

Newspaper contexts

The content of newspapers tended to be aimed at masculine communities of political preference in the world of commerce, politics and law: for most of the century, women were not catered for as a market by daily newspapers and their representation in editorial was often not very positive. Thus, for any gendered enquiry into this theme, there is an obvious starting point – newspaper ownership by and for men – by-and-large male managerial leadership defined the taste of readers of the opposite sex. In Europe, a political press catering for an educated upper-middle class male readership was still thriving. In early 1860s Britain, for instance, the venerable *The Times* of London (euphemistically referred to as 'The Thunderer') was still creating reverberations aimed at influencing a narrow, establishment-oriented political elite, and continued to dominate the newspaper market, despite the short-lived success of a largely illegal (un-stamped for tax) 'Radical Press' during the 1840s (Chapman, 2005a: 32–40, 48, 57).

In France an equivalent hegemonic power to that of 'The Thunderer' was wielded by a group of 'grands seigneurs' daily press: their verbatim accounts of parliamentary debates had also tended to cater for the interests of male political elites. Women, of course, were generally not expected to be stimulated by the interminably long broadsheet details of shipping, shares, financial ventures, legislative debates and court proceedings that provided the staple diet for European (male) daily newspaper readers. By comparison, as early as the 1830s and early 1840s, the American press was already extending to a new, more inclusive lower class readership with more concise, catchy and popular penny dailies, even if there were scarcely any female owners or female journalists. In France, Emile de Girardin had first argued for more popularism in 1836 (Chapman, 2005a: 35), but it was not until 1863 that a successful popular daily, *Le Petit Journal*, finally emerged during a period of repression.

Le Petit Journal blazes a trail in popularism

Arguably popular journalism has had a continuous presence throughout modernity, or even earlier if its ancestry is traced to the oral culture of seventeenth century ballads in Europe and America (Bird, 1992). This chapter records in more detail how Europe's first pioneering popular mass circulation daily manifested aspects of a tabloid style *before* the word tabloid was widely applied and before the process of 'tabloidization' (see later) became a recognizable trend. What was the nature of these early tabloid characteristics in Europe's pioneer mass circulation daily? Were women recognized as a new readership? Was there any evidence of simplistic, graphic and emotional writing styles, or of subject matter aimed at women?

Although it was not until the early twentieth century that the critical use of the term tabloid entered general usage (Greenberg, 1996), the word tabloid was first adopted as a pharmaceutical term for tablet medicine in 1884, and was used later by Northcliffe to describe the size of small newspapers. Scholars have discussed tabloid properties such as the spectacularization and simplification of news that can be discerned in a range of contemporary media (Franklin 1997; Sparks, 2000; Turner 1999) but historicization of these aspects is less clear. Of course, newspapers have always aimed to produce readers by creating a selection of news tailored to particular customers for the purposes of influence and/or profit, and *Le Petit Journal*'s appeal to a female French audience was unashamedly mainstream and popular. Founders of *Le Petit Journal* Alphonse and Moïse Millaud understood that appealing to women readers made good business sense and also that a paper needed to be both attention grabbing and readable.

Le Petit Journal's pioneering popularism was characterized by a trend towards the introduction of feature style content that had previously been the reserve of women's magazines and other weekly periodicals, for women were visible in the growing periodicals market.[3] This was achieved using an editorial tone and style that managed to be simultaneously spicy yet suspicious of change with a politically cautious editorial tone. Ironically, during the 1860s, government authorities favoured the propagation of such apparently innocuous content by the 'petits seigneurs' (non-political, popular daily papers, exempt from the tax on political papers) as a means of weakening the political influence of the anti-government 'grands seigneurs' and of maintaining the social conservatism of women. A veritable army of 60 civil servants was employed specifically to keep records on newspaper activities, business affairs and coverage. Ministry internal correspondence reveals an admission that the strategy failed: both categories of newspapers increased their circulation, despite costly attempts to launch government sponsored newspapers in competition (AN, F18 / 295). Thus, at a very early stage in their development, mass circulation dailies were encouraged by this legislative and structural business categorization to offer distractions from politics.

The Millaud brothers' painstaking efforts to render literate civilization accessible to country folk during the 1860s took *Le Petit Journal* to even the most rural of areas, using the newly launched railway network and local depots. By 1866 15,000 people either directly or indirectly earned a living from the *Le Petit Journal*, but fluctuations in circulation and revenue threatened their livelihood. Direct daily street sales (as opposed to the stability of annual subscriptions that were prevalent) meant that each edition had to uniquely appeal. As the consumer decided to buy or not on a daily basis, the management of *Le Petit Journal* was obliged to seek new attention grabbing tactics for making profits.

The commercialization of newspapers created a different kind of relationship between the press and their readers: increasing sales were attributed to the talent of owners and editors in discerning what the public wanted, then selling it to them. Proprietors were thereby thought to *stand in* for the public as representative of them – the 'Fourth Estate'. The assumption of a leadership role in the representation of other social groups as part of a broader responsibility for public sphere communications was an important motivation on all sides of the political spectrum at a time when women and the European working class more generally remained politically disenfranchised.

The distinction between high and low – between 'petits journaux' and 'grands seigneurs', or popular versus quality journalism – has conventionally provided a normative definition for the media in relation to the public sphere (Meijer, 2001). In France, this was mirrored by an emerging distinction between high and low markets in the literary world – with the low market as the new category. Within this landscape the serialized novel was positioned by newspaper entrepreneurs as a bridge between literature and newspapers. The advantage of the serialized novel was that it offered the paper complete editorial control over forward planning to ensure a steady and regular build up in circulation.

Layout and writing style

Although by 1866 more copies of *Le Petit Journal* were printed in Paris than of all 19 political dailies combined (Palmer, 1972: 97, 100), it would be wrong to imagine that, in appearance, *Le Petit Journal* resembled a modern tabloid newspaper. *Le Petit Journal* widened conventional readership by introducing content and a format that were deemed to appeal to women and the *'petite bourgeoisie'* in less accessible rural areas. Advances in the technology of typesetting and layout later in the nineteenth century meant that types and layout gradually became more visually attractive with headlines and subtitles (Chapman 2005a: 57–8), however, there was still a distinct absence of modern day presentation. Its appearance lacked the 'professionalism' of sub-editors' layout and design that is enabled by the modern day production techniques of recent technology, but nevertheless daily newspaper content was clearly changing.

In terms of writing style, the conventions of 'modern' journalism such as editing of copy, summarizing, quoting and interviewing had yet to emerge (Chapman, 2007: 480). There was little evidence of the present day characterization of news style as 'objective', balanced, with standard practice to use quotes from more than one point of view and source, and the evolution of information within the article using an 'inverted pyramid' structure and no attempt to differentiate between 'comment' and the factual reporting of events (Chapman, 2005b: 7). These aspects of journalistic techniques are supposed to represent elements of the modern, American inspired, 'news paradigm',[4] but were clearly absent.

In 1863 *Le Petit Journal* articles often had a spicy and enthusiastically prurient flavour, written in an intimate conversational in style, but were also longer, more random, less formulaic and therefore predictable in approach than in 1896. Reporting style changed gradually between

1863 and 1896: news became more consistent on certain themes, and concise, while lead articles became more discursive and didactic. Any interviews tended to consist of official statements from figures in authority or verbatim reports of court proceedings. Although women are often quoted in accounts of legal hearings, the paper steered clear of directly interviewing women. More generally, the 'elite' press in Europe at that time saw the interview as an intrusion into privacy and the French were slow to take on board these techniques because politicians preferred to retain verbatim coverage. Even in 1896 most news articles were sequential in style with 'as it happens' reporting topped by a short headline. For example, on 2 January 1896 the paper printed the President's 'thank-you' speech to those gathered at an official diplomatic reception at the Elysee Palace: to the modern eye, this verbatim account reads very much like a state-of-the-nation speech – one of the very few American speeches today that is reported verbatim.

Content and readership

Le Petit Journal achieved its success with women readers through its combination strategy of introducing feature style content, adoption of a 'modern' commercial approach and a cheap sales price of a 'sou' (centime/penny). This trend was criticized by contemporaries for its 'immorality' (Roberts, 1999: 307). The propensity for trivia apparently inherent in the newspaper and periodical genre had become a common complaint among literati ever since Rousseau identified that journalism was a labourer's task and that a periodical was 'an ephemeral work, without merit and without utility, which cultivated men avoid and despise and which serves only to give women and fools vanity without instruction: its fate is to shine in the morning at the toilette and to die in the evening in a cupboard' (Zeldin, 1977: 494).

Given this way of thinking, it comes as no surprise that a contemporary account describes *Le Petit Journal*'s approach as one that aimed to articulate what everyone was thinking, even if this meant being bold enough to appear stupid (Lermina, 1884-5). Another contemporary pamphlet argued that men were not afraid to leave the paper around for their womenfolk to read, for it contained nothing harmful or offensive (Desvaux, 1868). Emile Zola, who wrote for *Le Petit Journal* early in his career, was more cynical: he considered that it 'flattered' the people (Mitterrand, 1962: 26).

As France changed constitution from a conservative empire to a more liberal Third Republic the social, economic and political climates in which women could further their cause began to improve. For Mary Louise Roberts the focus for analysis of women during this period should be positive: 'Although performance of gender had (at least potentially) both a conservative and a subversive effect, I give analytic weight to the latter' (Roberts, 2002: 15). Certainly the new optimism of France's Third Republic was exemplified by the *Le Petit Journal* launch of *La Mode miniature féminine illustrée* in 1872. Yet Rousseau's words appeared to have had some resonance for, according to Samra-Martine Bonvoisin and Michèle Maignien it was a trivial female, not a feminist, magazine (1986: 16). This was followed by the launch of an illustrated Sunday supplement in 1884, promoted outside the headquarters with enormous banners as a public event.

Such spectacle formed only a part of the 'modern' commercial strategy of founder Moïse Millaud that also, crucially, involved the setting up of an extensive distribution network, as mentioned earlier. An army of 1,200 vendors, employed exclusively to sell his popular daily, were provided with a horn and a whistle to complement their loud voices, which they used to shout the title of the latest serialized novel featured in the paper. They were told in 'Instructions pour MM.les Marchards du Petit Journal': 'Please offer *Le Petit Journal* to everyone who buys a broadsheet ('grand journal'). Every time you have to give change, offer *Le Petit Journal* instead. Nearly everyone will accept' (BN, 1863: LC2 3011, February–June).

A contemporary assessment of the demand for the paper points to the fact that women and peasants had to be encouraged to read it and that *Le Petit Journal* 'obliged the latter to become interested in current affairs' (Lermina, 1884-5). The potential politicization of women is not mentioned. The timing of the publication of this comment is significant, as it coincided with new Third Republic reforms in 1884 that widened educational access (see later) , from which this very readership could benefit. Significantly, the launch of *Le Petit Journal* more than 20 years previously, during the Second Empire period of repression, testifies to an early concern with its educative function, even if this was dominated by a business motivation (Chapman, 2011b).[5]

The approach can be characterized as a 'form of cultural discourse'[6] – one definition of cultural citizenship discussed in the previous chapter. This line of enquiry recognizes that news serves a purpose beyond conveying politically relevant information. Millaud himself referred to his readership as 'les petits gens' (Palmer, 1972: 93), but nevertheless applied a great deal of marketing flair to the ongoing task of promotion. Demand increased so phenomenally that in 1867 Millaud was forced to invest in state of the art technology to increase production, namely the Marinoni designed rotary press that printed up to 40,000 papers per hour – 'un modèle sans rival' (ANR: 65AQ: A211, 257/2). By 1869 circulation had reached almost a half a million, and a celebratory banquet was held at which the 240 staff present toasted their female readers (Morienval, 1934: 230). Anglo-American scholarship claims erroneously that *The Daily Mail* was the first daily to hit mass circulation of a million, when in fact *Le Petit Journal* hit this target in 1887 – much earlier and before *The Daily Mail* was even founded.

Readership, the serialized novel and fact/fiction crossover

The serialized novel was central to this success, for it symbolized the connection between the increase in female economic power and their emergence as a force within the 'petits journaux' of journalism history. In *Le Petit Journal* there was always a serial at the bottom, the *rez-de-chaussée* or ground floor of the front page, and usually a second one inside. The trajectory of the feuilleton is a long one: competitor dailies also invested in serialized novels, from 1897 onwards *La Fronde* (see Chapter 3) also carried one on page three (BL: MF19 NPL) and a twentieth-century survey found that twice as many women read serialized novels as men (Zeldin, 1977, 2: 519).

Chalaby has correctly pointed out that in Britain and the United States the press developed independently from the literary field, but that this was not the case in France (1996: 303). However, what he fails to recognize is that popular literary based models such as that found in *Le Petit Journal* could help a paper become commercially viable, demonstrating that the Anglo-American route to modern newspaper consumerism was not the only one. The path of newspaper development mapped out here comprises a journey towards financial independence based on popular literature and human interest information, covertly sponsored editorial for business and the arts, heavily peppered with opinion, and envisaging women as an important section of the readership.

In fact, through to the twentieth century, women were the main consumers of the 'feuilleton' or serial novel (although it also appealed to men, particularly at its inception during the 1830s when the female reading public was not so large). The front page of the paper always consisted of 'faits divers' (human interest snippets), a 'chronique' (opinion column) plus a major serialized novel that was continued inside and ran for weeks on end, frequently accompanied by a minor serial on page three. These, according to Adamowicz-Hariasz, 'began the cultural democratization of French society – from the bottom up' (De la Motte and Przyblyski, 1999: 160) symbolizing the connection between the increase in female economic power and their emergence as a force within the popular press. Morienval recounts how much care Millaud took to ensure that the endings of serials happened at the right time, allowing for a sufficient build up of suspense to increase sales, and in the right way, allowing for the sensibilities of the female readership (1934: 223). This is supported by Palmer: 'care was taken not to offend those generally considered the majority readers of its serials: women' (1972: 97). Yet in later years this care was tempered by a definite taste for horrible murders and stories of violence, as presented later in the findings.

Among the papers seized from the Imperial family at the fall of the Second Empire was a report from the Ministry of the Interior suggesting that the Emperor's office could supply portraits of parliamentarians and a novel, written to favour the army, for serialization in *Le Petit Journal* (Zeldin, 1977: 519). At the time, the move was denied by those concerned, but even as a mere suggestion it demonstrates the importance of the *feuilleton*.

One of the first writers to create a big hit for *Le Petit Journal* was Ponson du Terrail, author of *Rocambole*. Du Terrail's talent was to serve up exotic amusement for non-travellers (especially women) who did not have the stamina for Flaubert and Baudelaire. His story outcomes (and those of other authors) were advertised on street posters, billboards and vendors nationwide with tantalizing word puzzles over the course of up to six weeks, one or two words at a time until the point became clear : 'Will he?', then 'will he speak?', followed by 'will Feringhea speak? He cannot decide . . . He will speak in a few days . . .', then 'he's going to speak' and finally 'Feringhea has spoken'. In this case Millaud was applying his considerable marketing flair to creating, arguably, the first catch phrase throughout France (Palmer 1972: 95), while simultaneously satisfying the public's thirst for suspense and the 'horrible details' of 'Les Thugs' – a story about religious fundamentalist gangs who committed murders in India, a sure-fire best seller!

By 1880 *Le Petit Journal*'s circulation was already four times that of its rivals, but the literary serials never increased circulation by more than 50,000, whereas salacious crime coverage such as that of the serial murder case 'Affaire Troppman' in 1869 easily doubled that figure. In fact circulation increased on a daily basis with reports of yet another discovery of a dead body. Indeed, the entertainment value of the gory, long running 'Affaire Troppmann' was so good for circulation that it prompted investment in new capital intensive production methods – namely the

Marinoni rotary press that printed a higher volume of copies much faster than previously. Direct daily street sales (as opposed to the stability of annual subscriptions that were far fewer) had made the paper 'the slave of topicality and sensational crimes' (Palmer, 1972: 103), whereas the serial provided regularity and continuity.

Nevertheless, the consumer's decision to buy or not on a daily basis meant that the management of *Le Petit Journal* was obliged to seek new attention grabbing tactics for making profits. Thus, during the very first month of publication of *Le Petit Journal*, writers were instructed by founder Moïse Millaud to create a fictional sense of entertainment in crime coverage. Alphonse Millaud had given instructions to one of his writers, Victor C., criticizing him for writing as a cold spectator without emotion. His editorial orders were published in the paper, so that intentions were transparent to readers: reporters must simultaneously evoke empathy, intense emotion, fear and excitement. 'I want you to quiver with rage at the assassin's dripping knife and to shudder with pity at the victim's fate' (BN: *Le Petit Journal* Micr-D-135).[7]

In 1864 Timothy Trimm (real name Leo Lespès[8]) – Europe's first ever 'celebrity' tabloid columnist – wrote about the rationale of female consumption of crime stories. What the flamboyant Trimm had to say was taken seriously by his readers, and his front page opinion *chroniques* became habit-forming. In fact fans flocked daily to watch him compose the column outside his habitual Parisian cafés as Trimm performed (usually on anything that came into his head) with ostentatious flourishes of the quill and an encyclopaedia to hand for facts. Trimm valued female readership, and he claimed that *Le Petit Journal* readers consisted of a public that was intelligent, manifesting traditionally female qualities of generosity and spontaneity towards crime coverage (15 October).

Female curiosity about graphic crime and catastrophe was deemed by Trimm to be natural, healthy and legitimate due to female emotions of sympathy and compassion (*Le Petit Journal*, 18 September 1864, 15 March 1863, 9 May 1864). Readers would probably have reacted in this way to, for instance, the particularly graphic story imported from an American paper of New Yorker Mrs. Parr. She suspected her husband of having an affair with their pretty young ward. When she found the girl alone, she grabbed her by the waist, forced her backwards and poured sulphuric acid onto her face and neck. The ward was horribly disfigured and lost the use of her right eye. Later, Mr. Parr forced the door open and found his wife in convulsions of agony – she has poisoned herself with prussic acid. She died in front of him (*Le Petit Journal*, 21 July 1863).

Trimm was eventually sacked for demanding too many wage increases and from a proprietorial standpoint star reporters were expensive and difficult to deal with. Furthermore a regular flow of gory drama in real life could not be guaranteed, whereas the advantage of the serialized novel was that it offered the paper complete editorial control and forward planning. By 1868, 15,000 people either directly or indirectly earned a living from *Le Petit Journal* but fluctuations in circulation and revenue threatened their livelihoods.

Demand for serials was not restricted to *Le Petit Journal*: in 1884 *Le Matin*, created to compete with *Le Petit Journal*, decided initially to only print human interest stories, but within a few months, it was forced to introduce 'feuilletons' as a result of reader requests (Quefféléc, 1989: 78). These conflicting elements in the format produced a tension in the pages of *Le Petit Journal* that actually resulted in a mutual synergy: an overlapping fact/fiction style of writing between reports and novels. The feuilletons contain a similar use of prose, speech and opinion to lend an air of authenticity to the fiction, but it is the factual pieces, not the fiction that contrast so starkly with modern writing. This was a characteristically French daily newspaper style of hybridization, appearing at a time when the Anglo-American model for journalism style was moving to a shorter, more succinct, information based 'inverted pyramid' approach to news writing. According to Michael Palmer, both serialized novel and factual pieces shared the same formula for success: 'Fiction was given the appearance of fact' (Palmer, 1972: 95, 1983: 27).

Fact/fiction crossover increased after 1863 as the editorial team attempted to identify the style of their paper with their assumed female readership. On 19 July 1863 a lead story by 'Georges' was composed to bring an element of drama bordering on gossip to a somewhat trivial event – an example of mistaken identity by a gentleman towards a female in a Paris street. He thinks she is a thief. The woman is alarmed and says she does not know him; it is a case of mistaken identity. The writer goes on to explain the story in dramatic style using prose, speech and opinion. He also goes on to cite the history of tales of mistaken identity (BN, LC2 3011). In this edition, the accompanying 'feuilleton' was on the subject of a fire, but 30 years later a higher level of thematic synchronization between the subjects of leading news stories and the serialized novel emerged.

Thus, on 30 July 1896 Thomas Grimm's lead news story of the education of young girls/orphans of decorated soldiers was a typical opinion piece. Opinion embellished the facts, but the vision of female destiny was somewhat gloomy. The unattractive-sounding schools in the news article were followed by a 'feuilleton' on the same front page narrating, in a news-like way, a heroine's odious marriage, spiced with victims and domestic torture, but clearly designed to appeal to women. The cultural implications of the fact/fiction crossover were highlighted by Crubellier's question: 'Are reality and fiction so basically similar that the reader accords credibility to the latter that the former deserves, and to the former power of emotion that is communicated in the latter? (1991: 188)

At a time when French newspapers were at their most diverse, a distinction was emerging between high and low markets in the literary world. As Adamowicz-Hariasz notes : 'After the creation of the popular press in 1863, as an attraction that sustained their interest, the *roman-feuilleton* initiated and subsequently accustomed members of lower social classes to a new cultural practice: the daily consumption of information provided by a mass circulation press' (De la Motte and Przyblyski, 199: 181). In the climate of 'somnolent prosperity and silent misery' during the repressive Second Empire readers became tired of politics and welcomed the distractions of the addictive, exotic fantasy provided by 'feuilletons' (Préfecture de Police: Ea109).

Moïse Millaud's insistence on the need for dramatic journalistic style and his concern to manipulate the timing and nature of content in serialized novels, as well as Trimm's attempts to categorize female readers' taste, are examples of what James Carey described as 'rituals of identity formation'. He used this to argue that for newspapers to broaden their social and economic base, it was drama not information that was required (1989: 20–1). This tendency to frame events for a target audience increased during the second half of the nineteenth century due to increased pressure for space, prompted by the need to accommodate advertising, and an increased flow of news due to improved technologies in transport and communications. *Le Petit Journal*'s reports gradually became fashioned into 'stories' in the form of short (tabloid) snippets or 'faits divers'.

'Faits divers'

Le Petit Journal's new emphasis on 'faits divers',[9] especially crime coverage, accompanied the introduction to front (and inside) pages of pulp serialized novels. There was clearly a demand for such material, as *Le Petit Journal* became the first daily newspaper in Europe to achieve mass circulation with a 'modern' commercial approach and a cheap sales price of a 'sou'.

In fact, attempts to present the accumulation of wide-ranging human interest stories became a function of daily sales: 'By offering numerous categories of information, however disparate, the chances that one or another of them might correspond to a particular consumer's desire tended to increase' (Terdiman, 1985: 133). Each edition had to have a unique appeal. The ultimate demonstration of news trivia is exemplified in the 7 September 1896 edition of the paper. Positioned in the same edition as a lady's game to while away the hours at home (a kind of DIY cut out cardboard prism that acts as a visual trick to reverse vision) there was a lead story on dogs and cats, written by a journalist aptly given the nom-de-plume of Felix. From the article we learn (inter alia) that Baudelaire was a cat lover.

Unfortunately an increase in framing and tabloid style snippets of quick news ran the risk of equally speedy judgement, and as Pickering has observed, 'When people do judge others too quickly, they often do so according to the available stereotypes' (2001: 42). By 1896 the phrase 'faits divers', used initially to denote news items, was now associated more firmly with curious, violent or shocking news (Shaya, 2004: 42). 'Faits divers' had assumed tabloid properties.

Consumerism

Clearly, the tabloid properties identified so far – emphasis on the serialized popular novel and snippets of information, with a predilection for attention-grabbing crime coverage, written using fictional techniques, and aimed at female readers – all need to be assessed within the more general context of newspaper development. In the case of *Le Petit Journal* this was characterized by the encouragement of marketing, spectacle and consumerism. According to Hobsbawm the trend towards consumerism (which was not new – it had been established in Britain during the previous century) was not confined to bourgeois women: the advertising industry realized that it had to focus on the mass consumption desires of even fairly poor women (2005: 218).

It was Hippolyte de Villessmessant, founder and editor of *Le Figaro* who compared his newspaper to a department store that contained something for everyone, and it is no historical accident that the staggering success of *Le Petit Journal* with its clear commercial ethos coincided with the advent of the department store, first invented in France. The headquarters of *Le Petit Journal* became a consumer spectacle in its own right: the public could enter 'le palais de Petit Journal' and see the wonders of the cylindrical printing machines in motion through glass windows and visit the sales bazaar (Morienval, 1934: 202). By 1869 the newspaper's physical presence in the capital – the huge, impressive new headquarters – ostentatiously symbolized a Haussmanesque pretension to power and influence and also acted as a consumer identity that made its mark on the landscape.

Newspaper buildings formed part of a physical 'embourgoisement' that accompanied the symbolism of the female consumer and reader. Haussman was famous for his demolition of 117,000 houses in the centre of Paris, to create a functional and healthy city: the fine architecture is still predominant in Paris today, but it had the effect of driving the working classes further out geographically, and making Paris a bourgeois city. Similarly, in *Le Petit Journal*'s illustrations, female readers are depicted as distinctly respectable and bourgeois.

There was a symbiotic relationship between department stores as advertisers and the newspapers that published articles about products from the stores and welcomed the income: 'Spectacle and entertainment, on the one hand, the world of consumption on the other, were now truly indistinguishable' (Miller, 1981: 173).[10] Both parties shared a sense of the drama related to consumer spending and its incumbent culture, first analyzed by Karl Marx in *Das Kapital* (1867, vol. 1) as a form of 'commodity fetishism'. The Bon Marché premises at Sèvres-Babylon on the Left Bank soon became a cultural attraction as a centre for its own events, including concerts, art gallery displays and other large-scale special performances and an in-house print works and promotional department for what in modern terms would be called 'marketing'. As Miller says of the world's first pioneering emporium, 'The Bon Marché was like a great consumption empire, drawing to its center a cosmopolitan throng, conquering its provinces with its promotional legions, and then reaping the tribute from its outlying territories' (1981: 61).

Le Petit Journal also conquered the provinces, using the new railways for distribution. The intention was to target the new female consumers, as an extension of their bourgeois domestic role, by encouraging women to leave the home to purchase the necessities to provision it (Tiersten, 2001: 23) through consumer information supplied by newspapers. It was hoped women would emerge from their homes well informed by newspapers. Richard Terdiman also compares newspapers and department stores, arguing that the department store played a crucial role in propagating the habits of newspaper culture: 'Here in the emporium, as with the experience of reading the newspaper, the practice of a culture was profoundly modified, and a new articulation of social space and of individual needs, desires, and expectations was produced for nineteenth-century French people' (1985: 135).

Women were critical to this enterprise. The female as consumer was reflected in contemporary French literature by Zola, de Maupassant and others: in Zola's *Au Bonheur des dames* Denise Baudu, newly arrived in Paris from her provincial village, walks in amazement through the first department store that she has ever seen (Chapman, 2011b: 41–58). By the mid-nineteenth century women were also visible as consumers in the growing periodicals market. *Le Petit Journal's* illustrations depict female readers as upright bourgeoisie, precisely the category of female consumer referred to by Veblen.

However, writers such as Zola, de Maupassant and others reflected contemporary concern about the appeal of the advertising spectacle: even some journalists blamed visual culture for the degeneration of civic order and for manipulating hidden, irrational ideas. As the self-interest of the female domestic consumer was perceived to be threatening civic virtue (cartoons depicted women shoppers as capricious, gullible or demanding), they were encouraged by a range of social organizations to use their material position for the furtherance of moral and public causes – hence the 'virtuous' women who was charitable became the ideal role model in news stories.

In recognition of the ethical responsibility this entailed, women were encouraged by a range of social organizations to use their material position to further moral and public causes (Furlough, 1991). As French women did not obtain the vote until 1945,[11] feminist historians have argued that they actively contributed to the public sphere in a range of other ways such as social, charity and pressure groups (Reynolds, 1986). Ethical purchasing organizations were motivated by the view that advertising aimed at women was dangerous and irresponsible. Even some journalists criticized the appeal of the advertising spectacle itself, blaming visual culture for the degeneration of civic order (a concern with civic order emerges in content analysis relating to crime, as we shall see) and for manipulating hidden, irrational ideas. Thus, satirical illustrations in newspapers depicted women shoppers as capricious, gullible or demanding (Livois, 1965).

Parallel to this thinking ran an editorial interest in consumer-based subject matter aimed at female readers as the climate in which women could further their consumer interests began to improve. The new optimism of France's Third Republic was exemplified by *Le Petit Journal's* launch of *La Mode miniature féminine illustrée* in 1872. This was followed, in 1884, by the launch of an illustrated Sunday supplement, promoted as a public event with enormous banners outside its headquarters. Another form of promotion was newspaper stunts – copied later by Lord Northcliffe in *The Daily Mail* – which also helped to increase circulation. In 1891 *Le Petit Journal* created the Paris-Brest-Paris cycle race and in 1894 inaugurated the first motor car race, the Paris-Rouen Horseless Carriage Competition (Concours des Voitures sans Chevaux).

Methodology

Particular focus is given in this chapter to two years: the launch year of 1863 and also to the golden age of the popular press, especially 1896 when the *Le Petit Journal* was riding high as an established and successful brand name. How far were financial considerations coloured by masculine perceptions of what female audiences wanted and by the largely right-wing and later centre-right (Bonapartist) political sympathies among the newspaper's high profile editorial team? The year 1896 is significant in three ways: first, in that year the life of the company in terms of its legal standing was boldly extended by the shareholders to 1950 – symbolic of the paper's own confidence in its institutional strength; second, in Britain Lord Northcliffe, copying the success of *Le Petit Journal*, decided to launch a similar paper – *The Daily Mail* – inspired and heavily influenced by the success of France's first tabloid; third, this happened on the eve of a very different sort of newspaper launch (in 1897) namely that of France's *La Fronde*, owned by a woman and also produced and entirely staffed by women, both examined in the next chapter.

A decision-making role by men for female readers, in the absence of female journalists, editors and proprietors, begs the question: how were female readers catered for? Is it likely that gendered aspects in popular newspapers, when examined in the light of the business development of *Le Petit Journal*, would point to a conservative effect? This hypothesis was investigated by using a range of primary sources, as there are no discreet gendered archives classified as such, no memoirs for the founders or subsequent proprietors of *Le Petit Journal* and no surviving company archive. However, there are company annual accounts, liquidator's reports, bankruptcy records and other contemporary accounts, in addition to detailed police archives of relevant press leaders and their activities. It is one of newspaper history's little ironies that the more repressive the regime, the more controls on and monitoring of the press, and the more abundant the police records. Thus, I have used the papers of the Ministry of the Interior at the Archives Nationales (AN) in

Paris and Roubaix (the labour and business history archive; ANR), and the Préfecture of Police (PP), in addition to quantitative content analysis of the newspaper itself, taking a 30 per cent sample – that is, one in three of all editions in the years 1863 and 1896.[12]

A comparison between the paper's early days and its golden age in the 1890s serves to identify a number of significant trends for gender and newspapers that are also manifest in other countries, and at other points in history. The analysis that follows of old newspapers, of contemporary official archival sources such as government and police reports, plus other contemporary accounts of and commentary on *Le Petit Journal*, augmented by secondary contextual histories, combines to suggest that masculine imagination and symbolism was coloured by men's politics (not women's), men's perceptions of what sort of content sold newspapers (not women's) and by the financial considerations in the (male) world of business. *Le Petit Journal*, as the avatar of France's popular press can be analyzed by using various indicators of female influence. In terms of content analysis of the daily newspaper, quantitative measurement demonstrates that it is possible to differentiate between subject matter involving women and aimed at female readers that involved some form of interest in citizenship (public sphere activities, charity and community work), as opposed to consumer-oriented articles.

There is always, within newspapers, an ongoing assessment of editorial priorities in terms of the space allocated to certain types of content, so the consumer influence can be contrasted with another approach that favours non-consumer content, namely articles with implications for membership of society, and the attendant rights and duties. In the findings presented in Table 2.1, citizen-centred pieces (or citizenship), was defined accordingly, whereas consumer was defined as any aspect that involves spending money.

As female purchasing power (i.e. consumerism) has already been identified as a growing trend that was facilitated by newspaper advertising and the growth within the *Le Petit Journal* brand of consumer orientated

Table 2.1   *Le Petit Journal* 1863 and 1896. Percentage of female-oriented articles representing citizenship or consumerism – taken from a 33 per cent random sample

	Articles on women	Citizens (%)	Consumer (%)
Sample A 1863	418	76.3	23.6
Sample B 1896	656	80.9	19.3

journalism, editions were analysed separately to measure this in terms of the percentage of consumer orientated pieces. All stories that had overt sales offers/competitions/ads and the *feuilleton* (serialized novel) were categorized as consumer.

At first consumer articles appeared alongside news coverage in the daily paper, but by 1896 consumer content may have moved to the *Le Petit Journal* weekly supplements, such as *Illustré* and *La Mode*. This would account for the reduction in consumer-oriented content in 1896. However, the creation of these separate consumer-style weeklies provided opportunities for cross promotion, such as this notification in *Le Petit Journal*: 'Announcements to our readers – female subscribers receive *La Mode* dress patterns for 50 centimes, non-subscribers pay 75 centimes' (26 May, 1896: 3). The hope was clearly that women readers would subscribe to the *Le Petit Journal* brand as a total package.

Advertising

Newspaper serialized pulp fiction delivered female readers who appealed to advertisers as consumers. Advertising was important as a vehicle for both influencing women and identifying them as a cohort within the public sphere. Yet Zeldin's claims that 'publisher and advertiser were considered to be in league' and that 'with time advertising did indeed develop into something of a conspiracy, because so much trouble was taken to conceal its true character from the consumer' (1977: 512). The focus here is not so much on the method by which commercial income was obtained but rather on the fact that those in power were recognizing women as consumers while simultaneously and system-atically excluding them from their circles.[13] As explained earlier, the strength of the discursive public sphere during the nineteenth century was constituted by a growth in political and commercial groups, clubs and associations – from which women tended to be excluded. The activ-ity of bourgeois women usually centred on domestic organization and control of the purse strings for this, plus unpaid charitable, cultural and voluntary affairs. Advertising, through its various promotional appeals, provides a snapshot of this.

There were no display ads in the 1863 papers, but by 1896 a large por-tion of the newspaper was given over to poster advertising. The larger ads catering for women were paid for by Galéries Lafayette for furnish-ings, Menier for chocolate and *Le Petit Journal*'s own promotions for both *La Mode* and the supplement. Many pharmacies advertised rem-edies for stomach ailments and haemorrhoids. These ads were aimed to appeal to the female reader so that she could keep her family healthy. Singer regularly advertised their sewing machines, encouraging thrift and efficiency. Various bookshops advertised their latest popular reading lists coupled with offers on prints of famous paintings and sculptures of both Renaissance masterpieces and religious objects, notably the Virgin Mary. Regular ads for hair salons encouraged women to look their best. In addition there were the usual private ads of cartomancers. The 'virtuous' female in nineteenth century society sought to improve herself. In fact this is by far the largest type of approach represented in *Le Petit Journal* advertising: hair ads, improving literature/art/furnishings/modest fashions, and stomach medicines for the butter rich diet of the upwardly mobile! Expensive travel and lavish fashions also appeared as a strong feature of advertising.

Whereas in 1863 there were hardly any advertisements and very little content aimed at women, by 1896 both had increased exponentially, with the number of poster/box ads quadrupling and the extent of fact/fiction crossover doubling. The culture of advertising was endemic within the layout of *Le Petit Journal*, manifested in ways of thinking and support for causes that suggests 'product placement', in modern parlance. The 'attentive' reader (Zeldin, 1977: 517) would have recognized certain patterns of promotion as part of a process of what Crubellier (1974: 184–6) refers to as 'standardization' (by which he means a repetitive consistency in the organization of types of content and in its presentation) that contributed to a feeling of identification between reader and paper. In short, the identification of the serialized novel – always on page one – as a medium that appealed to women is well known, but its commercial significance, the newspaper context that surrounded it, and its resonance as a factor for the 'commodification' of women is an aspect that has hitherto been neglected.

Advertising in *Le Petit Journal* provides evidence that a readership of women was a recognized force. When Millaud died in 1871, he left the paper almost bankrupt. However, the fortunes of *Le Petit Journal* recovered as the paper accepted commercial donations in exchange for financial coverage and back page poster advertisements (les annonces-affiches), differentiated from the 'l'annonce anglaise' classified ads. The French advertisements amounted to a kind of publication notice board service over which the newspaper exercised no editorial control, according to Zeldin (1977: 517). Companies frequently placed them as a pay-off to prevent journalists writing critical articles or reviews about their products.

Even George Sand invited a journalist to lunch in order to obtain a favourable review of one of her novels, but of course she was experienced in the workings of newspapers (Chapman, 2007: 479–95) and would have been well aware that the majority of lower paid journalists were in the pay of theatres or publishers. The classic example of the advert as 'pay-off' is the story of a retailer who stopped advertising: the newspaper retaliated by carrying an article that the store was stricken with the plague, carried by its imported Oriental carpets. The store then decided to start advertising again! (Zeldin, 1977: 516).

Business orientation[14]

Although financial considerations prompted a cautious and socially conservative representation of women and perception of female readers, in many ways *Le Petit Journal* in 1863 reflected the prevailing political climate as a creature of the times. By 1867 circulation already exceeded that of all other Parisian newspapers combined, and an annual dividend of 72 francs 56 centimes was paid to shareholders, but this was based on a fictive company profit (ANR: AQ65A211). Meanwhile the company's debt to Marinoni for printing continued to rise (ANR: 65AQA211).

The original company, registered in the names of Moïse and Alphonse Millaud in 1863, had also comprised other titles, and included, inter alia, a separate printing enterprise and a bookshop. It was these, rather than *Le Petit Journal*, that had caused Alphonse to go bankrupt in 1866. In 1868 investors were asked to agree to the establishment of a limited company, with 4,000 shares, but the additional investment of 4,000 shares was illegal (ANR: 65AQU257/1; 65AQA211). Alphonse Millaud and co-director M. Silva were sentenced to four years in prison for deception of the public, and M.M. de Girardin, Jenty and Gibiat started a new *Le Petit Journal* company. This change of ownership had two effects in terms of attitudes towards women and female influence. First, it brought the paper closer to active politicians and financiers, especially those in Bonapartist political circles; second, de Girardin's long-established literary reputation, for he had authored several works focusing on women, made female subject matter in editorial more likely.

The launch of *La Mode du Petit Journal* represented an acknowledgement of the new market value of women – a 'commodification' of the female readership. The brand's expansion with new property development, an extended newspaper format, a new fourth edition, and the recently launched colour supplements (also one on agriculture), all amounted to over 410 million copies during 1895 and contributed to a mood of excitement, reminiscent of the1880s when *Le Petit Journal*'s circulation had first hit a million (ANR:65AQU257/2).

The huge room booked for the 1896 annual general meeting of the Société de Petit Journal was insufficient to accommodate shareholders who, full of excitement, spilled over into the galleries and neighbouring rooms of L'Hotel Continental. The AGMs of high profile companies such as La Société du Petit Journal became newsworthy and sometimes dramatic events in the Parisian social calendar.[15] These events were attended by bourgeois women as well as men, for their involvement as managers of the family household expenditure 'afforded women a new degree of financial and psychic independence and physical mobility' (Tiersten, 2001: 23).

Central to the golden age of capitalism in France and Britain was the role of banks and in France it was customary for them to donate lump sums to newspapers in order to secure positive coverage of financial services, using the popular press to reach a mass market via agents who charged a hefty commission. Léon Renier, for instance, distributed half a million francs a year to *Le Petit Journal* and two other newspapers, and later in his role as a director of the news agency Havas, tried to consolidate all the financial advertising in the country into a monopoly. Zeldin maintains that no bank could even consider raising money without bribing the press (1977: 522).

'Puff' or advertorial journalism

Unattributed but paid for 'advertorial' and promotional articles were so extensive that a contemporary book was published on the theme of how to 'read' newspapers – every article was paid for by someone (Zeldin, 1977). Interpretative research is made more difficult by the widespread existence of covert ads within 'advertorials' that are not named as such. Direct recommendation to investors by publishers or editors in articles boosted share prices, and promotion increased with the encouragement of finance (Zeldin, 1977: 513). Conveying information about a product or cause was big business, and this could work either for or against women, depending on the provenance of the money.

Puffs, hidden 'advertorials' (when they can be detected) and advertising in *Le Petit Journal* all provide evidence that a readership of women was a recognized force, especially by de Girardin who was a long-term supporter of universal suffrage, free education and women's rights. He published *La Liberté dans le marriage par l'egalité des enfants devant la mère* in 1864 and also wrote a play 'le Supplice d'une Femme' in collaboration with the Dumas brothers, to whom the success was attributed.

In 1880, the year in which de Girardin, as part of the paper's editorial and financial management team, was strengthening the existing structural business links between *Le Petit Journal* and his Banque Nationale by moving the paper from its 2 million franc 'Hotel de Petit Journal' building to more modest shared premises with the Banque Nationale and his newspaper *La France*, he was also writing as Thomas Grimm about the progress of women's education. This was one of de Girardin's favourite themes and timely because of imminent legislation, namely the Camille Sée education law that granted compulsory state education for girls at high school level, becoming law on 21 December 1880. The reform was seen as a means to safeguard against past practice of compulsory marriage.

De Girardin also expounded on aspects of women at work, attacking working women for neglecting their maternal duties, but went on to propose a remedy – the setting up of additional crèches. It so happens that the first of these have been sponsored by benefactresses: an indirect advertisement for investment (21 October: 1). The practice was common: 'Like politicians addressing the mass electorate, financiers used the popular press to reach a mass market' (Palmer, 1972: np).

Between 1880 and 1888, *Le Petit Journal* received more from the Panama Canal company than any other newspaper – 696,751F (an average of 77,000F a year), including 7000F as a direct payment to Cassigneul, who was the son-in-law of director Marinoni (Flory, 1897: 302). This was somewhat ironic given the paper's opposition to the canal (Mollier, 1991: 389). In the case of *Le Petit Journal*, the influence of one particularly corrupt bank (with Emile de Girardin as President) extended further than the norm, in that the liaison included structural, organic and political influence. In 1873 *Le Petit Journal* was bought by the business partnership of Gibiat, Jenty and de Girardin, with interests in seven newspapers, ensuring that, according to police reports, the newspaper would be 'destined to become a Napoleonic organ' (Préfecture de Police: Ba 1094, Ba1096). The Banque Nationale owned shares in *Le Petit Journal* and the names of other directorships in both organizations were virtually interchangeable. Established in 1878, the Banque Nationale increased its shareholdings and capital from 4 million to 30 million francs.

On the day of the bank's AGM in 1882, de Girardin died suddenly. This was precisely the moment when the bank's shareholders were due to discover the realities of the failed banking venture and hence their own personal losses. During his last days de Girardin had been accused of spying for Germany[16] and was forced to flee from Paris to avoid publicity. He was replaced by Charles Jenty, already in charge of *Le Petit Journal* as the general administrator. The timing of this dramatic scandal was particularly sensitive, as not only was the Banque Nationale being criticized for investing too heavily in newspapers such as *Le Petit Journal*, but it had also become involved in the Panama Canal Company financial scandal, issuing 590,000 shares to match an equal number issued by de Lesseps. The following year the bank was declared bankrupt (Préfecture de Police: Ba1096).

It is clear from the above that *Le Petit Journal's* editorial comments about women appeared within a fairly conservative political context. Although *Le Petit Journal* has been considered by some scholars to have shown its support for the republican parties during the 1870s and 1880s (Shaya, 2004: 63), this claim does not take into account the oscillations in political affiliations, or the fact that even as a supporter of the Republic, its politics remained centre to right. In 1871 Marinoni stood as a republican candidate for the National Assembly, but by 1885 he had changed his political affiliations and *Le Petit Journal* changed politics with him. There is also ample evidence of Bonapartist sympathies among the leading editorial personalities. In 1872 de Girardin had published letters and thoughts in *Le Petit Journal* in defence of Thiers (5 December 1872) and on the subject of the dissolution of the National Assembly. Commenting on this, police reports noted that he was still a devoted Bonapartist, evidenced by the fact that he stood for election in Paris the following year, supported by Bonapartist newspapers.

However, by 1874 *Le Petit Journal* was reported to have turned Republican because it was losing readers as a Bonapartist orientated newspaper (Préfecture de Police: Ba1096). Although de Girardin withdrew temporarily from editorial activity during 1875, and stood as a republican candidate for the Chamber elections in 1877, later becoming a Gambetta supporter, his pre-1874 Bonapartist politics caused Republicans to fear a comeback by Prince Napoleon in 1880, supported by de Girardin (who was his uncle), *Le Petit Journal* and other press (Préfecture de Police: Ba1096).

By 1885, Marinoni was running a high expenditure candidacy for the Chamber as a conservative Bonapartist and by 1896 was making a public stand as an anti-Drefusard, with all the anti-Semitic implications of this stance (Préfecture de Police: Ba1173).[17] The relevance here to the representation of women in *Le Petit Journal* is that by 1896 the paper was lagging behind social and political trends in respect of female citizenship rather than providing a lead. Remnants of Bonapartist 'one nation' politics seemed increasingly inappropriate to the *Germinal*-style class campaigning, industrial unrest and newly established labour organization of the period, and to the phenomenon of 'new women' and suffragist politics. *Le Petit Journal's* talk of eliminating class distinctions and uniting the classes nationally in readership has been referred to by one writer as 'the journalistic equivalent of Baron Haussman's renovations of Paris' in the 1860s (Shaya, 2004: 71). Similarly, in *Le Petit Journal's* illustrations, female readers are depicted as upright bourgeoisie – precisely the category of female consumer referred to by Veblen.

Analyzing women as news sources

Politics during the 1880s and 1890s was participatory, diverse and significantly class conscious, so contemporary males, even in Bonapartist circles were discussing the phenomenon of the 'new woman' that was seen to change the position of women in society (see Chapter 3). By 1896, women's increased mobility, thanks to railways and the bicycle, and new openings in employment with industrialization and economic change – all seemed to point to a challenge to gender relations and a gradual weakening of the patriarchal regime, reinforced by divorce reform and improved educational opportunities. Yet, although contemporary males were discussing the phenomenon of the 'new woman' during the 1880s and 1890s (Roberts, 2002; Schwartz 1998; Shapiro, 1996; Rioux and Sirinelli, 2002; Terdiman, 1985; De la Motte and Przyblyski, 1999), professional women were frequently depicted negatively, along with suffragists and female consumers (Tiersten, 2001: 23). The 'new woman' who aspired to a measure of independence, whether in education, her career, her sexuality, in politics or in the cultural sphere, was a pivotal figure around which much of this 'fin de siècle' anxiety coalesced as the commercial press communicated conflicting images of female consumers, new women, suffragists and professional women reformers (Roberts, 2002).

There was ample coverage of women's civil rights legislation and divorce reform around the time of legislation, and on women's issues more generally, including the first ever 'International Women's Rights Convention' that was held in Paris (25 July–9 August 1878). Divorce reform furthering the civil rights of women was passed on 27 July 1884 – this also provided plenty of scope for copy. Usually it consisted of front page opinion pieces by *Le Petit Journal's* leading (male) journalists, sometimes in the form of a discourse. During the summer of 1884 a debate ensued on the implications of divorce reform – how would the new law be applied by courts and tribunals (28 July)? Should women have the right to take out mutual insurance in their own names? What would the implementation of the act mean for France (1 July)?

Women's events and issues were taking centre stage, exemplified by articles on the feminist congress of 12/13 April 1896. Like modern day media coverage of politics, reports tended to focus on divisions and conflict or drama. They debated employment issues, and equal political rights of men and women. On humanitarian and international issues, they called for general disarmament and the neutralization of the Alsace-Lorraine region, but speeches on co-education were interrupted and in general the conference was reported as a long, emotionally over-excited tirade. Toward the end of the article the reporter documented a verbal attack by men and women on a Dutch woman speaker for being a 'savage', not speaking adequate French and giving the wrong impression of the country.

This sort of coverage exemplifies the fact that, for most scholars, tabloids are associated with the emergence of 'sensationalism' as a means of attracting mass circulation. This is characterized by a lack of seriousness accompanied by a taste for trivia, scandal, celebrity, superficiality and entertainment (Gripsrud, 2000; Sparks, 2000). In *Le Petit Journal*'s case, decisions were made by men about what the female audience was likely to be interested in, and defined fairly conventionally in representations that were sensational and increasingly negative. By 1896 the reality was that the politics of class conflict was evidenced by the new practice of May Day rallies and marches, the abundance of political and interest groups and various socialist parties, and the fact that the trade union movement (so realistically depicted in Zola's 'Germinal', for instance) was gathering increased support in the midst of strikes, organizationally consolidated by the new *Bourses du Travail* – a structural initiative aimed at the coordination of labour activities at the local level throughout the country.

Representation of women in society as either housewife or harlot has been explored by James McMillan (1981), and in Victorian society, as Pickering points out, these have been referred to as 'the fragrant angel in the house and the fallen woman in the street. This is sometimes represented in historical analysis as the Madonna/whore dichotomy, but it is the . . . same impossibly split model for female behaviour and identity' (2001: 5, 7). The role of newspapers in reflecting or encouraging this appeal is less commonly analyzed in detail – especially over a period of time in order to identify changes in attitude.

Longer term trends can be measured by a combination of inductive numerical (quantitative) and deductive (qualitative) methods, using a range of basic indicators of modern newspaper populism, first suggested by Maurice Crubellier (1974: 184–6): crime coverage, personalized human interest, standardization of text (that we construe as crossover between fact and fiction) attempts to attract readers through games and polls, and evidence of professionalization through by-lines and images. Quantitative measurement enables an appreciation of evolution, in this case between the selected years for content analysis of 1863 and 1896. It also facilitates an empirical assessment of the relative importance of each of the above newspaper characteristics, giving us the ability to compare and contrast relative quantity and hence editorial importance, at a glance.

Table 2.2 presents the number of female-centred articles as a percentage of total articles, according to Crubellier's indicators mentioned here. Women's influence on editorial can also be measured according to the increase between 1863 and 1896 in the percentage of words devoted to aspects of coverage in which women are mentioned, by differentiating between certain styles of literary presentation and content. The only one of Crubellier's indicators that does not demonstrate an increase in feminizing influence between 1863 and 1896 is 'evidence of professionalization through by-lines', despite the fact that more generally, the mainly middle class new 'women's market' generated an increase in jobs for female professionals. In fact, probably the largest body of new female professionals was aspiring journalists, but as freelancers or part-timers they were usually not given by-lines and there are no employment records. According to Veblen (1899), women could earn up to 150 pounds sterling a year as journalists by supplying the Australian press, but there is no comparable evidence of this category of work in the case of *Le Petit Journal*. Once more, women's history remains hidden.

Close reading of article content in *Le Petit Journal* reveals that most subject matter consists of certain categories of news matter. In terms of their representation women tended to be represented in extremes: 'victorious', 'virtuous', 'vicious' or 'victims', although in the early days of *Le Petit Journal* a range of articles did not fit these categories. On the positive side, 'victorious' and 'virtuous' were exemplified by an obsession with female royalty and on the downside, women of fallen virtue or criminals who were 'vicious', and the weaker sex as 'victims'.

The findings in this chapter act as a means of testing Pickering's theorization of stereotyping and as a springboard for consideration of

Table 2.2 Coverage of female-centred articles, *Le Petit Journal* 1863 and 1896

Year	Crime as lead (%)	Human interest (%)	Fact/fiction (%)	Games (%)	Poster ads (%)	By-lines (%)	Images (%)
1863	8	12	10	0	4	0	0
1896	15	18	20	3	16	0	7

Table 2.3   Changes in the space devoted to women, by type, *Le Petit Journal* 1863 and 1896

Groups	Status	Increase in coverage (%)
Victorious	Royalty, aristocracy	18
Virtuous	Aspiring to improve their status	13
Vicious	Criminally inclined	10
Victims	Stories of suffering	8

the nature of stereotyping in *Le Petit Journal*. He differentiates between categories and stereotyping – neither of which are permanently fixed: 'Stereotyping may operate as a way of imposing a sense of order on the social world in the same way as categories, but with the crucial difference that stereotyping attempts to deny any flexible thinking with categories. It denies this in the interests of the structures of power which it upholds. It attempts to maintain these structures as they are, or to realign them in the face of a perceived threat. The comfort of inflexibility which stereotypes provide reinforces the conviction that existing relations of power are necessary and fixed' (2001: 3).

The female presence in each of the four 'V' categories of content mentioned above was calculated as a percentage of the total number of news articles. As the amount of text increased between 1863 and 1896, so these categories also increased their share of coverage and their prominence on the page (based on a 30 per cent sample). The paper in general increased its word count by 30 per cent from 1863 to 1896 as the number of columns was enlarged from four to six. Articles exhibiting feminizing influences increased with the increased word count. The proportionate increase in the nominated categories is significant when it exceeds any automatic increase that would be anticipated as a result of the increase in the number of pages. By 1896 technological improvements had facilitated the introduction of certain tabloid characteristics such as games and images. Poster advertisements were also prevalent.

In terms of their representation women tended to be represented in extremes: 'victorious', 'virtuous', 'vicious' or 'victims', although in the early days of *Le Petit Journal* this was not the case. Table 2.3 provides details of the space provided to each of the categories.

Victorious

Female representation as victors constituted a celebrated elite of privilege. Such women were victorious because they benefitted from an elevated social status. When Queen Victoria visited France with her household entourage, family and dogs, the Scottish and Indian elements provoked a bizarre fascination. By 1896 it had become clear that the voyeuristic cult of royalty rivalled the twentieth century deification of Diana, the Princess of Wales.

Virtuous

The virtuous woman was closely allied to the victorious one – both were elevated to heights of approbation as role models, not so much in the quantity of articles as in the use of language for this category. Stories about virtuous women excited the Christian, educative morality that lent itself to popularization in this new style newspaper. Such was the story of Jeanne de Chanal, a brave nun who defied a German general and saved a town: '[She] was as modest as she was brave and devoted. She never wanted to talk about herself' (12 February 1896: 2). On 29 November 1896 the paper carried a news article 'On the virtue of women' by Pierre Giffard that was loaded with description, reflection, opinion and quotes about how women should comport themselves. Male opinions on this appeared frequently in the pages of the paper.

Vicious

One way that women should *not* comport themselves was with vicious behaviour, and crime coverage provided ample anecdotal evidence of what readers should avoid. On 23 July 1863 (3), a 'vicious' woman was convicted for stealing and for breaking a ban to enter Paris; she claimed she had lost her way. On 20 June 1896 (4) under a heading of 'Fille Criminelle', a girl plotted to kill her father for not allowing her to marry a house servant, who assisted her in the plot. Women of fallen virtue also provided good stories – in fact coverage of prostitution rivalled de Maupassant's obsession with the subject.[18] This was paralleled by contemporary anxiety about the production and consumption of popular newspapers, organized 'around common, late-nineteenth century images of women such as the mad reader and the prostitute' (De la Motte and Przyblyski, 1999: 310). However, the press generally preferred to depict the prostitute as working towards redemption, for such representation appeared more magnanimous: then such women could be described as unfortunate 'victims'.

Victims

This is easily the largest category shown in Table 2.3. Chalaby refers to a syndrome of 'miserabilism' on the part of journalists who 'made a good living out of others' misery' (1996: 317). Certainly the pages of

Le Petit Journal abound with such examples – usually about women. On 23 July 1863 the paper carried a story about an assassination attempt on a Madame Legendre by a man who climbed through her bedroom window 'with the intention of catching her and satisfying his desires'. When she resisted, the man struck her so many times that she lost consciousness and could not remember where her injuries came from. Vivid descriptions of injuries were common, even in the case of the mysterious death of a six-month-old baby on a bench at the Gare de Nord, reported on 13 January 1896.

Similarly, although by 1896 the tone of *Le Petit Journal*'s emphasis on 'virtuous' was now more inclusive in that there were more stories about women who sought to improve themselves in society by doing good works, they were depicted as either 'victorious' or 'virtuous' in a conservative way. Typically, positive elements in a story were diluted by comments that decried recent attitudes. An article on 30 January 1896 announced that the paper thought it would be a good idea to name girls' schools after famous women: however, editorial comment within the article pointed out that it was the men who became the real heroes. The prevailing morality was always that women should be good wives and mothers, as the way to true happiness.

Girardin's articles and the educational trajectory of *Le Petit Journal* may well have contributed to the national mood for reform, but it would be wrong to see the paper's publicity in this respect as necessarily progressive. Positive elements in educational stories (and on other aspects of female citizenship that also increased in numbers) were sometimes diluted by criticism of recent changes. Despite recent educational reforms, the implication in 1896 was that too much (higher level) knowledge was a bad thing for women. It was no surprise, therefore, that on 4 March 1896 an article described how 'university madness overtook our unfortunate French families, pushing thousands into ruin and into misery by taking on their over intelligent daughters'.

The influence of Rousseau, as expressed in *Emile*, was still evident: 'The whole education of women ought to be relative to men. To please them, to be useful to them, to make themselves loved and honoured by them, to educate them when young, to care for them when grown, to counsel them, to make life sweet and agreeable to them – these are the duties of women at all times, and what should be taught them from their infancy' (1906: 263).

A reduction in what can be construed as positive coverage (virtuous, victorious) and a rise in negative coverage (vicious, victims – usually crime reporting) is reflected in the measurement above. Finally, these same categories are presented as a proportion (indicated as a percentage) of all articles (see Table 2.4). The changes between the two years suggest an increased focus on categories (as opposed to disparate articles that do not fit into these categories). This could be construed as an increase in stereotyping, as defined by psychologist Gordon Allport: 'an exaggerated belief associated with a category. Its function is to justify (rationalise) our conduct in relation to that category' (1954: 191). On the 'good' side, women were depicted as 'victorious' and 'virtuous', exemplified by an obsession with female royalty; on the downside, women of fallen virtue or criminals were 'vicious' or as the weaker sex were 'victims'.

These figures suggest a slight decline in 'good news' (virtuous, victorious) but a marked increase in 'bad news' (vicious, and victims) items, with a rise in victims, an axiomatic feature of crime coverage, that was boosted by high profile court cases such as the 'Affaire Troppmann'. Delporte claims that the masses recognized themselves in the media products that had been constructed for their consumption (1998: 120). Society gossip about the rich and famous, usually royalty, fed the public's curiosity and allowed for the kind of reader identification with celebrity that is so resonant today. Trimm's amateur theories on the psychological profile of female readers suggest empathy towards the victims of horrific crimes, yet within Carey's perspective of 'rituals of identity formation' (1989: 20–1), there is a discernible change in editorial tone between earlier years and 1896.

However, these longer term changes are still accompanied by an ongoing inconsistency in attitudes towards women. The latter is identified by Pickering, for whom 'the distinctiveness of category mismatches' should be viewed as: 'a characteristic of modernity' in stereotyping (2001: 7). In 1863 the creation of a community of readers, as identified by the *Le Petit Journal* editorial team, centred on content that was not offensive to women, but by 1896 the overarching belief that the female

Table 2.4 Coverage of women, by editorial type, *Le Petit Journal* 1863 and 1896

Women's status	1863	1896
Victorious (%)	11	8
Virtuous (%)	15	14
Vicious (%)	12	11
Victims (%)	32	48
N/A (%)	30	19
No. of articles	415	655

readership wanted graphic crime stories had led to prurient and critical coverage that collectively added up to an increased volume of negative representations of women as victims and as irrational criminals.

Conclusions – the emergence of gendered tabloid properties

The evidence in this chapter has some resonance with contemporary arguments by scholars such as Franklin (1997), that the diversion of audiences away from issues of political relevance to a 'soft' tabloid focus on human interest, sport, scandal, celebrity and entertainment challenges the ability of current affairs to provide debate as a function of citizenship. Although *Le Petit Journal* did not yet carry sport, and its definition of celebrity was restricted mainly to foreign royalty (in republican France) and upper-class women, nevertheless by the end of the nineteenth century a tension was emerging in content between a more traditional approach and more recent, controversial forms of female representation, epitomized by discussions about, and literary interest, in the phenomenon of 'new woman' (Caine, 1997: 136–44).

A reduction in positive coverage (virtuous, victorious) and a significant rise in negative coverage (victims) confirm the importance of crime and prostitution in the news stakes as tools to increase circulation. Whereas by 1896 more specialist periodicals and journals carried feminist debates on personal morality and private conduct linked to political demands for emancipation (Roberts, 2002; Reynolds, 1986), in *Le Petit Journal* such issues were transformed into individual tales that were presented as either 'good' (virtuous, victorious) or 'bad' (victims, vicious). The vehicle for this trend was a textual narrative (usually 'fait divers') that was frequently sparked by a supply of individual court cases, or by the spectacle and moral example of royal or 'society' events and charity.

The example of France's first popular daily suggests that nineteenth century newspapers manifested 'tabloid' aspects before the phrase came into common parlance, but does this evidence amount to early 'tabloidization'? The latter is usually defined by scholars as a twentieth-century process of more widespread infiltration of the everyday concerns of non-elite readers (including women) into the news media, but for Turner the present usage of the word exemplifies a 'moral panic' apropos women, and a 'widely accepted label for a set of established debates about contemporary shifts in media content, production and consumption' (2004: 76, 78). He believes that the term is so widely applied that its analytical utility is threatened – but this had not yet become the case during the nineteenth century pioneering years of the popular press. Thus, to be more precise, *Le Petit Journal* provided an early example of some – but not all – tabloid properties, but was a precursor of 'tabloidization'.

The effect in the case of representation of women was not to contest bourgeois societal values. *Le Petit Journal* was *not* a site for resistance to cultural hegemony. The success of *Le Petit Journal* was built on risky and often illegal business dealings that had the effect of over-prioritizing financial considerations, resulting in a cautious and socially conservative perception of women, both editorially and as consumers/readers. Rather the evidence here supports the view (Grabe et al., 1999: 636) that tabloids support society's dominant values by presenting spectacular examples when such norms are transgressed. This was the case with the paper's main tabloid property – crime and the negative depiction of women.

The proprietors of *Le Petit Journal* recognized from the beginning that crime sold newspapers – indeed this same assessment was by no means new – it had already been made in England with coverage of the Bow Street Runners prior to Sir Robert Peel's establishment of a police force in the 1830s, and in the United States by penny press coverage of high profile murder cases (Chapman, 2005a). The fact that *Le Petit Journal* reprinted articles from the American press, while in Britain *The Daily Mail* lifted them from *The Telegraph* and from *Le Petit Journal*, would indicate that there was a shared transnational interest, at least to some extent, in crime coverage. However, more detailed quantitative analysis is needed in order to explore the wider gendered implications of this trend in terms of female representations and perceptions of the new female readership.

Research in this chapter clearly indicates a fairly traditional perception of women, and the argument is not simply a case of twenty-first-century values being imposed on a nineteenth-century phenomenon. In 1863 the paper appeared to be a creature of its time – a reflection of Second Empire Bonapartism (Eveno, 2003: 22). Textual analysis suggests that it was far from apolitical, even in the early days, although the government at this time formally incentivized a 'non-political press', led by *Le Petit Journal*. It is difficult not to conclude that the more overtly politicized the paper became, the more representation of women suffered. By adopting a more traditional view of women's needs in order to gain mass appeal, mass circulation dailies offered the potential for distracting attention away from radical ideas about women, explained in more detail in the next chapter. Although women's suffragist events such as international conferences were reported, there was no open or direct support for the enfranchisement of women, or for other radical female organizations.

It seems that conservative, speculative and sometimes corrupt business influences on *Le Petit Journal* form a backdrop to editorial content with increasingly negative forms of representation of women, motivated by the financial incentive of larger circulation. An obsession with financial 'bottom lines' such as circulation, dividends and profits underwrote a whole range of cautious values towards women and how they should be both represented and catered for, influenced by the political support of *Le Petit Journal*'s various directors and proprietors for the Bonapartist centre and right.

The contribution of the serialized novel as a tool for profit making is clear and the quantitative analysis of citizenship versus consumerism indicates that the latter is evident in several other forms: puff journalism, bank donations and cross ownership. These findings amount to a form of popular conservative feminization, a phenomenon that has the effect of dating tabloid properties to an earlier period than previously indicated by historians, and can be defined by the following characteristics: coverage of trivia rather than female citizenship; negative and graphic representation of women in crime coverage; political support of *Le Petit Journal*'s various directors and proprietors for Bonapartist centre and right; an obsession with financial 'bottom lines' such as circulation, dividends and profits; a patronizing leadership role in defining the taste of readers of the opposite sex; and an encouragement of traditional upper-class and establishment values in novels and features.

Contemporary tensions between emerging female citizenship – both consumer and political – and more traditional views of female domestic interests in the context of the continuing realities of economic, social and political disempowerment (despite reforms) were not always reflected in the pages of *Le Petit Journal*. Writers in *Le Petit Journal* touched on issues such as divorce, childcare and education in editorials as well as in 'faits divers', but by and large did so in a way that reaffirmed traditionally gendered values through a preference for sensationalized morality tales.

Consumers initially gained purchase through a civic identity, shaped by political trends that were economically embedded in the culture of empire, but what was at stake in the double articulation of media as conveyors of consumerism and media products such as newspapers as consumer goods? Ways of championing the citizen and the consumer, as outlined in the next chapter, help the historian to position Alfred

Harmsworth's formidable and impressive achievements in newspaper publishing.

The next chapter also analyses how some women challenged the types of representation that have been depicted in categories here. In fact, Pickering, quoting Hall, calls for us to consider: 'shifting the focus of theoretical attention' away from the binary evaluative categories they involve and onto 'the process of classification itself' (2001: 202, Hall, 1993: 23). Arguably newspaper representation of women is a symbolic example of the interrelation in society between centre and periphery that requires further consideration of how classifications were either conformed to or challenged transnationally, and the processes that this involved. These are all ways that emerging aspects of cultural citizenship as well as cultural consumerism can be assessed.

3
France and Britain
Cultural Citizenship and the Rise of Consumer Society

The previous chapter examined *Le Petit Journal* as a case study, but these findings need to be tested in a comparative manner. The case study contained both quantitative and qualitative analysis in its investigation of early forms of cultural consumerism and citizenship. This chapter continues the combination of methodologies by comparing the French daily to *The Daily Mail*. The aim is first to explore how far the gendered values and approaches discovered in *Le Petit Journal* were discernible elsewhere; especially in the British mass circulation dailies of proprietor Alfred Harmsworth (later Lord Northcliffe).[1] An examination of the early days of *The Daily Mail* reveals the influence of the *Le Petit Journal*. It is clear that Harmsworth saw a readership among women, and crucially, a female advertising market – although the range of material that would appeal to female readers is much larger. It is as important to consider his rejections as well as his inclusions.

Second, a comparison between France's daily *La Fronde* (established 1897) and Britain's *The Daily Mirror* (launched originally in 1903 by Harmsworth as a paper produced for and by women) demonstrates the contemporary tensions between socially cautious 'conservative feminization' and *La Fronde*'s more radical concept of news produced by and for women. This chapter explores why and how *The Daily Mirror* experiment failed within its first three months, whereas the paper that had served as an inspiration, *La Fronde*, survived for longer. The existence of *La Fronde* in France, a daily that provided a bridge between serious debates about and by women on the one hand, and on the other hand, conservative feminization of most popular dailies, demonstrates an alternative way of catering for female readers and of using female production workers and journalists to provide the service.

The argument presented is that an alternative range of outlooks towards gender and newspapers as a consumer product was available – and was entering the mainstream agenda. Yet this claim needs to be qualified: many of the serious discourses of the period that provided regular fare in specialist journals and periodicals were missing from the women's pages of mass circulation dailies. It is only possible to appreciate the various approaches and processes of categorization in terms of what was included and what was not, by some exploration of trends, debates, longer term developments and changes in attitude – between periods, different sorts of print publications and countries, some of which are addressed in this chapter.

The influence of periodicals

Periodicals acted as a model for popular consumerism that the new mass circulation dailies could draw inspiration from. As feature articles and women's pages became popular and advertising aimed at female consumers also increased in importance, mainstream media demonstrated an ability not only to appeal to women readers but also to commodify them (Chapman and Nuttall, 2011: 254). The relationship between consumerism and citizenship as it impinged upon women needs further elaboration. Brewer and Trentmann refer more generally to 'potential synapses between consumption and citizen [that are] so often ignored' but make the point that these stabilize the idea and identity of the consumer, by connecting it with favourable views of society and politics (2006: 52). Women's magazines had long provided an alternative space that essentially reinforced female domesticity within a developing consumer-oriented environment. The earliest magazine devoted to women was the London-based *Lady's Magazine* (1770) (Chapman and Nuttall, 2011: 252–3). This was followed in 1798 by the *Lady's Monthly Museum*, launched by 'A Society of Ladies', and in the new century John Bell started *La Belle Assemblée* (1806). These three magazines, which merged in 1832, were aristocratic rather than popular but 'established the woman's magazine as the genre we understand today' (Beetham, 1996: 17). The first American example of a popular women's magazine was *Godey's Ladies Book* (1830–98). There had been other American publications for women, but *Godey's* was the first successful one, and 'the first to approach the now standard format' (Seneca, 2009). This included short stories, poetry, job advertisements and addressed personal issues. Most importantly, 'readers could become involved in the course and nature of the publication' (Seneca, 2009) because much of the content was reader-generated. It also included fashion plates but it was not until Ebenezer Butterick published the *Delineator* (1863–1937) 'that fashion magazines really came into existence' (Seneca, 2009). Later examples include the now famous *Ladies Home Journal* (1883–present) and *Good Housekeeping* (1885–present) both of which used reader's letters, questionnaires and product 'quality guarantees' as ways of maintaining reader involvement.

Newspapers like Britain's *Women's Penny Paper* (1888–90) used women to write about women but enjoyed little success. The *Women's Penny Paper* is now best remembered for its support of the suffrage movement, where it found its most faithful audience. *Le Petit Journal* and *The Daily Mail* can be seen as a counter-current to such newspapers as the *Women's Penny Paper* in Britain and *Truth* in America which, as much because of their content as their target readership, were largely marginalized as 'feminist' products.

Early periodicals and newspapers that were sold through subscriptions also contributed to the creation of a sense of reader community. This was exemplified by political journals that shared with political party subscription the ability to engender recognition by financial supporters that they – together – formed a group of like minded people (Leonard, 1996: 48). In the United States the dispersed and often difficult to reach population meant that subscription systems could be critical to the survival of publications concerned with socialism and women's rights, for instance. Agents travelled thousands of miles across the country giving speeches at public meetings, introducing new ideas and publicizing the newspaper that communicated these concepts. *Appeal to Reason* had an army of agents nationwide and sold close to one million copies (Chapman and Nuttall, 2011: 259). Significance for the creation of audience also arose from the fact that for journals such as *Ladies' Home Journal* – the most popular women's periodical in the United States by the turn of the century – subscriptions were often generated as a result of negotiation on price and editorial policy by club members (Chapman and Nuttall, 2011: 259). This kind of democratic involvement acted as a form of consumer-based political power, further enhanced by the fact that this particular journal published the work of muckrakers such as Jane Addams, who went on to win the Nobel Peace Prize. Investigative journalism, or muckraking as it was called in the United States, became a high profile example of the potential for gendered cultural consumerism.

Thus, women were already visible as a consumer force in the growing periodicals market – an influence that had extended to daily newspapers by the mid nineteenth century as advertising revenues gradually started to replace political party subventions as the chief source of revenue for the press. The process created a 'commodified' journalistic discourse that gradually began to replace the old fashioned Romano-Greek inspired public discourse of outdoor mass meetings (Chalaby, 1998: 66). The presence of advertisers in mass circulation papers was accompanied by an ideological shift in newspaper editorial content that began to include features, fiction, recipes, games and fashion, such that women were identified for the first time as consumers. Despite the fact that *Le Petit Journal* carried much fewer ads than *The Daily Mail*, the trends that it set (see Chapter 2) were being replicated elsewhere, and in general, the female as a consumer was much discussed by the second half of the nineteenth century.

Audience and the evolution of newspaper visual appearance

There is a stark difference between the visual appeal of newspapers from the early nineteenth century and the *fin de siècle*. Conventions of layout and style were only gradually established and it was the weekly rather than the daily press that became the seedbed of innovation. The *Illustrated London News*, for example, published in 1842, was the world's first illustrated weekly. Costing sixpence, the magazine had 16 pages and 32 woodcuts. Mid century saw the growth of the populist Sunday press in Britain with *Lloyds Weekly Newspaper* (1842), a competitor to the *Illustrated London News*, the *News of the World* (1843) and *Reynolds's Weekly Newspaper* (1850). These papers combined woodcut illustrations with sensationalist reporting of crimes and scandal. The first pictorial daily was the *Evening Illustrated Paper* of 1881. Three years later *Le Petit Journal Illustrée* was launched as an illustrative Sunday supplement, with a now iconic all visual front page. Early news photographs had to be engraved before they could be printed. The New York *Daily Graphic* published the first halftone reproduction of a news photograph in 1880 and by 1897 halftone photographs could be printed on presses running at full speed.

The significance of breakthroughs in visual technology is that, in conjunction with other contextual factors, the 'audience design' (Bell, 1994) of the newspaper began to reflect its readers' expectations as well as the paper's own cultural and political inclinations. By the end of the century the telegraph and an expanding railway network both ensured a quicker and more extensive circulation of information at a time when page space was also under pressure from the increased demands of advertising. Although printing technology had advanced significantly, the verbatim report – the mainstay of the serious paper – gradually became truncated and turned into what became known as a 'story': something that could be chopped about to fit the available space. As news styles developed, so also did ways of handling audiences. Decisions about what should be sacrificed and what should be published, as well as decisions about what version of events best suited a particular audience, all formed part of an emerging philosophy that was gradually formalized around concepts such as news agendas and news values. This compact with the audience came to underpin the news agenda and provided a powerful articulation of a paper's promise to its readers, in both its reporting and its opinions. Thus, on launching *The Daily Mail*, for example, Alfred Harmsworth instructed his staff to write in a plain, clear style for his lower to middle-class readership and later, in his account of the paper, attributed *The Daily Mail*'s success to its brevity and 'compactness' (Harmsworth, 1903).

New Journalism

The first 'New Journalism' was characterized by visual as well as content and business developments that laid the roots of the twentieth century's popular newspapers with the use of new technologies to produce more eye-catching layouts, complemented by a writing style that was popular and emotive. In 1895 this was described by Evelyn March Phillips, writing in the *New Review* as: 'that easy personal style, that trick of bright, colloquial language, that determination to arrest, amuse and startle' (Holland, 1998: 20). In Britain the visual change extended to front pages, and in some papers the old style of densely crammed advertisements gave way to an attractive design of content. In fact, changes in visual presentation that pointed towards a disconnected montage intended to seize reader attention while glancing through the pages were advertiser led/developed 'partly to accommodate illustrated and boxed advertisements, while the use of exclamatory and hortatory advertising slogans prefigured the use of striking headlines' (Holland, 1998: 20).

An increased attention to the visual was thought to appeal to women; certainly 'New Journalism' tended to have a levelling effect, representing a further move towards mass appeal, exemplified by entertainment and sensationalism and also by high profile campaigns and investigations. As W.T. Stead said, 'Society . . . outwardly, indeed, appears white and glistening, but within is full of dead men's bones and rottenness' (Chapman, 2005a: 75).

The main development in content at this time was a move from editorial towards more news, in an attempt to offer access to more and different types of information. Therefore, definitions of what constituted news and how it could be presented were also undergoing a fundamental shift. Significantly, 'New Journalism' became inescapably bound up with notions of the feminization of the press through more human interest stories and features and the rise of this phenomenon, both in the big cities in the United States and in Britain. This was an important factor in generating journalistic openings for women from the 1880s until World War I, because it broadened the topics covered in dailies, with those attributes that were deemed to distinguish the female from the male being similarly employed to distinguish the New Journalism from the Old. A milestone occurred when Pulitzer bought out the *New York World* in 1883. This paper was one of the first to include a women's page (Smith 1979: 159) for Pulitzer recognized the growing importance to advertisers of women as an economic force.

New Journalism was intimate rather than authoritative; it stressed the personal note in its reporting and, moreover, focused much more on the lives of ordinary people rather than pursuing the heroic public figure, while still tackling political affairs and public welfare, but by favouring the urban working classes (Chambers, Steiner and Fleming, 2004: 20). One pioneer was the editor of Britain's *Pall Mall Gazette*, W.T. Stead, who created a sensation when he mainstreamed the commercial formula by publishing a reworking of the melodrama of urban sexual adventure in a marathon exposure of child sexual slavery entitled the 'Maiden Tribute of Modern Babylon'.[2] The ensuing controversy was so great – in parliament, the law courts, public protests and in the pages of other press – that an estimated *one and a half million* unauthorized copies of his articles were distributed.

According to Judith Walkowitz, the way the press recounted sensational stories of sexual danger helped to consolidate a public sphere in which new social actors participated in the national political culture: 'In the pages of the daily and periodical press, protesting workers, platform women, girls in business and Glorified Spinsters (sic) appeared as telling and disturbing signs of modernity' (1992: 80). The mass culture of New Journalism signalled simultaneously a shifting of the public discourse on sexuality, and a fresh stage in the development of a mass market that was now segmented into multiple reading publics, including women – who were encouraged to communicate a new sexual subjectivity publically (discussed later). According to Walkowitz, 'In fact and fantasy, London had become a contested terrain: new commercial spaces and journalistic practices, expanding networks of female philanthropy, and a range of public spectacles, from the Hyde Park "Maiden Tribute" demonstration of 1885, to the marches of the unemployed and the match girls in the West End, enabled working men and women of many classes to challenge the traditional privileges of elite male spectators and to assert their presence in the public domain' (1992: 11).

Yet for critics such as the British novelist and essayist Matthew Arnold there were many dangers inherent in any alternative public sphere. Arnold believed that culture was the pursuit of 'sweetness and ligh', a 'study of perfection' (1987: 205) and a necessary bulwark against anarchy. The 'great aim of culture,' he believed, was to set 'ourselves to ascertain what perfection is and to make it prevail' (Arnold, 1987: 207). His distinction between traditional Old Journalism as 'organs of reason' (Arnold, 1987: 258–9) and the New Journalism as 'feather-brained' (Arnold, 1887: 638–9) was a factor that, according to Margaret Beetham, 'implicitly mobilized the vocabulary of gendered identity', as part of a more general 'feminization' of culture with domestic and private values assuming a new significance (in Britain) (1996: 122). It was feared by some contemporaries that such content would have a corrupting influence on the potentially impressionable and irrational female reader, as it was seen by some contemporaries to represent a form of immoral de-politicization of the press.

'New woman' and other fashionable new terms

In France, women were criticized as both political figures and as domestic consumers whose self-interest threatened civic virtue (Tiersten, 2001). The debate focused on issues that were first surfacing in the popular press, in fiction and in drama during the 1880s and 1890s. The phrase 'new woman' had burst onto the British literary and journalistic scene in 1894: even Mr. and Mrs. Harmsworth went to see a London play called 'The New Woman' (British Library: 62382). In fact, during the 1890s and early twentieth century the phrase was followed by other new words such as 'feminist', 'suffragist' and 'suffragette'. Although the 'new woman' was virtually synonymous with advocacy of female rights, nevertheless women themselves were divided over the scope of reforms.

Dominating much literary and social debate by the mid 1890s, the concept actually embodied much of the *fin de siècle* questioning of institutions, beliefs and assumptions, especially those connected with marriage, family life and sexuality. In gender terms, the effect of this high profile was to raise the question as to whether or not women wanted to reject marriage and family ties. Female reformers were particularly concerned about 'healthy reproduction', reflected by the social and scientific thinking of the period, and by the success of Josephine Butler's campaign against the Contagious Diseases Acts in later Victorian England. This demonstrated the centrality within the public sphere, especially among parliamentarians and members of the professions, of debates about sexual conduct (Walkowitz, 1992). 'Sexual conduct was, therefore, an explicit political issue for at least several decades' (Scott, 1999: 23). Furthermore, imperial expansion and social Darwinism resulted in a significant interest in eugenics (supported by many feminists as scientifically progressive because of the way it elevated the status of mothers and attacked the sexual double standard). Equally, sexuality was positioned at the core of personal identity by the emergence of sexology and psychoanalysis as articulated by thinkers such as Havelock Ellis. For female reformers, this was accompanied by a revival of interest in the personal stories and writings of earlier pioneers such as Mary Wollstonecraft (Caine, 1997: 138).

Discussion on the nature of 'feminism' followed on those concerning 'new woman': although definitions of both were fairly vague, it would be fair to say that feminist identity differed substantially from its twentieth century incarnation. Although it extended beyond social and political attitudes to personal life and identity, the nineteenth century meaning was liberally extended to those who simply supported educational improvements or other reforms for women. During this period there was also a revival of socialism as a word and as a movement, with a proliferation of organizations embarking upon a whole range of social, educational and recreational activities such as cycling groups, the newspaper *Clarion* caravans (see Chapter 5) and Fabian summer schools. For women, such activities connected socialism with private life, personal and political identities, and sexual relations. According to Caine, discussion of the latter 'brought a closer sense of the connection between liberation, comradeship, intellectual challenge and new lifestyles on the one hand, and social and political transformation on the other' (1997: 143).

Comparisons between *Le Petit Journal* and *The Daily Mail*

In contrast to the above *Le Petit Journal*'s appeal to a female French audience was unashamedly mainstream. During the period that *Le Petit*

Journal was building its circulation, the young Alfred Harmsworth (who was born two years after the establishment of *Le Petit Journal* in 1863) and his brother Harold, were starting to build the biggest periodical publishing house in the world. Harmsworth's early journalistic experience was gained with low circulation niche magazines such as *Youth* and *Bicycling News*. But, crucially, he was also an occasional contributor to George Newnes' weekly magazine *Tit-Bits*. It was the success of *Tit-Bits* that fuelled Harmsworth's ambition to set up a rival magazine and in 1888, aged 23, he published the first edition of *Answers to Correspondents*. The first weekly issue, priced at one penny, was an immediate success. Content included: Strange Experiences, Curious Facts, Tests for the Eyesight, What the Queen Eats, Swindling Advertisers, 100 Jokes. *Answers*, as it became known, sold over 200,000 copies a week at its height (Chapman and Nuttall, 2011:123). Eight years later, in 1896, he published the first edition of his new newspaper, *The Daily Mail*. This, together with *Answers* and the more recently acquired *Evening News* (London) formed the bedrock of what was then to become the largest periodical publishing empire in the world, Amalgamated Press.

At the height of his success, Harmsworth was launching a new magazine every six months, transferring both the ideas and profits from his periodicals into the world of newspapers. By 1919 he owned a chain of 31 newspapers including *The Times*, *The Sunday Times*, *The Daily Mail*, *The Daily Mirror* and *The Observer*, as well as six magazines and two wire services. Northcliffe's empire was essentially national but at its zenith he controlled a larger share of Britain's newspaper circulation than did Rupert Murdoch in the 1990s. Lord Northcliffe, of course, headed a predominantly print-based organization, despite opportunities for diversification into the new technologies of radio and film.

Harmsworth was much impressed by the business achievements of *Le Petit Journal*, headed in 1896 by Hippolyte Marinoni. The former's diaries record 'the wife and I are off to live in Paris for the month of November' (1894, British Library: 62382). In fact they made regular visits to *Le Petit Journal*'s headquarters to pick Marinoni's brains. Harmsworth diary entries about his social activities, closely linked to his perceived business needs, indicate a certain competitive identification with the Frenchman. Certainly there are comparisons to be made in terms of the political involvement of the proprietors of *Le Petit Journal* and *The Daily Mail*: both claimed to be financially independent of parties, but in fact were highly political, witnessed by their political experience. Harmsworth stood as a conservative candidate for Portsmouth in 1895. In 1871 Marinoni stood as a republican candidate for the

National Assembly and in 1885 as a conservative Bonapartist. By 1896 he was an anti-Dreyfusard (Préfecture de Police: Ba1173). Indeed, A.J. Balfour wrote to Harmsworth on 7 May 1896, 'you have taken the lead in newspaper enterprise, and both you and the Party are to be heartily congratulated', and on 18 July 1899 he offered thanks for *The Daily Mail* support in the St Pancras by-election (British Library: 62153). Northcliffe's political affiliations are well documented (Thompson, 2000: 35), even if the implications of his outlook for early gendered content are not.

On 15 November 1894, while staying in Paris Harmsworth visited the printing of *Le Petit Journal*, with the comment: 'didn't think much of it' – although the world famous Marinoni-invented rotary presses had long been a tourist spectacle available for public viewing through glass windows. He seemed to have been more fascinated by *Le Petit Journal's* editorial obsession with crime coverage as a good seller, for he also took a tour of Parisian 'criminal quarters' accompanied by a policeman. On 17 November 1894 he spent the afternoon at the *Le Petit Journal* offices, and a few days later went to the Opera as a guest of Marinoni. The following day, and again a few days later Mr. and Mrs. Harmsworth dined at the Marinoni house. On 26 November he lunched at a restaurant 'with Marinoni's party'.

He and his wife left Paris on 28 November, with a diary recording 'everything going well'. Back in London, he and his brother Harold drafted a plan for a new daily on 6 December (British Library: 62382). Harmsworth returned to the *Le Petit Journal* offices for two separate visits in November 1895 and a further visit on 18 April, 1896 – very close to the 4 May launch of *The Daily Mail*. Significantly, he made no mention in this early period of any other French newspapers, only *Le Petit Journal*, presumably because, since the early 1880s, the circulation of *Le Petit Journal* had always been four times that of its rivals.

In Britain, *The Daily Mail* was the first popular half-penny daily newspaper to include elements to appeal directly to women. 'The Daily Magazine' appeared in the first issue and was sub-headed, 'An Entirely New Idea in Morning Journalism'. The jaunty typeface drew attention to the light-hearted nature of the page and 'A note from the Editor' confirmed that it was 'a practical attempt to provide something more than mere news' and furthermore 'the style of the "Daily Magazine" is to be entirely different to the other parts of the paper' (*The Daily Mail*, 4 May 1896: 4). Magazine writers and novelists were featured and although the 'magazine' was 'designed to interest both sexes' Alfred Harmsworth was at pains to point out that 'movements in woman's world . . . are as much entitled to receive attention as nine out of ten of the matters which are treated of in the ordinary daily paper. Therefore, two columns are set aside exclusively for ladies' (*The Daily Mail*, 4 May 1896: 4).

The marketing and distribution methods of *Le Petit Journal* seem to have had a lasting impact on Harmsworth. For instance special 'Daily Mail' trains were introduced in order to take the paper to the provinces in record time, first from London to Manchester, and subsequently to the West Country (1904, British Library: 62225). Forty years earlier Millaud had conquered the provinces using the railways and his own newly established regiment of 1,200 newspaper vendors who cycled from the stations out to villages armed with a horn and a whistle. After the launch of *The Daily Mail* and its extension to a 12-page format, the paper claimed that it reached one house in every seven in Britain, thanks to its system of special trains (British Library: 62922A).

The so-called Northcliffe revolution turned the British press into a business branch of the consumer industry. He did not invent popular journalism in Britain – many developments in style and content were influenced by American and French models and change was inevitable, given contemporary economic and social forces (Ward, 1989: 40). Yet it was Harmsworth (later Lord Northcliffe) who took advantage of these new developments by turning the commercial potential of journalism into a reality. He produced newspapers and magazines that were cheap and entertaining.

Other Northcliffe literature acknowledges influence from the United States and France, but usually not in detail: 'Newspaper men talked with admiring despair of the enormous circulations of the popular New York and Paris journals, and wondered why the same results could not be obtained here.' Accounts tend to underplay the long stays of Harmsworth and his wife in Paris, but refer instead to 'visits to 12 countries and the Dominions' (McKenzie, 1921: 14) and to advice from W.T. Stead (Brendon, 1982: 113). Harmsworth himself was somewhat patronizing about French influence: 'While the French are learning news management from us, we might acquire from them something more in the way of graceful charm and *verve* in writing' (Harmsworth, 1903: 183).

Despite the influence of *Le Petit Journal*, the kudos is still with Harmsworth: 'Alfred had always championed the rights of women – in his own peculiar way. He had pioneered their mass readership of newspapers, and he continued to define the market' (Taylor, 1998: 80). F.A. McKenzie's Associated Newspapers pamphlet, euphemistically entitled 'The Mystery of the Daily Mail' (the mystery being its success) claimed that up to the launch of *The Daily Mail*, female readers were not considered by morning dailies, so women did not read them. 'That condition of things definitely ended on 4 May 1896 . . . Today, thanks to the lead of the first number of the *Daily Mail*, the daily Press of the world, at home and abroad recognises that women readers exist' (McKenzie, 1921: 16).

Harmsworth certainly encouraged female readers more strongly by introducing some of the populist features of the evening and Sunday press into daily morning journalism, but as with *Le Petit Journal*, female interest was defined conservatively. *The Daily Mail* displayed a mast head slogan 'The Busy Man's Paper'. This was an admission that the majority of the original readership was male: people such as clerks who envisioned themselves as 'tomorrow's £1000 a year men' (McKenzie, 1921: 16). Northcliffe's diaries, correspondence and other more recent studies outline how he created systems to facilitate changes – but these were changes that were already happening elsewhere, or, 'were likely to have happened anyway in some form or other' (Catterall et al., 2000: 10).

As an editorial tool for profit making, the 'feuilleton' had been central to the success of *Le Petit Journal*, symbolizing the connection between the increase in female economic power and their emergence as a force within the popular press. *The Daily Mail* also featured a serialized novel, lifting the word 'feuilleton' from *Le Petit Journal* for use as a heading, thereby acknowledging the appeal of fiction to the female reader. In the 4 May 1896 launch edition the story involved royalty from the exotic country of 'Servia' (British Libray: LON LD6NPL). Content tended to be unashamedly 'feminine', featuring well-to-do women being saved by, and falling in love with, gallant gentlemen. A pamphlet of Northcliffe's claimed that before *The Daily Mail*, 'journalism was only a few aspects of life. What we did was to extend its purview to life as a whole', although it is worth remembering that all newspaper 'realities' are a construct influenced by news values and rules of presentation (Catterall et al. 2000: 10, 12). Although it would be true to say that it was the commercial press, epitomized by Lord Harmsworth and *The Daily Mail*, which found a way of exploiting female emancipation for profit, nevertheless the Associated Newspapers record of Harmsworth's achievement in this respect tends to minimize any business and advertising contribution before *The Daily Mail*.

In its first edition *The Daily Mail* promised to cover women and politics: 'Movements in the women's world, that is to say, women and politics, dress, toilette matters, cookery and home matters generally, are as much entitled to receive attention as nine out of ten of the matters which are treated in the ordinary daily paper' (McKenzie, 1921: 17). In fact, coverage was scant for 'movements' and for 'women and politics'. Textual analysis confirms that content consisted mainly of cookery, dressmaking tips, features and serial fiction (Bingham, 2004: 18–19, 27). Equally, by 1896 *Le Petit Journal* was lagging behind social and political trends in respect of female citizenship rather than providing a lead. In news comment the political sympathies of *Le Petit Journal* fluctuated along a scale from centre to right, as demonstrated in Chapter 2. Yet in both countries this was a time of class politics, industrial unrest and newly established labour organizations (see Chapters 4 and 5), suffragist politics and the phenomenon of 'new women'.

Readers, stunts and advertisements

There are also similarities between *Le Petit Journal* and *The Daily Mail* in the attitude of both proprietors to readers: just as Millaud had referred to his consumers as the 'les petits gens', so too the 'little people' was also the somewhat patronizing phrase later used by Northcliffe in correspondence with *The Daily Mirror* editor Alex Kenealy (30 November 1910, British Library: 62234). Northcliffe's various stunts owed much to the ideas of *Le Petit Journal*. In 1891, for example, *Le Petit Journal* created the Paris–Brest–Paris cycle race and in 1894 inaugurated the first motor car race, the Paris–Rouen Horseless Carriage Competition (Concours des Voitures sans Chevaux). Equally Northcliffe used stunts to sell his papers. In 1906, for example, the *Mail* offered £1,000 for the first flight across the English Channel and £10,000 for the first flight from London to Manchester.

Editors gained added value if a female journalist conducted a stunt, because any achievement would seem extra daring. Most famous, of course, in this respect was the American Elizabeth Cochrane who wrote as Nellie Bly, joining the *New York World* in the early 1880s. Her infiltrations for the purposes of social investigation often led to policy changes: she feigned madness in order to reveal mistreatment of mental asylum patients, worked in stores and factories to investigate employment conditions, and was arrested in order to investigate conditions in women's prisons. In 1889 the *New York World* sent her around the globe in order to beat the record of fictional Phileas Fogg in Jules Vernes' *Around the World in Eight Days*.

A similar sense of showmanship to Pulitzer's seems to have prompted a somewhat patronizing claim that 'stores and kindred advertisements in *The Daily Mail* are to many women readers the most interesting matter in the paper' (McKenzie, 1921: 108–9). If adverts were indeed so readable, it may well have been because they often displayed prevailing cultural norms: empire products (fabrics, soaps, perfumes, bric-a-brac and fashion accessories, for instance, were promoted in both France and Britain as an exotic form of consumption (Chafer and Sackur, 2002; McClintock, 1995) reflecting the widespread acceptance of colonialism and the arguments of many historians that cultural imperialism was integral to the economic and political landscape of middle- (and upper-) class European women (Burton, 1994; Cooper and Stoler, 1997; Blanchard and Lemaire, 2003). In Britain, *The Daily Mail* openly fanned the flames of 'Imperialism', as the new patriotism was called, inspired by Joseph Chamberlain and Cecil Rhodes and by the melodramatic Jameson Raid in December 1895, just before the paper's launch. Harmsworth was handed a circulation gift by the Jubilee of 1897, when 'pride of race reached so unseemly a pitch' that even Rudyard Kipling was moved to rebuke his compatriots for over enthusiasm (Jackson, 1988: 14–15).

During the twentieth century net investment costs for a newspaper came down as a result of the income from advertising, which was necessary for financial stability. Within this climate, editors were obliged to continue a trend that had first surfaced during the nineteenth century: their papers needed to appeal to as wide an audience as possible in order to retain valuable advertising. Alfred Harmsworth and his brother Harold, (later Lord Rothermere), understood this. The former, something of a showman himself, announced that sales of *The Daily Mail* on its first day of publication, 4 May 1896, had topped 700,000 copies. Yet he had no real way of finding out the truth of this statement at such short notice. However, Harmsworth certainly took concerted action to introduce 'modern' systems: this was reflected in a *The Daily Mail* article headed 'advertisers' gold mine' explaining that the paper's extension from 10 to 12 pages in order to accommodate advertisers' demand (ever since the paper became the first to publish its circulation figures), would mean more adverts and editorial (British Library: 62922A). By 1913, the first four pages consisted entirely of illustrated advertising, including a large number of display advertisements, with articles starting on page five (British Library: LON LD6NPL).

The situation changed when Harold introduced net sales certified by chartered accountants. 'Real net sales, achieved after the newsagents' returns had been deducted from copies distributed, were a badge of achievement and influence. They made possible a rate card for advertisers which told them reliably how many readers they would reach for a given expenditure' (Baldasty, 1992: 60). The Audit Bureau of Circulations (ABC) in the United States is its modern incarnation. This innovation by the Harmsworths essentially changed the relationship between newspaper and advertiser and 'as political patronage waned and advertising grew, advertisers who patronized the newspaper came to expect advocacy on their behalf. They frequently demanded that newspapers be loyal supporters of their business ventures. In short, another illustration of how advertisers propelled the commercialization of news' (Baldasty, 1992: 60). Certainly the editorial content aimed at women and Harmsworth's insistence on domestic and fashion oriented subject matter could be conveniently associated with advertising products, now that circulation statistics were being published to support the appeal of the latter. The principles of brevity and clarity were clearly evident in the journalism promoted by Harmsworth. This brevity made room for a much wider mix of articles and also allowed for an expansion of advertising, especially as the display advertisement was coming into its own as a visual enhancement of the page and as a valuable source of revenue.

Evolution of emphasis and tone

Comparisons between *Le Petit Journal* and *The Daily Mail* can be extended if more systematic textual analysis is added to qualitative material in order to compare and contrast the two papers' approaches to 'conservative feminization'.[3] This will help to illuminate mainstream gendered values and approaches in both countries. Quantitative analysis can reveal processes of change in representation for both papers: in *Le Petit Journal* between its origins and what it had become by 1896, and *The Daily Mail* between the period of experimentation and the early post-launch period (see Table 3.1). On the latter, Northcliffe later stated: 'For months before May 4th we produced a great many complete private copies of the paper. In some of these, I remember, were inserted all sorts of grotesque features with which to delude any of the enemy who might be awake, and we saw to it that he got those copies' (Clarke, 1950: 80). Thus, on 17 February a large 'grotesque' political cartoon appeared on page one – a style that was replaced by advertising from 4 May.

'Grotesque' distraction aside, the value of a comparison between the dummy run and the early days of the final launch resides in the fact that trends can be discerned including the way that Harmsworth wanted the newspaper to evolve through a preliminary experimental process of trial and error in production terms. Significantly, editorial effort to cater for

Table 3.1   Comparative analysis of citizenship versus consumerism as percentage of total articles on women

	Articles on women	Citizenship (%)	Consumerism (%)
Le Petit Journal 1863	418	76.3	23.6
Le Petit Journal 1896	656	80.9	19.3
Daily Mail 17 Feb–3 May 1896	307	76	24
Daily Mail 4 May–31 Dec 1896	2007	96	4

women increased considerably after the launch date, demonstrated by a staggering increase in the number of articles with some female interest, with 25 per cent of the total on 15 May. Nevertheless, female content was still lower than in *Le Petit Journal*. *The Daily Mail* had now created 'Women's Realm' – a two-column slot that symbolically lifted the editorial importance of women. In addition, one or two of the six or seven articles in 'News From Around the World' tended to be female oriented, although 'borrowed' frequently from French papers, (including *Le Petit Journal*) that were also mined for stories to fill 'La Vie Parisienne' column – an indication that Harmsworth looked to France for society glamour, gossip and social trivia.

   In *The Daily Mail*, 'virtuous' and 'victorious' upper-class female role models became more prominent than in *Le Petit Journal* and the tone more educative and positive. The emphasis on self-improvement was defined by Northcliffe in class terms: he assumed that his target readership of lower-class women would want to emulate their upper-class sisters and take an interest in the society gossip. Thus, education consisted of domestic tips, celebrity (royal and aristocratic) activities and fashion. A reader would undertake self-improvement through good works (charity), learning sophisticated recipes, learning some French phrases, how to dress elegantly and by pondering over questions to do with leisure rather than politics or how to change the world. In fact, apart from charity, the biggest proportion of 'virtuous' stories concerned female leisure issues: should the sexes swim together in the sea? (6 August). There were 120 letters on the subject. Significantly, there were three times more cycling stories than stories on women's suffrage. How would bicycling affect young ladies' health? (5 September); what were the advantages of cycling skirted as opposed to sporting knickerbockers? (28 September) Harmsworth and his wife cycled regularly

(British Library: 62382). Positive coverage in *The Daily Mail* was tempered by a conservative tone: on 4 May it was reported that a legislative initiative was to set a limit for barmaid work of 66 hours per week. The 'scandal' of overworking was (apparently) prompted by a new female 'aversion to domestic service' – a complaint that is repeated in an article lifted from *The Telegraph* on 8 December commenting that it is 'nearly impossible to get a general' (maid). Servants want to be addressed as 'miss', be called 'ladies' help' and wear hats rather than muslin caps. What was the world coming to?

For *Le Petit Journal* there was a reduction in positive coverage (virtuous, victorious) and a significant rise in negative coverage (vicious, victims – usually crime reporting), confirming the importance of crime and prostitution in the news popularity stakes as tools to increase circulation. Whereas in more specialist periodicals and journals, feminist debates on personal morality and private conduct were linked to demands for emancipation, in the two popular dailies analyzed here, such issues were transformed by journalistic news values into individual tales that were presented as either 'good' (virtuous, victorious) or 'bad' (victims, vicious). The vehicle for this depoliticizing transmogrification was a textual narrative (usually a 'titbit', 'snippet ' or 'fait divers') that was frequently sparked by individual court cases for the latter, or by the spectacle and/or moral example of royal or 'society' events and charity for the former. The previous chapter explained the rationale for categorization of article content about women into four basic story types: on the negative (crime coverage) side, victims and vicious, and on the positive (successful role models for society) side, virtuous and victorious. This categorization is appropriate for content analysis of both papers (see Table 3.2).

Harmsworth believed so strongly in the commercial viability of *The Daily Mail*'s successful role model of the society woman as an image to

Table 3.2 Comparative analysis of virtuous, victorious, vicious and victims articles, *Le Petit Journal*

	Le Petit Journal 1863 (%)	*Le Petit Journal* 1896 (%)	*The Daily Mail* 17 Feb–3 May 1896	*The Daily Mail* 4 May–31 Dec 1896
Victims	34	49	43	52.8
N/A	30.4	18.7	19	16
Virtuous	16.4	14.4	17	14.2
Vicious	12.3	11.2	14	11
Victorious	10.7	7.7	7	6

captivate readers and hence sell newspapers and advertising, that he carried it forward to his new *Daily Mirror*. However, the success or otherwise of newspaper developments depended on how they were adapted in the light of contextual factors in national development and culture, and, more immediately, on the willingness of readerships and advertisers to support new ideas. Such factors are exemplified by the way that the *Daily Mirror* in Britain and *La Fronde* in France were developed.

La Fronde and the *Daily Mirror*

This comparison is significant for an indication of the varying and frequently conflicting facets of cultural citizenship and the evolution of consumer society that had emerged by the early twentieth century. It is clear that Harmsworth saw a readership among women, and crucially, a female advertising market – but the argument presented here is that there were choices concerning the editorial approaches that could be used to interest women. His concept was to create the 'first daily newspaper for gentlewomen' and according to Kennedy Jones (1983) the idea was based on *La Fronde*.

The very different editorial approach of *La Fronde* – produced entirely by women –points to an emerging versatility in female influence on early mass circulation dailies and permits some conclusions about performance of gender during the crucial formative period of the evolving market. The *Daily Mirror* was to be staffed mainly by women journalists in a similar manner, but unlike *La Fronde*, not also by female production staff – and there turned out to be distinctly contrasting editorial philosophies. Whereas *La Fronde* provided a bridge between popular but socially cautious dailies and the specialist publications in which new ideas were discussed the *Daily Mirror* continued the conservative feminization of *The Daily Mail*.

As mentioned in Chapter 2, the radical and feminist inclinations of French women manifested themselves in some of the earliest examples of 'alternative' political newspaper and magazine communications anywhere in the world, especially during the late 1830s and the 1840s. Yet it was not until the 'Belle Époque' (1897) that a mass daily newspaper was launched by and for women. Contemporary feminists were aware of the negative depiction of women and reacted by trying to generate a public discourse on progressive ideas and role models (Roberts, 2002). Thus, in 1897 Marguerite Durand established *La Fronde* as a daily newspaper produced entirely for, and by, women, with a brief to cover current affairs and politics as well as discussions of gendered issues.[4]

Marguerite Durand was a former actress and self-proclaimed feminist with solid journalistic experience on *La Presse* and *Le Figaro* and she managed to ensure that *La Fronde* was much talked about in France and abroad in the run up to the first edition, especially the provocative nature of the title and the issue of how a group of women could manage to produce a paper.

The 'frondeuse' tradition of journalism had originated during the seventeenth century rebellion against Mazarin, and literally meant a 'slingshot' – a female David against the male Goliath. *La Fronde* ran from 1897 to 1905, financed by a donation of 7 million francs from the high profile Jewish banker Gustave de Rothschild. It was revived in 1914 and again in 1926. The original aim was to create a new Dreyfusard paper – it first appeared only weeks before Zola's 'J'Accuse' when the Dreyfus Affair issues of anti-Semitism and army corruption rocked France. *La Fronde* published 'feuilletons' and was based on the model of mass daily newspapers, except that the only man in the entire building was the caretaker: it was written, edited and typeset by women, paid the same wage as men.

The paper acted as a forum for late-nineteenth century feminist ideas on politics, education, trade unionism and the female world of work. Politics, social issues, sport and gender identity in French culture, were all discussed. Durand 'had an intuitive sense of what would work for that political moment' (Roberts, 2002: 247) and in her view this meant also covering content themes *without* obvious gender considerations. *La Fronde* journalists wanted to prove that female reporters could write about so-called 'male' topics as well as the men themselves were able. In fact, Durand had to go to considerable lengths to secure special permission for her female reporters to enter the parliament, law courts and other all-male bastions of power.

The problem of identity for *La Fronde* was that it appeared neither feminist nor feminine. Attempts to present a diversity of representation led to confusion over the approach women's journalism should take. One day the paper would carry an article demanding political rights for women, and the next day an article saying these rights were useless (De la Motte and Przyblyski, 1999: 304, 333). To show its sense of equality the paper dated each edition according to a variety of different calendars – the Jewish calendar, the French Revolutionary calendar and the Gregorian calendar (Chapman and Nuttall, 2011: 254). Articles were long, conscientious, well-informed, austere and edifying (*Le Temps*, 25 December 1897). A contemporary article about what men thought of *La Fronde* complained that the style of writing was not sufficiently 'feminine' – that is, insufficiently delicate and light hearted. In the words of the weekly *L'Illustration* (15 January 1898), the paper provided 'not feminist theses, but exclusively feminine opinions on politics and the news of the day'.

Clearly there were choices concerning the editorial approaches that could be used to interest women, and a comparison between *The Daily Mirror* and *La Fronde* facilitates a greater appreciation of the contemporary tension between competing images of women, and hence also of editorial choices concerning representation of women that were available by the *fin de siècle*. The contrast with *The Daily Mirror*, supposedly based on the same concept of by and for women, was a stark one. The verdict on the original version of the *Daily Mirror* is that it 'was essentially a stunt' for which Harmsworth 'neglected to do the spadework . . . an unmitigated disaster' (Taylor, 1998: 81, 82). Yet the promotion was extensive. '"No newspaper", said Northcliffe "was ever started with such a boom. I advertised it everywhere. If there was anyone in the United Kingdom not aware that the *Daily Mirror* was to be started he must have been deaf, dumb, blind, or all three' (Cudlipp, 1953: 8).

Harmsworth carried forward his version of 'conservative feminization' from *The Daily Mail* to the *Daily Mirror*, covering (with male editors) 'Fashion, Beauty Culture, the Nursery, the Garden, and the furnishing and adornment of the home' (sic). In the *Daily Mirror* stories inclined towards an 'unholy alliance of crime, bathos and self improvement' (Cudlipp, 1953: 8) – 'Beauty and the Bath', 'A Page of Interesting Books' next to stories such as 'Baby in a Dustbin', 'Cut Off by Tide' and 'Divorce by Dagger'. According to Hamilton Fyfe, who was made temporary news editor, Harmsworth gave instructions such as: 'You must make the *Mirror* suggest that it is produced for people in Society; for those who first adopt new fashions; for those who have leisure and large means' (1930: 93). Expensive fashion styles and recipes for the rich were the order of the day. 'He had invited the British public to a diet of *consommé aux nids d'hirondelles*, followed by sole in white wine with mushrooms and truffles; the readers were told how to make these lavish delicacies. Also recorded in the first issue, but only briefly, was an inquest on a 14-year-old orphan girl of Oswaldtwistle who lost one eye and went blind in the other. She had been sacked from the mill and had committed suicide during temporary insanity, for the child had no prospect of earning her living again. The paper for gentlewomen made no comment' (Cudlipp, 1953: 10). Later on Harmsworth berated editor Thomas Kenealy (1904–15) for content that was 'below the intelligence of the average fourth housemaid' (British Library: 62234).

Female journalists

Durand appointed a galaxy of brainy, high-profile, high-achieving, well-educated professional women such as: Séverine (Caroline Remy, who had a national reputation as a reporter); Clemence Royer – a scholar, translator of Darwin into French and the first woman to teach at the Sorbonne; Daniel Le Sueur (Jeanne Lapauze) – playwright, novelist and one of the first women nominated for the Légion d'honneur; Jeanne Chauvin – one of the first women admitted to the Parisian bar as a lawyer; Blanche Galien – the first female pharmacist in France; and Augusta Klumke – the first female astronomer to join the Paris observatory.

However, contemporary attitudes more generally were still ambivalent towards female journalists: the appointment of such a galaxy of stars was truly radical. Indeed, in the earlier nineteenth century, the labels 'reporter' or 'editor' implied a man (Onslow, 2000: xii). Examples in the previous chapter demonstrate that editors and proprietors viewed women as consumers and sometimes subjects for news, but not producers of news. The growth of advertising aimed at women prompted the recruitment of female journalists to write articles that it was deemed (by male editors and proprietors) would appeal to female readers, and around which further promotions could be placed. 'Women were hired as "women journalists" to attract female audiences' (Chambers, Steiner and Fleming 2004: 15).

Records of female employment are slim, but the programme for the Pageant of Women's Trades and Professions, 27 April 1909, is a good indicator of suffrage attitudes towards the profession of journalism at the time. Among the various work areas, the heartfelt entry for journalists points to the conservatism of editors and proprietors (Tickner, 1987: 101): 'With perhaps two exceptions, no woman on the inside staff of a London daily has secured a good and remunerative position . . . There are many women who earn a good livelihood by writing on dress, doing shop notices, and supplying society news, but these are outside the true sphere of journalism.' Indeed, Mary Howarth, as editor of the ill-fated, all female version of Northcliffe's *Daily Mirror*, was only paid £50 a month – a modest amount when one considers that, by 1952, Northcliffe's nephew Cecil Harmsworth King talked of an editor of a daily being paid almost as much as a Prime Minister (Cudlipp, 1953: 10).

According to Lucy Brown (1985: 77–8) women journalists predated women's pages – but their numbers were small, so the critical mass of female numbers in Fleet Street was too few to matter, despite the fact by 1911 that there were 14,000 people employed in the profession in Britain (Searle, 2004). Thus, the Society of Women Journalists (established 1895) sought to improve the status of the woman journalist rather than challenge the men on their own terms (Lee, 1977: 116). In fact, writing, journalism and teaching were the main jobs that provided opportunities for women to rise above a humble background, to survive as a widow or to overcome the problems of a broken marriage. Journalism was attractive for a number of reasons: no formal entry qualifications were needed; the job provided interesting human contact; and it contained an element of variety in the work tasks.

However, there were compromises to be made. It is precisely what happened when women strayed from the allocated career path, or when that path proved inadequate in various ways, that is germane to the development of cultural citizenship. Such a line of enquiry is not pursued in order to denigrate the women's pages of dailies, the content of which tended to fall largely within the remit of domestic consumer subject matter. Such pages provided an entry point for women into journalism and a legitimate space for the discussion of women's issues.

Examples of women who managed to take a different route by entering and succeeding within the male world not only acted as role models and pioneers but also provided evidence of emerging trends and changing contexts that are central to an understanding of both the tensions and the possibilities of the period. Harriet Martineau's achievements – over 1,600 leaders for the *Daily News* between 1852 and 1866 – not only provided an inspiration to future generations, but also informed men on so-called 'masculine' topics. It was Florence Fenwick-Miller who speculated: 'I wonder how many of the men who have presumed to say that women are "incapable of understanding politics" or of "sympathizing in great causes", received a large part of their political education, and of rousing stimulus to public-spirited action, from those journalistic writings of Harriet Martineau?' (Fenwick Miller, 1884: 194). Margaret Fuller who, after two years as literary editor of the *New York Tribune*, became America's first woman foreign correspondent was equally remarkable (Allen, 1979). The stories of individuals also provide evidence of the under exploitation of journalistic talent:[5] Susan Carpenter, for instance, was the first woman to work for the Press Association, but she was channelled into 'women's interests', spending much of her time moving from hairdressers to Court dressmaker to get details of the outfits to be worn at Court occasions (Onslow, 2000: 51). The choice of whether or not to conform to such constraints placed female journalists in a dilemma if they refused to be sufficiently 'feminine' in their work, they could be criticized as deviant, but if they accepted the constraints they could become professionally marginalized.

Editor of the *Pall Mall Gazette*, W.T. Stead, became one of the first in Britain to employ a female journalist when he employed Hulda Friederichs as chief interviewer in 1882 (Carter et al. 1998: 21). Although Frances Power Cobbe in an 1888 article for the *Women's Penny Paper* (3 November: 5) praised the lightness and 'pace' of the woman writer as being more appropriate to journalism than the male virtues of solidity and strength, many of the insults were precisely because women were beginning to carve out careers for themselves in various branches of the profession. Yet the fact that journalism's default definition was a male gendered one acted as a significant impediment: 'By marking out the gender of women journalists as odd and abnormal while treating the gender of male journalists as neutral, male editors created an effective barrier to women's success' (Chambers, Steiner and Fleming, 2004: 24).

Most women journalists were freelance, undertaking a range of periodical work rather than employment for just one title (Onslow, 2000: xi). Florence Fenwick-Miller's *Illustrated London News* columns were the exception rather than the rule. Although most early female journalists were middle class and very well educated, they were undermined not due to their class, background or any innate inability to do the job but because they were considered to be 'emotional rather than rational, given to seeing matters in personal not abstract terms . . . and absorbed with the trivial and domestic' (Pugh, 1980: 8). In the process, female journalists were often portrayed in disparaging tones, from the 'Jennie Jot-it-down' or 'Rita Rite-it-up' with her 'complete absence of such adult literary ingredients as grammar, style and common sense' (Marks, 1990: 85) to the 'manly' woman who seemed to come in for particular opprobrium. 'If there is anything the [Englishman] hates and ridicules,' wrote a correspondent to the *Girl's Own Paper*, 'it is a masculine, unwomanly woman' (Forrester, 1980: 34). The 'Frondeuses' were also laughed at for so-called masculinity, and portrayed visually as butch cross-dressers who mimicked men in a male profession (Livois, 1965).

Durand and Harmsworth clearly differed on the way female journalists were employed, as well as in their vision and in their politics. Harmsworth's suggestion for aspiring female journalists was more pedestrian: 'There is no better beginning, if the novice is really expert in shorthand and typewriting, than an appointment as secretary to the editor' (Harmsworth, 1903: 66). When it seemed that *The Daily Mirror* had failed, he was quoted as saying, 'it's taught me that women can't write and don't want to read' (Fyfe, 1949: 115).

In Britain, the 1841 census listed 15 women 'authors, editors and journalists' but by 1881 there were 660. However, this growth is small in the light of the fact there were over 2,000 newspapers in Britain by then (Brown, 1985: 77–8).[6] In 1863 there were no female journalists in *Le Petit Journal* by 1896 there was still only one reference to a female journalist – 'Mamselle Chiffon' – probably a pseudonym for a group of male contributors (ANR: 65AQU257). This is likely, given the paper's track record of adopting a joint pseudonym of 'Thomas Grimm' for a group of five male editors who collectively replaced Timothy Trimm's column after he left. *The Daily Mail* referred to 'Janet' in the dummy runs, then Mary Howarth became editor of the two female columns. Thereafter articles appear by 'Lady Charlotte' and it was announced that 'Mrs. Mann' and 'Mrs Mannington-Caffyn' were to join the team after the expansion to 12 pages (British Library: 62922A).

Contemporary accounts of the conduct of women journalists on first day of *The Daily Mirror* publication, 2 November 1903, tend to be patronizing and cynical. It was said that female staff suffered fainting from the pressure, and several burst into tears. Harmsworth sent in champagne to revive them. Kennedy Jones monitored and changed much of their copy, including a column heading 'Our French Letter' that had to be renamed 'Yesterday in Paris'. He later told colleagues '"You can't imagine the things I had to blue-pencil", continuing, "Two people acting at Drury Lane got married and went on acting as usual – they didn't go away for a honeymoon. The paragraph about this ended: "the usual performance took place in the evening"' (Cudlipp, 1953: 1). One of the sub-editors given the task of correcting the inappropriate language commented that the exercise was something of a 'French farce'. Another added that 'in a French farce, they would be beautiful' (Taylor, 1998: 82).

Such disparaging anecdotes epitomized a commonly held contemporary view that women were not suited to the rough and tumble of daily newspaper journalism. Edward Bok, editor of *Ladies' Home Journal* was not alone in his opinion that 'a girl cannot live in the free-and-easy atmosphere of the local room or do the work required of a reporter without undergoing a decline in the innate qualities of womanliness or suffering in health' (quoted in Steiner, 1992: 10). Yet there was also a general view at the time that women made the best interviewers, and women who managed to rise within this male world were inevitably very good at their jobs. Flora Shaw, foreign correspondent for many years of the *Times* of London, was said by a contemporary to probably be better informed on colonial affairs than almost any other London journalist, and any other woman, except the Queen (Onslow, 2000: 53, 54).

Blaming women

As discussed earlier, 'new woman' was 'perceived to have ranged herself perversely with the forces of cultural anarchism and decay' (Dowling, 1978: 440), thus was also associated with the perceived danger to religion of Darwin and his *On the Origin of Species*, with the challenge to economic liberalism and the free trade ethos by socialism and the rise of labour, and with the cultural decadence of the aesthete, symbolized by Oscar Wilde. All of these associations represented threats to notions of Victorian maleness and manhood and to the more stable mid-century notion that the women's issue was confined to politics only because of its connection with education.

In France too, commercial newspapers communicated conflicting images (Roberts, 2002, de Grazia, 1996) of female consumers, 'new women', suffragists, professional women and the charitable imperial missionary reformer. Confusion combined with a circulation decline to thwart *La Fronde*. After the end of the Dreyfus affair, France experienced a decline in newspaper sales. *La Fronde's* impact and circulation were at their highest during the first six months. In its first week it sold 200,000 a day, then went down to 50,000. *The Daily Mirror's* circulation also declined: from 276,000 on the first day, it gradually descended to 24,801. Harmsworth misunderstood the requirements of the new market he himself had encouraged. Women did not want their own daily paper, 'or at least the respectable, socially aspiring conservative women he sought did not' (Bourne, 1990: 33) especially if it served up a diet of trivia and domestic content that could be obtained from magazines elsewhere. When it appears to be failing, Harmsworth famously stated: 'I will make women read it' (Clarke, 1950: 84), but within four months of its launch, Fyfe was instructed to dismiss the *Daily Mirror's* women editorial staff and replace them by more experienced male reporters from *The Daily Mail*. 'They begged to be allowed to stay. They left little presents on my desk. They waylaid me tearfully in corridors. It was a horrid experience – like drowning kittens' (Pound and Harmsworth, 1959: 278).

Harmsworth's masculine commercial instincts about what he assumed women readers wanted were temporarily destabilized by the failure of the all-female daily paper, but Harmsworth claimed that he had seized victory from the jaws of defeat (Pound and Harmsworth, 1959: 278). In fact what he successfully recognized was that advertisers were ready to pay for female readers, but there were three failed attempts to attract female readers, including the *Women's Times* as well as the *Daily Mirror*

(Tusan, 2005: 14, 99). The editorial concept was to bring upper-class cookery and fashion habits to the aspiring lower-middle classes (readers were given a 'leaderette' in French (Cudlipp, 1953: 90)). From a gendered perspective, 'The aim appears to be to include "feminine" values without handing over any power to women' (Holland, 1998: 21). It was also a business miscalculation that cost Northcliffe £100,000 in losses.

On 28 January 1904 the *Daily Mirror* was re-named the *Daily Illustrated Mirror*, 'A Paper for Men and Women', and the price was lowered to a half-penny. Three months later, on 28 April, it became the *Daily Mirror* again: 'An Illustrated Paper for Men and Women' – a daily picture paper. The *Daily Mirror* was saved by halftone photos, adapted to the speed of newspaper printing, when it became the first morning daily newspaper to be proclaimed a picture paper. Then it went through a number of incarnations before the proprietor, enobled in 1905 as Lord Northcliffe, found a successful formula. Keanaly put the paper on its feet and turned it round.

According to *Time and Tide* in 1920, Northcliffe failed to draw in women readers because of his lack of attention to issues such as female employment and education (Rhondda, 1920). Yet Northcliffe appeared to be unrepentant on the issue of content for women: just over a month before his death in 1922, he was still advising the Australian newspaper magnate Keith Murdoch on editorial management of the Melbourne *Herald* stating that the women's page should be 'feminine'. 'Glad to see a little hairdressing for a change', he commented on 6 July 1922 (Northcliffe, 1921–22: NLA Ms 2823/3/7).

Press barons and transnational gendered considerations

According to one of Northcliffe's former editors, Kennedy Jones, the decision to start *The Daily Mail* was prompted 'when Harmsworth found that *Le Petit Journal's* mixture of lively news, gossip and political attack was selling 650,000 copies a day and making a profit of about £150,000 a year' (Williams, 1969: 81). *Le Petit Journal* developed the concept of 'faits divers' in the 1860s: founder Alphonse Millaud had understood that appealing to women readers made good business sense and that a paper also needed to be both attention grabbing and readable. Later Alfred Harmsworth in Britain and the Yellow journalists William Randolph Hearst and Joseph Pulitzer in America also favoured the 'titbit' of information and the human interest story over the traditional daily fare of political and business reporting.

Despite the lack of 'syndication' systems between countries at this time, news articles were pirated and reproduced. The fact that *Le Petit*

Journal reprinted articles from the American press and *The Daily Mail* lifted them from *The Telegraph* (and *Le Petit Journal*) suggests that the approach to 'conservative feminization' was shared by other contemporary newspapers. There is some evidence that late-nineteenth-century and early-twentieth-century pioneering press barons from different Western countries compared notes on newspaper development, but how successful was the transfer of ideas, given cultural and contextual variables? Connections and interchange between Harmsworth and Marinoni have already been discussed, but they existed also between the former and Pulitzer.

At the latter's invitation, Harmsworth guest edited a special edition of the *New York World* to mark the beginning of the twentieth century. Pulitzer's purpose was to give Harmsworth the opportunity to demonstrate his concept of the 'tabloid' newspaper – new in size and new in style, and specially designed for the fast pace of twentieth century living (Chapman, 2005a: 79–80). Later, between 1920 and 1922, a pattern of knowledge transfer, imitation and adaptation emerged between Northcliffe and Keith Murdoch in Australia, when the former imparted his vision and editorial priorities for a 'popular daily' via dialogues and written exchanges on newspaper popularization. In a speech given by Northcliffe in Rockhampton during his travels in Australia during 1921, he points to the attention given to female readership in evening papers, because 'The paper is taken home, and by the time the man gets home, he has probably finished reading it and it becomes the property of the woman of the household. Hence the prosperity of evening newspapers (sic). It is calculated that eight per cent of advertised goods are purchased by women or that women have some part in the decision to purchase . . . Look at the windows of your stores, the advertisements in your newspapers, and you will realize what a power woman is where the purse is to be opened' (Northcliffe, 1921–22: NLA, Ms 2823/3/7).[7]

Yet the British press baron's perception of what content was needed for women had always been limited. As part of his advice to Murdoch about how to run a successful newspaper, he also sent the latter copies of daily notes issued to *The Daily Mail* newsroom journalists, entitled 'Message from the Chief'. On Thursday 4 May 1922 the instruction was, inter alia, 'The Skirt (sic) discussion must be continued' (Northcliffe, 1921–22: NLA, Ms 2823/3/7). The discourse was on the length of women's skirts. In a list of instructions to Murdoch, each with a heading ('Advertisements', 'Circulation', 'Staff', etc), the penultimate heading is 'Women'. The instruction notes: 'Run a page every day. Dresses, cookery, social gossip. Enough' (Northcliffe, 1921–22: NLA, Ms 2823/3/7).

The power of female consumerism, in the eyes of a proprietor who in his time, owned and ran a media empire larger than that of Keith's son, Rupert Murdoch, in the 1990s, was clear (Chapman, 2005a: 91). However, Northcliffe gave no advice on the nature of coverage for political movements or women's collective organization at a time when many were active in Cooperative and labour movement groups.

The power of political consumerism

Knowledge of the nineteenth and early-twentieth century female consumer has been derived primarily from retailers and social movements. In this context, Brewer and Trentmann refer more generally to 'potential synapses between consumption and citizen (that are) so often ignored' but make the point that these stabilize the idea and identity of the consumer, by connecting it with favourable views of society and politics (2006: 52). The phenomenon of 'conservative feminization' referred to in this and the previous chapter was fulfilling this very function: coverage in *The Daily Mail* and *Le Petit Journal* of consumer- and citizen-oriented news items provided a popular respectability to aspects of female activity in the public sphere that in periodicals and more specialist publications, tended to be conceptualized in a more radical way by other political periodicals and more specialist publications.

As previously established, in terms of content analysis of the daily newspaper, it is possible to differentiate between subject matter involving women and aimed at female readers that involved some form of interest in citizenship (public sphere activities, charity and community work), as opposed to consumer-oriented articles. Crossover between politics and consumerism provides the fertile ground for the potential 'synapse' referred to above, especially in terms of women's direct action in this field, which I will discuss later.

At the very time Harmsworth was complaining about the inadequacies of female journalists and readers, there were already examples, such as in the United States and elsewhere in Britain, which demonstrated the potential influence of the use of journalism by women to further consumer rights. Readers and activists were being made aware that well-reported information, told in a non-emotional even-handed fashion by a woman, could address the most important issues and confront powerful people and industries. The achievements of Ida M. Tarbell[8] act as a milestone in the development of cultural citizenship because they demonstrate the potential of both the printed word and the consumer at this time – for both Tarbell and Rockefeller battled for the hearts and minds of the public. In fact, Ida M. Tarbell became a beacon for women who wished to pursue a career in journalism due to her extraordinary achievement with the Standard Oil story. Her reporting helped contribute to legislation that broke the corporation's monopoly control of the oil industry. In short, she took on the richest person in the world, John D. Rockefeller, and won – through meticulous reporting and a fact-based narrative. Her singlehanded defeated of the most powerful business leader of the time and her exposé of Standard Oil for *McClure's Magazine* in 1904 set a new benchmark in investigative reporting and was one the central pieces of journalism produced by the US 'muckrakers' of the early twentieth century. Eventually Tarbell produced 19 articles for the magazine and the resulting book entitled *The History of the Standard Oil Company* was published in two volumes in 1904.[9]

Tarbell hoped that John D. Rockefeller would be drawn into a debate with her but all he did was command that her name never be mentioned in his presence. Standard Oil mounted a vigorous national campaign to try to discredit the book and its conclusions. Rockefeller donated huge sums to charity in a bid for public support and Standard Oil distributed five million copies of an essay 'extolling the benefits of monopolies, and published a book supporting Rockefeller which they distributed free to librarians, ministers, teachers, and prominent citizens throughout the country' (Jensen, 2002: 30). Ultimately his campaign failed and Congress passed the Hepburn Act in 1906 that effectively abolished oil company rebates. That same year a Bureau of Corporations was formed for the purpose of investigating the oil industry. It concluded that Standard Oil had been obtaining preferential treatment from railroad companies for some time. The Attorney General filed a suit under the Sherman Act accusing Standard Oil of 'conspiring to restrain and monopolize interstate commerce in petroleum' (Jensen, 2002: 30). The corporation was found guilty and fined US$29 million. Standard Oil was broken up into 38 separate companies – some still trading; Mobil, Exxon, Chevron and Amoco.

The journalistic achievements of Tarbell on a consumer rights issue of accountability need to be appreciated within the context of the development of contemporary thinking in that field, not only in the United States, but also in Britain, France and within an empire context. If alternative forms of consumer organization that demonstrated consumer power in action were not dealt with in popular dailies, they were certainly covered within the pages of the labour movement's own papers. In Britain these included well-established newspapers like *The Clarion, The Common Cause* and the US *Appeal*, and a whole host of others in

Britain that served to solidify women's own organizational ability, such as the Co-operative Women's Guild, Women's Franchise League, Women's Labour League, Women's Liberal Movement, Women's Trade Union League, Women's Citizenship Association and the Women's Christian Temperance Union.

Such was the organizational potential of women using their own print publications, that by 1903 the Co-operative Women's Guild in Britain was waging a national campaign in opposition to tariffs and consumers' co-operative shops formed the world's first mass co-operative movement. William King founded a monthly periodical called *The Co-operator*, the first edition of which appeared on 1 May 1828. This gave a mixture of co-operative philosophy and practical advice about running a shop using co-operative principles. Specific suffrage organizations such as the Women's Social and Political Union (WSPU) had their own suffrage journals, and other feminist newspapers such as *Freewoman* and *Feminist Review*, are looked at in more detail in Chapter 4. The political clout of consumer direct action was demonstrated in Britain by female suffrage supporters of the 'The Women's Tax Resistance League' (1909–17), who had their goods seized and auctioned by the authorities. One leader, Clemence Housman spent a week in Holloway for non-payment of taxes in 1911.

Votes for Women, the paper of the WSPU in Britain gave unequivocal editorial support to advertisers, promising to deliver to them the business of readers. Reader-consumers in turn were urged to support shops that advertised – especially promotions by Oxford Street stores – and readers were also encouraged to visit shops to solicit advertising for their paper (Tusan, 2005: 154; DiCenzo, 2000: 122). Readers were encouraged in their identity as consumers: they could also purchase WSPU souvenirs in the form of china, stationary, novelties and jewellery. In fact they could even purchase the services of a special interior decorator to furnish rooms in the Union's colours (DiCenzo, 2000: 121) Amazingly, when the *Suffragette* was advocating arson and window smashing of West End Stores, these companies still advertised in the paper – it comprised 22 per cent of advertising in 1912 at the height of the violence (Harrison, 1982: 282).

For women, consumer politics provided another means of empowerment – referred to by Nancy Fraser as women's 'counter civil society'. This was especially the case in France where suffrage was thought to present a threat to both the security of the Third Republic by creating further divisions among supporters, and to the strength of working class unity that was deemed to be a higher priority by socialists and the labour movement. The strength of the co-operative movement was also mirrored in the United States. In France it received an intellectual boost in 1904 with the publication of *Consumers' Co-operative Societies* by Charles Gide, an eminent French professor of political economy and defender of empire. Gide was to become a tireless champion of the co-operative movement – both agricultural and consumers' co-operatives – in the early part of the twentieth century. His ideas also provided the intellectual defence for female activism in France in the field of consumer organization and for female influence in French working class co-operatives. His book acted as the bible and an inspiration for Theresa Billington-Griegs's *Consumer in Revolt* (1912).

Such was the scale of activity, and public communications in this area in France that the social catholic influenced Ligue Sociale d'Achêteurs launched its own press advertising campaign (Furlough, 1991). This latter use of newspaper advertising carried a larger significance as consumers were encouraged by a range of social organizations to use their material position for the furtherance of moral and public causes. Examples of benevolence found their way into the pages of *Le Petit Journal*, for instance, even if the organizational strength of the public movement in France in favour of non-selfish spending did not.

Conclusions

One of the aims of *La Fronde* was to raise public consciousness of ways in which female identity was represented in French culture, and to widen its scope, giving women a greater visibility in representation. The paper's initial impact shows that female readers were open to considering a variety of journalistic provision, including the discourses on 'new women'. Durand and Harmsworth clearly differed on vision and politics and on the way female journalists should be employed. By adopting a more traditional view of women's needs in order to gain mass appeal, mass circulation dailies offered the potential for distracting attention away from radical ideas and collective female protest – at a time when these phenomena were relatively common. The government of the Second Empire formally incentivized a 'non-political press' for this very reason. Were female readers of *La Fronde* less likely to become politically anaesthetized by trivia? *La Fronde* was said to be *the* newspaper for school teachers, but any impact on their politicization awaits further research. A powerful visual record summarizes Durand's attitude towards education as a liberating force for working-class self-improvement: in a sponsored lithograph, a group of women overlook Paris from the heights of Montmartre, and the middle-class women show their working-class sisters the socially uplifting benefits of education as they point towards the Sorbonne (Dufau, 1898).

Yet in Britain Northcliffe later banned suffragette coverage, instructing his *Mirror* editor 'except in an extreme case, print no more of them' (British Library: 62234), whereas the *Illustrated London News* carried regular discussions of suffragettes and citizenship issues in the women's page (British Library: MicB.51). Mass circulation dailies full of human interest, domestic subject matter, and the all-important serial novel – aimed at an expanding female readership – demonstrated their own category of 'conservative feminization' in the way that they used female-based content to address their readers. In later years, a division arose between the tabloid style lighter, more entertaining address that was referred to as feminized 'soft news' and more information oriented content.

The importance of *La Fronde* lies in the fact that the paper tried to bridge this emerging gap at a time when this was needed, and in doing so, Durand and her female team combated what Huyssen has referred to as 'the persistent gendering as feminine of that which is devalued' (1986: 53). The paper's initial impact shows that female readers were open to considering a variety of journalistic provision, including the discourses on 'new women'. In other words, a cautious editorial approach was not necessarily warranted.

There were three trends that contributed to cultural citizenship by and for women: recognition of women as readers and consumers; women as journalists; and women as contributors to news content, through their actions in society – particularly in public affairs. Clearly none of these developments were achieved quickly, smoothly or without challenge. Contemporary tensions between emerging female citizenship – both consumer and political – and more traditional views of female domestic interests in the context of the continuing realities of economic, social and political disempowerment (despite reforms) were not always reflected by *Le Petit Journal*, *The Daily Mail* or the *Daily Mirror* and even in *La Fronde* they emerged as editorial contradictions. This demonstrates that 'conservative feminization' and alternative views are not a twenty-first century revisionist construct but rather an acknowledgement of the political nature of the conflict between more traditional and fairly new forms of female representation. The success or otherwise of newspaper developments depended on how they were adapted in the light of contextual factors in national development and culture, and, more immediately, on the willingness of readerships and advertisers to support new ideas. Coverage in *The Daily Mail* and *Le Petit Journal* of consumer- and citizen-oriented news items provided a popular window to aspects of female activity in the public sphere that in periodicals and more specialist publications tended to be conceptualized in a more radical way by other political periodicals and more specialist publications.

This chapter has explored something of the scope of ideas, processes of formulation of attitudes that influenced the categorizations identified, together with analysis of specific examples. These all combined to lay the conceptual ground for both cultural citizenship and cultural consumerism. Contextual factors from the 1880s onwards such as the influence of 'new women' and of 'New Journalism' show that battles to win the hearts and minds of consumers as citizens were now clearly on the agenda. They were aimed at a female readership within a broader framework of discourse and experiment, demonstrating that there were a range of editorial choices during this formative period in the representation of women.

The choice of paths for women within the public sphere was also beginning to emerge, and France was at the forefront of progress in women's education. From 1868, for instance, women were admitted into the Medical Faculty, 11 years before the University of London accorded the same right in Britain. Yet this progress in educational and professional prospects was not without contradictions, not least the generally held attitude that women were almost divinely destined for the domestic role. Even the phrase 'professional women', especially in the French language, was nuanced towards the traditional stigma that actresses and prostitutes suffered from as 'public women'. Newspaper messages were crucial in influencing the change in attitude that was necessary if women were to gain respectability and acceptance as professional workers.

At the end of the nineteenth century the interest in female activities was certainly evident in the media, but so were the tensions of the moment – all the more reason for critical scrutiny of the often contradictory performance of mass circulation dailies in their reporting of and attitudes towards women. Such tensions emerge in gendered press communications as they related to women organizing around labour and political protest, as analyzed in Part III.

The potential for change that public manifestations of female confidence represented is evident in a range of different media contexts. The example from the United States of female 'muckraking' demonstrates that the power of investigative journalism could be exercised by women as a way of furthering the power of the citizen and consumer.

The printed word, used by a woman, could change society. There were other ways as well, such as the act of taking to the streets of villages and towns – a bold step towards new forms of citizenship that is examined in the next two chapters. Part III adds fresh dimensions to the relationship between women's activities in the polity and the way they were communicated, both in terms of the countries, moments, the actions that women took and the kinds of mediation involved. The scope of historical dimensions to cultural citizenship will be widened in order to emphasize the influence of class and economic factors.

Part III
Labour Movement Roots and the Politics of Exclusion

4

French India

From Private to Public Sphere

This chapter examines the way in which print communications were used as a counter-hegemonic vehicle for class and women's activism in a colonial context. The relationship between citizenship and female influence in India reveals a discourse of awakening, with trends that differed from the domestic and cultural values underwriting the gendered consumer power and material acquisition in the Western world. In a colonial context direct action hit at the core of imperialist production with consumer boycotts and strikes that became the catalyst for a highly politicized manifestation of cultural citizenship. This is analyzed here by reference to French territories in India, through an examination of Tamil protesters' communications during the first major strike where print public communications were significantly adopted as a vehicle for collective awareness and self-expression.

The example is 'hidden history': the existence of direct rule from Paris over some very small parts of India has been largely forgotten. Women in French India were deprived in almost every way possible, ranging from their living standards through to their lack of basic civil and political liberties, including the vote. The absence of this latter right was something they shared in common with women in Britain and France. In this neglected corner of the French Empire, the local population – including peasant women – emerged for the first time from the private to the public sphere as an organized force, a factor that has largely been ignored by historians.

A symbiotic relationship between print communication and social movement developed through the use of advocacy journalism, and it reveals important traces of early cultural citizenship in a subaltern context. This was characterized by important class actions that also produced collective gender awareness. Events from 1935 to 1937 formed the roots of a structured women's movement that emerged in 1947, and also the origins of an organized nationalist movement, the activities of which were covered extensively in *Swandanthiram*. As far as that paper was concerned, the struggle for citizenship was all about class, power, hegemony and counter hegemony.

Scholars recognize that Indian women were not simply passive subjects: 'Through their development of a feminist consciousness they were active agents in processes of change at the height of colonial rule' (Anagol, 1998: 99). This involved taking significant steps towards a move from private to public spheres. As with the radical feminists in late Victorian England, consciousness manifested itself through collective action, with class action taking precedence. Exemplifying the relationship between class and gender, which was also evident in the British labour movement at the end of the nineteenth century and into the early twentieth century, this synergy and cross-fertilization on issues relating to working and political rights became a feature in counter-hegemonic communications in colonial India.

The purpose of subaltern communications in French India was to communicate what was happening throughout the community, but also to influence authority. Leaders hoped to encourage gender awareness as a means of widening support for protest – they needed women to be politically active. How did the involvement of women in protest relate to the press? In Pondicherry opposition newspapers were sold, circulated and read aloud throughout the province as a means of enhancing solidarity. They were destroyed before the authorities could seize them; but authors of rebel communications also wanted their dissenting voice to be heard by the territory's ruling elite in their own language in order to influence their policies. Campaigning in Pondicherry is evidenced by the fact that from time to time during 1935–37 *Swandanthiram*[1] contained French language articles as well as Tamil, or an occasional entirely French version would appear, clearly targeting the 3 per cent of the population who used the language.

Similarly, trade union leaders wrote numerous letters of protest and sent telegrams to the governor and to the minister for the colonies, that they translated into French. Letters, reports, telegrams and newspapers all represented attempts to express opposition to the existing power structure. Protests were simultaneously conducted via propaganda in *Swandanthiram* and leaflets in Tamil explaining the overtures that were being made by leaders on behalf of the local working class. In fact, the same text was usually produced in a range of communications. The purpose was to convince both the authorities and the previously passive indigenous population of the need to gain basic civil and political rights such as a labour code, press freedom and equal political enfranchisement – all as a prerequisite to freedom from colonial direct rule. Within this context, women expressed their own forms of solidarity, discussed in this chapter.

In British India there were earlier examples of female influence during the escalation of the civil disobedience movement after the Amritsar Massacre and during Gandhi's second 'swadeshi' movement, but by the 1930s women's participation was more prominent and widespread throughout colonial territories. How far did indigenous communications contribute towards the origins of anti-colonialism in French India as an example of a politicizing move from private to public sphere via print communications and as an empowering voice for women? Collective organization focusing on industrial action provided valuable politicization and awareness of the significance of public communication for many women, who also became active in women's pressure groups and political parties, and later assumed post-colonial leadership roles (AITUC, 2009).

This chapter establishes a triangulation between public communications relating to industrial direct action, freedom movements and manifestations of gender awareness on the part of protagonists. How compatible are these findings with existing scholarship? Colonial discourse analysis has come to accept that the relationship between colonizer and colonized is complex (Bhabha 1983), with writers such as Suleri (1992) talking of an 'anxiety of empire' on the part of the colonial power – an anxiety that clearly emerges in French colonial communications. Similarly, Spurr (1993) in his study of colonial discourses within journalism, writes of contemporary 'instability' that is not just manifest in colonial and post-colonial divisions but is also evident within systems and writings about them. Instability and anxiety on the hegemonic front was matched by women's growing confidence as public participants in change.

Research methods for female protest and communications

From the standpoint of research methods, it has been necessary to adopt qualitative analysis, because of the fragmented and disparate nature of surviving sources. Historical records are mainly on the establishment side. The plentiful reports and correspondence of the Governor and staff communications are preserved at the 'Archives Nationales d'Outre Mer' in Aix-en-Provence, but these are, as Confer suggests, 'archives of sovereignty' (1969: 120–6). The police service kept an enormous number of files on individual activists such as the strike leader V.S. Subbiah, who also wrote a memoir. In addition, the police translated every Tamil leaflet and publication, but only limited runs of newspapers have been preserved, mainly because of the difficulty for proprietors and editors, faced with censorship and jail sentences, of maintaining publication given their low or non-existent budgets, raids on newspaper offices, arson and other attacks.

The regional archives in Pondicherry hold the individual papers of some local politicians, and some press cuttings. There are no files on individual women and to find any mention of them in other files amounts to a needle in a haystack search. Conversely, indigenous left-wing political organizations encouraged women to participate. Tamil pamphlets and books published by the AITUC (All India Trades Union Congress) in Pondicherry have also been used. According to AITUC, after the Tamil *Swandanthiram* was distributed and read (sometimes aloud to groups of workers), it would then be destroyed before the authorities could seize it (AITUC 10 December 2009, pers. com.). Nevertheless, advocacy journalism such as that of *Swandanthiram*, when not thwarted by controls, was able to take an organizational lead through a crucial function of disseminating information to otherwise isolated communities and by creating solidarity among its audience, including women. An AITUC pamphlet (nd) records the roles of female activists in later years, mainly post-1947. The Subbiah memoirs draw attention to female participation in the 1930s strikes and the subsequent freedom struggle.

Context and background

Pondicherry is the main focus of this case study. The state and town was the principal centre of population of France's five Indian 'comptoirs' (or trading posts) with a total population of around 800,000. In terms of overall influence in India, Annasse (1975: 134) provides the following statistics for French territories in 1940: Pondicherry had a population of 258,000 and the other main towns were Karikal (84,000 inhabitants); Yanaon on the Coromandel coast (6,800 inhabitants); Chandernagor, not far from Calcutta in Bengal, with a population of 38,000; and Mahe on the Malabar coast (population 14,000). Settlements covered 510 square kilometres, with a further 4 square kilometres and 2,000 people spread across 12 enclaves or 'loges'. A large proportion of French Indians were Brahmin, with an important Catholic minority and also a Muslim minority, mainly in Karikal. Textile workers in and around Pondicherry were mainly untouchables. There were four indigenous languages, with Tamil predominating in Pondicherry and Karikal. Predictably, the local economy was dependent on British India; contraband in precious stones and gold to British India was prevalent and one of the best sources of income was the salt tax revenue from Britain. Employment centred around textiles, rice, coconut, sesame oil and animal bone powder production, light engineering and Indian crafts (Annasse, 1975: 135).

It was the textile industry in and around Pondicherry that became the focus of political action, from which the communication of traces of gendered issues emerge. The years 1935–37 have been selected for more detailed analysis here because they reveal a saga of severe economic exploitation, violence and political struggle – a trajectory of social conflict in the public sphere that has since become a forgotten episode in the history of a neglected corner of the French Empire. During this episode evidence of gender awareness linked to heightened and significant newspaper usage emerged for the first time. Most importantly, these trends also represented the origins of the movement towards independence.

The rhetoric of anti-colonial politics was already evident in the press. In 1935 the use of the newly popularized word 'imperial' was so mistrusted in newspaper rhetoric because of its association with the challenge of Bolshevism, that the French colonial ministry sent out an order to seize all copies of the Socialist paper *le Populaire* when the paper arrived at the ports of all France's overseas possessions: the offending piece was dated 29 August with an article headed 'Contre le brigandage colonial' (ANFOM: FM:1AFFPOL/1386). This crude censorship order appeared, of course, in the Indian case against a backdrop of a dramatic acceleration in political consciousness and the spread of communist ideology, most notably in Bengal (with a small French settlement at nearby Chandernagor). The Communist Party was not yet established in Pondicherry.

Although censorship existed in both British and French India, French territory in India was mainly known to the British as a safe haven for escaping revolutionaries and exiled nationalists; their newspapers were secretly printed in Pondicherry when banned by the British (Barrier, 1974: 36). This tradition of asylum for revolutionaries and their publications such as the Tamil *India* can be explained by France's anti-British feeling, plus the somewhat contradictory belief that she could not expel them without going against her own historic principles of liberty, equality and fraternity. The longer term consequence was that revolutionary papers provided a heritage of dissent that the local nationalist movement was later to evoke. A. Ramasamy, in his *History of*

Pondicherry, acknowledges that print publications played an important role in the dissemination of ideas, preparing the population for the 'fight', as well as a more obvious function of providing a means of communicating programmes and progress by the movement (1987: 161).

Prior to 1935, the main press criticism of the system flowed from the pages of the satirical monthly *Sri Soudjanarandjani* that published in French and Tamil. In 1920 the paper vociferously denounced conditions in textile production – Pondicherry's only heavy industry – after an illegal strike failed. Workers, including women, experienced a 12-hour day, although workers in British controlled Madras did no more than 10 hours and were paid more.[2] Although the newspaper also regularly published Tamil language nationalist poetry by Subramanya Bharati, whose writings became a symbol of cultural identity, it was not consistently anti-French: in 1930 it praised security forces for doing an 'impeccable' job (15 November–15 December). Other Tamil papers made a stand from time to time: the *Puduvai Morasu* argued for the abolition of the caste system and for the liberation of women, and *The Basumati* reported on textile strikes in Madras during 1927 (ANFOM: FM:1AFF-POL/332).

Escalating reverberations from British India were paralleled by internal criticism of the system in French 'comptoirs', as the youth organization expressed solidarity with Gandhi's civil disobedience campaign. As early as 1930, the governor had warned, in reports to Paris, that young people with some education but no jobs could become vulnerable to recruitment for anti-colonialism (ANFOM: Inde/E15). In addition, governors' reports show some awareness of weaknesses in the constitutional system that was likely to give rise to anti-colonialism. As elsewhere, French territories were governed by institutional integration with mainland France, despite local hostility to the politics of assimilation. Republicans still hoped that cultural assimilation would follow. Instead, the caste system acted as a class barrier for both sexes: corruption and control of the electoral system by the higher castes were both well entrenched. In the governor's opinion the system of government entailed burdensome administration – making the possibility of reforms more remote. Typhoid and cholera were endemic; the territory had no proper sewage system, lacked water management and electricity (ANFOM: Inde, E16/1934). The more vulnerable lower classes suffered from long-term economic disempowerment and by the 1930s were becoming politically alienated. In this context it is no surprise that class issues took precedence over gender.

How are these tensions reflected in existing scholarship? Originally Pondicherry had been occupied in 1674 by the French trading business

Compagnie des Indes orientales. From 1742 to 1754 (during the time of Dupleix), French influence extended to almost two-thirds of southern India, but by 1815 this had been reduced to a handful of mostly coastal trading settlements following half a century of fighting with the English. Thus the 'comptoirs' always represented a vestige of the 'first' French colonial empire – an 'empire manqué', or symbol of what could, or *should* have been.

Those historians who have taken an interest in French India have mostly gravitated towards the period of decolonization from 1947 onwards (Pitoeff, 1991; Neogy, 1997; Chaffard, 1965; Decraene, 1994), while some concentrate on the fortunes of French citizens post independence (Miles, 1995; de Comarmond, 1985). Arthur Annasse (1975) and Jacques Weber (1996, 2002) have addressed the history of French India for the earlier period, but the latter does not emphasize economic and social factors as part of his thesis that the colonial system made the wrong decisions on institutional rather than cultural assimilation. None of these historians mention gender factors as an influence on the interaction between ideology and economics – a relationship that is crucial to any appreciation of changes in the public sphere in French India.

Class, gender and counter-hegemonic communications

The way that women's shifting visibility from private to public spheres happened, it is argued here, reflects the roots of anti-colonialism communication – at a time when neither gender nor empire were high on the political agenda in France, largely because the Left set a higher priority on campaigning against the threat posed by fascism. Yet the realities of economic hardship in a few Indian outposts seemed peripheral to concerns about the Axis and the Comintern in the theatre of Western Europe. However, the formation, followed by the electoral victory, of the left wing Popular Front boosted the hopes of labour interests in Pondicherry that their demands for basic civil rights, industrial reforms and higher wages would receive more sympathetic attention than they had previously in mainland France.

Thus, in the years 1935 to 1937 the feelings of a disempowered and previously passive textile workforce were articulated publicly for the first time on a significant scale. With no public voice due to a lack of political organization and basic civil liberties such as the legal right to strike or hold meetings, and with press censorship, the indigenous Tamil speaking population – including peasant women – nevertheless emerged for the first time from the private to the public sphere as an organized force. Using their own clandestine newspaper '*Swandanthiram*' (meaning 'freedom') and their own printing press as a vehicle for mobilization and to cement community support, workers campaigned for a labour code that had been granted in mainland France during the nineteenth century.

Colonial neglect was by no means new – in 1906 Henrique-Duluc told his fellow deputies in Paris that workers worked 14-hour days on 'des salaires de famine' (a famine wage) of 40–45 centimes per day for men, 25 for women and 5 for children who were as young as eight years old and working 11-hour days (AAN-S.O., 1906: 1215). He was referring to the largest mill 'Rodier' (also called 'the Anglo French Textile Co.') where British investors had been lured by the total absence of legislation controlling hours, pay and working conditions (Weber, 1996: 333).

In 1933 Pondicherry young people grouped together to form a branch of Tamil Nadu Harijana Seva Sangh, a social welfare network dedicated to the abolition of the caste system. Harijana Seva Sangh then invited the organization's founder – Mahatma Gandhi – to visit. In his 1934 speech to the crowds at an outdoor rally held near Pondicherry, the Mahatma invited resistance to the inequalities of the caste system, in the name of the French constitution's traditional revolutionary principles of 'liberté, egalité and fraternité'. Ramasamy has correctly noted how visits from nationalist leaders raised spirits and encouraged the message of freedom (1987: 160). Pratibha Jain's (1985) argument that the Mathatma's nationalism was a social and economic programme, rather than simply a political one is clearly relevant to French territories, where he gained much support. Furthermore, the approach gave women new recognition through a politics of inclusion. Harijana Seva Sangh and its concept of self-help social welfare were relevant to both gender and class. Although throughout India (and Europe) women formed a significant part of textile workforce this was the first organization to take an interest in textile workers, both male and female (who were mostly untouchables): evening classes were instigated and secret trade union branches were formed.

By January 1935 Harijana Seva Sangh had helped to organize a work stoppage. Following the suggestions by communist activists over the border in the British sector V.S. Subbiah, who was a leading fundraiser for the organization, and had started *Swandanthiram* as a monthly (previously the paper had also been sold in British India, but had been censored) relaunched his paper that same year as a weekly for the Pondicherry area only.

In terms of early communist influence, George Lieten (1982), for instance, has demonstrated that for the first time the communists played an active role in the large scale Bombay textile mills strike of 1928–29, but does not mention similar conflicts in Pondicherry in the 1930s, nor the gendered element. Yet when the Pondicherry Communist Party was established in 1943, the 1935–37 textile strikes were evoked as the main formative event in the movement's history, with further relevance here, as the development of the workers' public voice within such a climate can be characterized as a form of advocacy journalism.[3]

Thus, industrial relations became an important vehicle for female activism and political expression on a class basis. The nature of indigenous communications was directly connected to basic disempowerment and lack of civil, political and economic rights, despite the fact that the authorities systematically suppressed all formal attempts at protest – including those during 1936, the year of left wing victory in France. While workers in mainland France were celebrating the formation of Leon Blum's Socialist Popular Front, 130 armed troops in Pondicherry were ordered by the governor to occupy the biggest textile mill that had been taken over by strikers, leading to a battle referred to as 'Pondicherry Shooting Day' in which 12 died and 20 were injured. This tragedy turned out to be the dramatic high point of protracted textile conflicts with mass picketing that spanned a two-year period (1935–37), involving three mills and 10,000 strikers, many of whom were women.

The textile industry conflict reached a peak in 1936, escalating into a general textile strike that coincided with similar ones in mainland France with the same worker demands: an eight-hour day, collective agreements, wage increases and paid holidays. In France such reforms were encapsulated into the Matignon Agreements in the wake of the coalition Socialist, Communist and Radical parties' Popular Front electoral victory. The same principles were eventually agreed in Pondicherry, but with one exception: workers also demanded a civil right that they had never had – the right to form trade unions. It was refused. Successive French governors took the view that trade unionism was an 'Anglo-Saxon' import, and that the previously passive workforce were unprepared for it. Governors also recognized in their reports to the minister that the seeds of anti-colonialism were sown within trade unionism. (ANFOM: 1AFF-POL/332). By denying trade union rights, the French rulers actually encouraged a nascent freedom movement that had not existed in any sizeable form previously.

Publicizing women activists

Despite the fact that picketing was illegal, the tactic became prevalent and was organized systematically, as Subbiah explains: 'Women workers were posted from the mill gates extending to the working class villages. When the blacklegs were taken to the mills, women volunteers approached them and persuaded them not to betray and disrupt the strike. Some of the women volunteers were armed with broom sticks, raised up as a symbol of their protest' (Subbiah, 1991: 64–5). *Swandanthiram* also reported how, faced with a French ban on public meetings, Subbiah marched 5,000 people, including female workers, six miles into British territory to hold a rally and thereby to circumvent France's ban on public meetings (Subbiah, 1971). Further agitation eventually led to the introduction of a labour decree on 6 April 1937, this included: the right to trade union recognition as well as age controls on the employment of children; reforms for female workers such as maternity allowance and the abolition of night work; the introduction of holiday rights; wage increases; and a reduction in the working day to nine hours, to be further reduced to eight by 1 January 1938.

When demands for independence started to emerge in local newspapers, the colonial authorities ignored them (Michalon, 1993: 24), although the Paris based *Le Courier Colonial* (4 June 1937) warned that propaganda and malicious rumours from abroad about independence were circulating in all of the colonies, especially North Africa. In fact, the extent of politicization was far wider, evidenced by the fact that crowds lined up to welcome back their leader Subbiah on his return from France, where he had lobbied for a more speedy introduction of the new labour code. *Swandanthiram* carried a front page photo of this example of the emergence of the local population into the public sphere, while Subbiah recorded: 'I was back again in Pondicherry. As I crossed Beach Road, I came across thousands of women workers standing in two parallel rows in an orderly manner. The more I advanced towards the town, I caught sight of milling crowds as if the whole of Pondicherry territory was mobilised. What did it show? . . . the unprecedented resurgence of the people following a significant victory . . . which had encouraged the will and determination . . . for national emancipation from the colonial yoke' (1991: 137). This was the beginning of female politicization, that by 1947 culminated in 10,000 people attending the first ever women's conference, held at Pondicherry's sports ground and reported exclusively in *Swandanthiram*, by this time the organ of the communist party.

The governor took the view that the labour code was 'prematurely imposed on an illiterate, credulous and impulsive population' (ANFOM: FM:1AFFPOL/709) and later called for it to be revoked. Meanwhile the new trade union branch mushroomed to 3,000 members, the biggest in Pondicherry (ANFOM: FM:1AFFOL/2888). Rodier management (the biggest of the three main textile employers) refused to recognize the new trade union and a further strike erupted. Workers' leaders then reacted by calling in the International Labour Office (ILO) in Geneva to settle the dispute. Characteristically, in Pondicherry and outlying villages industrial violence was followed by political violence. The controlling Franco-India Party, led by Mayor M. David, resorted to strong arm street gang tactics to retain support in the face of this new challenge to their power. This involved demands for franchise reform, propagated by a new party – Mahajana Sabha. As Subbiah said, 'Only Frenchmen and the privileged few had 50 per cent of our state and they dominated power in all these so-called democratic institutions. Therefore we demanded suffrage to all people over 21, including women' (Subbiah, 1971).

Press censorship escalates

In *Swandanthiram* (15 April, 1938) the defeated Mahajana Sabha Party accused the police and administration of collusion with the ruling Franco-Indian party in the systematic organization of 'banditism' and in 1938, *Swandanthiram* was banned once more, despite protests to the colonial minister by Marie Savéry, Mahajana Sabha president (ANFOM: FM:1AFFPOL, 709). The paper's Samudra printing works was also raided by the police and in 1939 their Liberty Press was targeted. The paper was normally sold by activists on street corners and in villages, but these people were also attacked by pro-French gangs. In fact in 1948 *Swandanthiram* sellers were murdered (AITUC, 2009).

It is clear that the new nationalist movement was able to benefit from criticisms of the French regime's corruption (Michalon, 1993: 246). As in British India protesters called for a boycott of the administration, legal system, police and taxes, and the independence movement in British India gave them support. How far was this agitation recognized in the French press? There was no tradition of working-class leadership in Pondicherry, so local organizers needed help – but instead of decrying colonial abuses, *l'Humanité* was beginning to turn the spotlight on Hitler. Although the pages of the CPF (French Communist Party) organ were full of attacks on colonialism in the early 1930s, right wing riots in Paris in 1934 provided a wake-up call to the dangers of fascism and its threat to bolshevism. Thus, by the end of the decade, fighting the fascists became the main tactical priority for communists worldwide, overriding any interest in gender and/or industrial conflicts.

Equally, France's ruling socialists (SFIO) seemed to be indifferent to such events. This can be explained by splits in the party at the time, with the faction that supported the colonial idea interpreting self-determination in a very limited way, and gradually imposing its support for political and cultural assimilation. In the face of communist propaganda, the SFIO. had moved to the right. The policy agendas of the SFIO and the PCF helps to account for the fact that when Subbiah and a French-speaking colleague travelled by boat and train from Pondicherry to Paris to gain support for their call for the introduction of a labour code, sympathetic French journalists could not believe their ears, commenting that their stories were too fantastic to be credible. Interestingly, it was the British consul who reported this to his French equivalent, based on evidence from the English security services who had intercepted correspondence including communications by the two female French journalists who, at the instigation of Nehru, were acting as hosts to Subbiah and his colleagues (ANFOM: FM:1AFFPOL/2888).

The use of censorship as a weapon motivated by fear on the part of authorities has usually formed part of the vicissitudes of publishing. Yet there are several aspects that make the French Indian example of 1935–37 distinctive. First, the severity of censorship; second, the gang violence and intimidation which, according to activists, was sponsored and condoned by the authorities; and third, the seriousness of economic exploitation in textiles. Not only were female activists at the receiving end of censorship accompanied by violent gang warfare, but more significantly, working-class, uneducated women were active participants in change on a collaborative basis, although no female leaders emerged until the immediate post-World War II period, unlike British India where educated higher caste women led the protests.

The existence of strong censorship meant that victims of acts of violence and gang warfare could not communicate their experiences within any public forum. Villagers on the receiving end of arson, for instance, faced the choice of either abandoning their homes and trying to cross the border into the British sector where they would have no entitlements, or defending themselves as a community. It was under these deplorable conditions that women emerged into the 'public sphere' to take unilateral action – literally as a baptism of fire in terms of collective action. When hired gangs of thugs roamed the villages around Pondicherry during the night, with the covert support of the authorities, female villagers would stand watch, keeping their fires burning. A smoke signal was used to alert women in neighbouring villages, so that cauldrons of oil would be ready to pour onto the attackers. Boiling oil and broomsticks brandished by female pickets were not conventional weapons, but these actions represented a form of politicization that brought women into public affairs as protesters for the first time. The broom became the symbolic icon of female Indian strikers in both Bombay and Pondicherry.

In this highly charged public sphere environment, a workers' victory (by 1938) gave a further boost to subaltern confidence. This was reflected in public discourses, despite bans, by a frenzy of newspaper publishing in French and Tamil. Even establishment papers such as *Dessobagari* came out with huge blank areas and one single word appeared in the middle of large expanses of white blank space – 'censuré'. *Swandanthiram* had sections totally blacked out and was banned altogether for part of that year, while Subbiah went into hiding once again: gangs had set fire to his house and the homes of many other worker activists were also burned down.

The threat of 'banditism' to press communications

The new political party that Subbiah had helped to initiate, Mahajana Sabha, was now referred to publically as 'the party of Congress' (*Madras Mail*, 7 July 1938), and by the end of the year most of their leading members were locked up in the overcrowded Pondicherry jail. The French governor still adhered to the view that Subbiah had no mandate and had been opportunist in introducing trade unionism to a population who were not prepared for it. The governor's reports also admit to the widespread acceptance of 'swaradjistes' (nationalist) methods such as the organization of volunteers, committees and cells at commune level, and the wearing of khaddar and Gandhi caps. A workers' proposal for the nationalization of one local mill, Modieliaupeth, was blamed on Nehru's ideological influence, while Subbiah's 'propaganda' was seen as having nationalist appeal, construed as hostile to European influence and increasingly aligned with the communist tendency of the Hindu Congress Party. In short, the governor was forced to admit that from 1936 to 1938 Pondicherry was 'un theatre de troubles' (ANFOM: FM:1AFFPOL/709).

In *Swandanthiram* (15 April 1938) the defeated Mahajana Sabha Party accused the police and administration of collusion with the ruling Franco-Indian party in the systematic organization of 'banditism': these complaints were repeated in letters and telegrams to the minister. In this dangerous and violent climate, women's actions were particularly brave. In 1937 and in 1938, *Swandanthiram* was banned once more, despite protests to the colonial minister by Marie Savéry, Mahajana Sabha president (ANFOM: FM:1AFFPOL, 709). The paper's Samudra printing works was also raided by the police and in 1939 their Liberty Press was also targeted. The paper was normally sold by activists on street corners and in villages, but these people were also attacked by pro-French gangs. The Mahajana Sabha Party retaliated with their own gang pressure to force the resignation of Franco-Indian party municipal councillors so that their own representatives could replace them (ANFOM: 1AFFPOL/ 2888). Yet significantly and for the first time the real issue was not who took total control of the system, but rather whether people wanted a French India or an Indian India (Weber, 1996: 335).

In Paris the Pondicherry siege had been condemned by the colonial minister as symptomatic of the indifference of his own authorities that had driven workers, in desperation, to insurrection. The government responded by sending Senator Justin Godart to conduct an enquiry into social and industrial conditions, with a view to extending France's new social legislation to the territories. A crowd of 6,000 people turned out to greet him at the port when he arrived to carry out his enquiry. Women were positioned prominently and in an orderly, separate fashion in the front rows, in the same way that they had patiently sat cross-legged in the front rows of the crowd that greeted Subbiah when he disembarked from the long boat journey that had taken him to France to argue the Pondicherry case for civil rights reforms.

After receiving representations from all quarters, Senator Goddart concluded in his report to Paris that the colony had been allowed to 'stagnate' for too long. People wanted more schools and the aboli-tion of all mention of caste within the administrative and judicial system (ANFOM: FM:1AFFPOL/716/3). Meanwhile on a visit to France, Jawahalal Nehru and Krishna Menon presented to ministers a dossier of information relating to the other side of the story – 'brutal repression' in Pondicherry. According to the Anglo-Indian press, this diplomacy, carried out during their visit to France, worked well (*Bombay Chronicle*, 1 August 1938). The governor was replaced: this was the third change of governor in two years.

With both sides under the public spotlight, created by 'Pondicherry Shooting Day' and the worsening friction in French territories, the rhet-oric applied via arguments in newspapers, reports, leaflets, telegrams and correspondence, points to certain ideological inconsistencies. Both sides evoked the 1789 mantra of 'liberté, egalité and fraternité'. For the authorities, it was a question of stressing the benefits of French rule (ANFOM: 1AFF-POL/2888). For subaltern activists the purpose of propaganda was to convince the previously passive indigenous population of the need to gain basic civil and political rights such as a labour code, press freedom and equal political enfranchisement – all as a prerequisite to freedom from colonial direct rule.

Subbiah had edited *Swandanthiram* for two years, but increasingly he was obliged to hide in order to escape violence and arrest. J.T.A. Arul took over. In correspondence to the minister in Paris, and in telegrams to Nehru, the newly formed 'Comité des Ouvriers de la France Inde' (workers' committee for French India) claimed in July 1938 that 10,000 workers had been forced to flee their homes because of gang violence and intimidation. Once more, workers were being laid off as the economic crisis once more took its toll (ANFOM: FM:1AFFPOL/2888).

Conclusions

Economic and political tensions that had manifested themselves sporadically since the early twentieth century, largely due to European neglect, had finally transformed into full-blown conflicts. The timing was such that they were fuelled by, and simultaneously gave rise to, nascent anti-colonial feeling, influenced by the situation in British India. It is clear that the combination of economic and political negligence led the indigenous population to organize themselves on a class basis, actively supported by peasant women in a way that represented a move from private to public spheres. From 1935 to 1937, and extending well beyond that date, press usage was connected to basic civil, political and economic rights.

Even the British who had already granted trade union rights, accused the French of social and economic neglect and of being 'feudal' and 'reactionary' (ANFOM: 1AFF-POL/2888): unsurprising, therefore, that gender awareness and use of newspapers was at a very early stage of development. On 14 February 1923, Albert Londres had written in *L'Impartial de Saigon* that in terms of economic reforms for the Hindus, the French had only introduced one-tenth of the British effort, yet in Pondicherry life was 'idyllic' whereas in British India 'hate' prevailed (ANFOM: AFFPOL2871). By the 1930s the political climate had changed: it was clear that the combination of economic and political neglect had led the indigenous population to organize themselves. In such a severe climate of economic deprivation, trade unionism was destined to grow, supported by the reality of inequalities that clearly challenged any perception of an idyllic life: even in 1936, mill managers were earning 20 to 40,000 francs a month, while workers were receiving 20 to 60 francs a week (ANFOM: AFFPOL2871). Female wages were at the bottom end of the scale.

With low levels of literacy, poverty and economic neglect, class consciousness came to the fore. This was accompanied by gender awareness through collective action, supported by the protesters' own publicity, written in a style that was intended for reading aloud as rhetoric to groups of people, many of whom were illiterate. Advocacy journalism, such as that of *Swandanthiram*, when not thwarted by controls, was able to take an organizational lead through a crucial function of disseminating information to otherwise isolated communities and by creating solidarity and politicization among its audience, including women.

After the end of World War II (when many anti-colonial activists actually fought for the French Resistance), 1947 proved to be the high point for female activism in Pondicherry: The milestone of a 10,000 strong women's conference aimed to form a new organization was front page news for *Swandanthiram* but it was ignored or minimized by most of the French and colonial press. Yet without the consciousness-raising effect of events between 1935 and 1938, such economic and politically motivated gender awareness and the associated publicity would not have been possible.

In French India, protesters had to produce their own publicity because they were excluded from the mainstream. This had the effect of creating solidarity for the nascent nationalist cause. These were not produced for or by women, but they aimed to include them and to encourage the politicization of women. In a context of economic neglect, poverty and lack of rights, class came before gender. With low levels of literacy and poverty class consciousness was integral to caste divisions. Gender awareness emerged from collective action, supported by the protesters' own publicity, written in a style that was intended for reading aloud to illiterate people. By disseminating information to otherwise isolated communities, encouraging solidarity and political awareness, advocacy journalism served a crucial function, although not specifically addressed to women separately or distinctly. Without the consciousness-raising effect of events between 1935 and 1938, later gender awareness and associated publicity would not have been possible.

Despite censorship, the struggle to communicate economic and social protest represented an extension of the scope of newspapers' role in the polity. Errors of omission are crucial to an appreciation of the colonial press where censorship was common, but one of the main contemporary complaints of British suffragettes about coverage in the popular press also centred on what was *not* reported. Issues of censorship and social exclusion were not confined to colonial systems. In so called 'democracies' this can involve editorial choice. The nature of mediation in turn raises questions concerning the extent to which the popular press either harmed or benefitted radical women's movements in the Western world. This is examined in relation to British suffragettes in the next chapter and is further developed in Chapter 6.

5
Britain

Collective Organization, Public Communications and the Vote

From a media perspective, subaltern civic agitation analyzed in the previous chapter was only just beginning to register in indigenous publications. In sharp contrast, the British mainstream press was clamouring for news about all things female. In 1914, looking back on his coverage for *The Daily Mail* of The Hague Peace Conference in 1899, journalist William Maxwell wrote: 'I was bombarded for several days with telegrams urging me to "describe the doings of the ladies!"' He responded that if they wanted this sort of coverage they should send 'a society reporter' to replace him. Eventually the editor intervened and instructed Maxwell to continue taking the business seriously. Nevertheless, Maxwell concluded from this episode: 'The ladies have exercised a subtle and powerful influence on journalism', although not specifying what kind of influence (1914: 1090).

Through examining a broad range of newspaper sources in Britain, this chapter analyzes the influence Maxwell notes in terms of collective organization of forms of cultural citizenship – their origins, their growth and the implications for women's suffrage. In order to answer these questions qualitative examination extends across a wide range of print publications. Thus, the scope of the issues from all sides and the scale of publicity can be appreciated.

The newspaper landscape for suffrage

The battle for press attention during the protracted suffrage campaign in Britain was a complex one that reveals much about the emerging relationship between women's citizenship and newspapers. The more formal, documentary approach of traditional press coverage was now under challenge form the popular press that treated political issues such as suffrage in a sensationalist way as a series of 'human interest' stories, evoking a sense of outrage and other emotional reactions on the part of the reader. This had an effect on the behaviour and attitudes of female activists who were beginning to think more openly that such press coverage constituted a 'must have' essential for campaigns. In 1910 Emmeline Pethwick-Lawrence commented in *Votes for Women* that 'In these modern times women who have a great cause to advocate come out into the open' (15 July: 689). This and the following chapter trace the development of this way of thinking as well as its implications and influence on emerging cultural citizenship.

How did supporters of women's suffrage promote the cause 'out in the open' using their own press and other newspapers? What were the reasons for, and the nature of, the evolution of a publicist orientation? There had long been a tradition in Britain for what is called today 'alternative media' – that is, non-mainstream publications. Women had communicated in their own journals and other specialist publications for a long time; debating policies, campaign tactics, ideas and social conditions. In turn, the mainstream press used such journals as a source for stories, and women's papers became the Fleet Street reporter's database for intelligence.

By the late nineteenth and early twentieth century newspapers of all kinds were thriving, with women reading them, writing for them (in small numbers, see Chapter 3) and making the news. Both pro- and anti-suffrage arguments were developed and rehearsed in three categories of newspaper: the movement's own journals (suffrage and labour), the political press (led by *The Times*), periodicals and the new half-penny and penny mass circulation popular dailies. In particular, the new half-penny mass circulation national dailies such as *The Daily News* and the *Daily Mail* had an appetite for sensationalism. This was fed by the desire of suffrage organizations to engage with the press, and the orientation towards publicity that women's organizations (especially militants) learned to develop.

Specialist women's journals in Britain reflected the complexities of the relationship between 'new woman' and feminism that was merely hinted at in most mass circulation dailies, for they included debates that were *not* covered or dealt with adequately in most of the popular press. One of these that found its way into the mainstream in August 1888 was a great debate started in the pages of Britain's *Daily Telegraph*, sparked by freethinker and feminist Mona Caird's article on marriage. She argued that conventional marriage had failed and that in future women should achieve economic independence and a spiritual union based on prior friendship, for with such comradeship and equality marriage could become a free contract. *Twenty seven thousand* letters poured in, despite competition from the rival publicity of the Jack the Ripper case that appeared on the same pages. For a month or so, the 'petty disputes and squabbles of middle class marriage were juxtaposed in apparent contrast to the degradation of East End prostitution' (Walkowitz, 1992: 168). The significance of this vibrant national newspaper debate can be better appreciated by noting the context in which it appeared. Rejection of marriage was a popular theme in novels such as Hardy's *Jude the Obscure* and others by Emma Brooks, Sarah Grand, Olive Shreiner, Grant Allen and George Gissing (Caine, 1997: 136). Frequently contemporary fiction also raised the question of sexual suffering, when innocent and ignorant women and their children faced congenital syphilis and infection due to their husband's excesses.

By the early twentieth century print publications of all sorts – penny and half-penny mass circulation dailies, evening and Sunday press, popular periodicals, political broadsheets and journals were all so well developed that the generation of ideas, organizational campaigns, a plethora of community groups, social, religious, economic and political interests could all jockey for the attention of a huge reading public. The main point of newspapers was to communicate ideas and persuade others in a range of discourses. Some writers opposed suffrage, but supported employment or property rights for women (Onslow, 2000: xii; Lewis, 1984). There was a division, for instance, between those who argued the phenomenon was merely a question of better education than in earlier times, and those who supported Caird by maintaining that what made the 'new woman' distinctive from previous generations was her rejection of marriage. There were suffrage supporters who did not demand any further action other than the vote, while others saw it as a preliminary to a far more fundamental reform of society; others were dedicated to single aspects of reform such as education.

Publishing by other organizations was widespread. Every socialist group established in Britain after 1880 eventually launched their own newspaper: there were over 400 (Hopkin, 1978: 295). As with these organs, women's papers also represented the opinions of readers who felt the mainstream press misrepresented, ignored or misconstrued ideas and proposed reforms. They used their own publications to refute what they perceived as these popular fallacies (Tusan, 2005; DiCenzo, 2000). *Woman's Signal* , for instance, in an article entitled 'The New Woman' (29 November 1894: 345), argued that mainstream periodicals such as *Quarterly Review* represented the 'new woman' as an anarchist in a way that was a slander and a libel, when in fact she was 'Puritan and not Bohemian', but with 'strength of body and mind'.

Debates in women's own newspapers showed the range, complexity and diversity of ideas. *Women's Signal* considered Mona Caird's ideas on marriage to be extreme, whereas *Shafts* supported her novel *The Daughters of Daneus* and serialized her essays on *The Morality of Marriage*. The latter journal, according to Caine, preferred discussions on language, issues of representation and meaning to campaigns, while *Women's Signal* prioritized the dissemination of information on campaigns and legislation (1997: 140, 141). Although such feminist writing has been the subject of extensive scholarship, the way that these activities influenced the gendered attitudes of the popular mainstream press has not.

Cross-fertilization between newspaper and periodical sectors

In origin, most of the arguments propagated in the press predated the suffrage campaign itself. Just as the anti-suffragists women who became famous at the end of the nineteenth century had all 'been trained in that anti-feminist stable of the 1860s, the *Saturday Review*' (Harrison, 1978: 104), so pro-suffrage women gained their experience from women's papers away from Fleet Street (Onslow, 2000: 2, 26) and from early campaigns in the labour movement with cross-fertilization taking place between suffrage movement newspapers and the labour movement press. Helen Swanwick wrote for the *Manchester Guardian* before becoming editor of the suffragist paper *Common Cause*. Helen Blackburn the editor of the *Englishwoman's Review*, supported suffrage during her tenure from 1881 to 1890. In this period social and political values of the 'belle époque' were subject to friction and upheaval, challenged not just by militant and constitutional suffrage campaigns but also by new industrial, economic and political forces such as increasingly powerful trade unions, intense labour unrest and industrial activity as well as political crises such as the struggle for Home Rule and the revolt of the Tories. Women's suffrage cut across party boundaries.

Activists relied on their own press for updates on progress, everyday workings, and policy, but reporting of events happened simultaneously in both branches of public communication, and women's organizations were only too aware that they needed to persuade the largely male domain of Fleet Street that in turn was the receptor and interlocutor for politicians wanting communication with the wider public. Most divisive issues were reflected in Fleet Street: here the worlds of politics and newspapers converged and overlapped, with individual organs gaining a reputation for being 'protectionist' or 'free trade', 'unionist' or 'home ruler'. The leader of the establishment pack was *The Times*, supported by the *Morning Post* and the *Pall Mall Gazette* (inter alia). The *Manchester Guardian*, the *Daily News* and the *Westminster Gazette* acted as stalwarts for the Liberal Party.

Women's suffrage was never included in the election manifesto of either of the two main parties. The tags 'pro' or 'anti' women's suffrage fluctuated according to changes in editorship and/or proprietorship and much depended on the individual editor – for example the *Fortnightly Review* suddenly became interested in female suffrage when John Morley took over in 1867. Such vacillations can be explained by the fact that individual editors harboured ambitions to influence opinion rather than to reflect it (Pugh, 2000: 15, 228, 230). Newspapers tended to be fickle in the way they were influenced by party considerations and changes in suffragist tactics, so there were also discernible changes in opinion within journalistic columns as the suffrage movement gained momentum. Strangely, there appeared to be little or no correlation between the strength of a party or faction and editorial support (Koss, 1981: 8), although the majority of national newspapers had conservative inclinations. Female journalists could also change viewpoint: Janet Courtney, for instance, had once contributed to the *Anti-Suffrage Review*, but ended up writing in support of women trade unionists (Onlsow, 2000: xii). Many sympathetic Fleet Street reporters such as writers in the *Manchester Guardian* later turned against militant suffrage tactics (see Chapter 6).

Yet it was not really until the early twentieth century that commentators were able to categorize newspapers into 'pro-suffragist' and 'anti-suffragist', by which time regular debates were held between female and adult suffrage supporters and with anti-suffragists for instance. By 1912 the *Common Cause* (NUWSS newspaper) was able to list the press according to pro, anti and neutral (4 January: 677), and considered that the majority were pro-suffrage. This contention is questioned in the next chapter.

However, in the early days of the campaign, any newspaper publicity, even if critical, served to raise women's profile, as women's organizations were dependent on press coverage. Critical press comment always had the effect of raising the issue in question and inviting feedback in the form of letters, so it is possible to argue that in the early days of the campaign even bad news was good news: the public profile of the cause was raised. Benefit in the early years from critical newspaper coverage goes some way to counteracting suffragette claims of press bias in later years, examined in the next chapter.

For women's suffrage groups, the task was to use journalism and public communications to strengthen the women's cause while simultaneously persuading four groups of people: MPs to give active support within Parliament; their own potential supporters such as the labour movement; the press; and the wider general public that was not directly involved but could be stirred from time to time by specific issues or events. This meant that women had to intervene in a range of public discourses in the fields of medicine, law and education, and not merely parliamentary politics.

Ideas were the lifeblood of persuasion. It was Mona Caird who stated in 1892: 'We are not governed by armies and police, we are governed by ideas' (1892: 829). Ideas permeated the organizational culture of social, legal and political institutions and practices from which women were banned or from which they suffered unequal treatment. Ideas were announced, explained, discussed, challenged, changed and/or defended in the pages of the press and periodicals: such was the range of ideas that the press always had plenty of material – even if they chose not to use it. There were arguments to be made on 'natural' (inherent) rights, and on expediency (social reforms), for instance. Whether these ideas could be converted into legislation was a different matter, but influencing the press was a necessary prerequisite for this goal.

Ideas could be flawed, but when it came to women's citizenship, the concept of the vote needed to be accepted within institutions and social practices if the position of women was to change. In the competitive environment for the 'feminist public sphere' (DiCenzo, 2011: 26) the concept of 'embeddedness' within national consciousness, aided by newspaper dissemination of ideas, was crucial. This process depended on newspapers, so effort was made to ensure newspapers were influenced in their favour. Certainly the main promotional motivation of the two main women's suffrage organizations – the NUWSS (National Union of Women's Suffrage Societies) and the WSPU (Women's Social and Political Union) – was to generate a constant flow of propaganda that kept the issue of the vote live in the public sphere.

Women's creative and extremely active use of the press for suffrage propaganda during the late nineteenth century and early twentieth century challenges the Habermasian assumption of public sphere decline by that time, and it also calls into question any blanket assertions concerning the inexorable decline of a political press in Britain. In fact women's newspaper efforts contributed to press diversity

(Chapman, 2005b: 104, 116–17). This effectively underlines theories of 'counter publics', proposed by Fraser, supported in the case of the United States by Ryan (1992: 259–88). 'Women were not only trying to gain access to the public sphere through political representation, but were also challenging the very definition of what constituted the public sphere of concern' (Dicenzo, 2011: 16). This point is evidenced in early campaigns that aimed to influence Fleet Street newspapers.

Early campaigns and their newspapers

When in 1866 John Stuart Mill presented a women's suffrage petition to the House of Commons, Emily Davis drew up a list of 500 newspapers and periodicals to which articles and copies of the petition were sent. This was the earliest, and very effective, example of an intensive press publicity campaign. The *Pall Mall Gazette* published details and although some newspapers took the opportunity to express opposition *The Times* remained silent (Bostick, 1980: 125–7). An amendment to the 1867 Reform Act followed, but was defeated, prompting the formation of the first women's suffrage committee.

A municipal franchise for British women was introduced in 1869, followed by further legislation for the right to vote at county, district and parish council levels. By the end of the century, female volunteers were used extensively by political organizations and pressure groups. No longer could it be said that they were emotionally unsuited to the rough and tumble of political life. On 19 November 1910 a *Times* Woman's Supplement 'How to Help your Party' claimed there were 50,000 women involved in campaigning before the January election of that year. After 1884, when the franchise was extended to most working class men, suffrage agitation for women had gone into decline – until the NUWSS was formed in 1897, with Mrs. Fawcett as president, as a non-party, non-militant organization that was consolidated from 16 constituent societies.

An eminently respectable organization, the NUWSS believed in civic rights, civil responsibilities, and aimed to create a parliamentary lobby, supported by their newspaper *Common Cause* (established in 1909), and hopefully, by enlightened public opinion in the country as a whole. Many of its members had also been active in other Victorian pressure groups, sharing similar procedural experiences such as lobbying for reforms, and in educational and electoral activities including the founding of journals, petitioning, writing leaflets, organizing local branches, holding meetings and conducting fundraising activities.

Among a host of other newspapers and broadsheets, *Votes for Women* was the organ of the Women's Social and Political Union (WSPU), the main militant group founded by Emmeline Pankhurst in 1903 and particularly active within the news from 1905. The communications of the NUWSS and the WSPU provide strong evidence for the assertion of Nancy Fraser that 'Counter-publics contested the exclusionary norms of the bourgeois public, elaborating alternative styles of political behaviour and alternative norms of public speech' (1992: 116). This is illustrated by the fact that the word 'feminist' was first used extensively by Dora Marsden, editor of *Freewoman*, in order to criticize the WSPU as being authoritarian, centralized and not intrinsically connected to feminism (Caine, 1997: 143–4). The first British article to attempt a definition of 'feminism' offered a range of ideas with a very broad zeitgeist and was written by 'Ellis Ethelmer', a pseudonym for Ben and Elizabeth Wolstenholme Elmy (Caine, 1997: 143–4). Many in the WSPU saw the vote as a first step towards the kind of spiritual and personal independence advocated by Marsden. Central to these arguments was the issue of sexuality (see Chapter 3). The WSPU favoured withdrawal of women from heterosexuality rather than sexual freedom per se.

When the editors of the paper Emmeline and Frederick Pethwick-Lawrence left the WSPU *Votes for Women* in 1912, the paper was renamed *The Suffragette*. Frederick brought inspired financial management to *Votes for Women*, and according to a supplement to *Votes for Women* (1 October 1909), in less than two years between 1907 and 1909 the circulation of *Votes for Women* rose from 200 per month to an impressive 30,000 per week – but he was in a distinct minority as a male.

Most suffrage organizational publications were run by women members who gained journalistic, editorial, organizational and management experience. Ownership and/or editorship of a newspaper opened up the power of public communication. Among the movement's own press, leading feminist thinkers were also sometimes newspaper editors, such as Lydia Becker who organized the Manchester Suffrage Society and edited the *Women's Suffrage Journal* until her death in 1890, and Helen Swanwick who started *Common Cause*. Barbara Onslow suggests that as women were excluded from parliament, they directed their energies at the press (2000, p. 170). Many also became active in trade union politics and labour movement communications.

The legacy of this earlier period for the suffrage movement was an important one: through the labour movement press women gained a sense of unity and collective solidarity.

Labour movement background

The emerging strength of women's suffrage in Britain was intimately connected with the simultaneous growth of unionism and labour movement organizations in the 1880s, 1890s and by the turn of the century. 'It is impossible to understand the social positions of women without understanding the ways in which the hegemonies of class (and race) are articulated with those of gender' (Tickner, 1987: 274). However, the majority of female trade unionists who supported suffrage chose to also work with men: a unisex approach was not unusual. According to Jacoby (1976: 155) this was a distinctive feature of the British women's trade union leagues that were class rather than gender oriented, compared to the United States. Yet as trade unionism grew stronger among women workers, it was paralleled by a significant growth in other women's groups, such as the Women's Co-operative Guild that had 100 branches by 1892. Articles and letters by members of this important organization were published in support of suffrage by *The Englishwoman's Review* as well as in *Co-operative News* – the latter had a 'Women's Corner' as early as 1883. During the 1890s *The Women's Labour News*, a suffrage quarterly, led the way in publicity, and the Women's *Trade Union League Review* also campaigned to create solidarity through its pages on the issue of working conditions. In addition, traditions of working class self-help education aided female citizenship: women often joined the Co-operative Library. Women from the Women's Co-operative Guild would read and debate books such as Ethel Snowden's *The Feminist Movement* and William Morris's *Dream of John Ball*.

However, by far the most widely-read platform for debating ideas about women and the arguments for and against women's suffrage in the 1890s was the *Clarion*, a weekly noted for its clarity and wit. This working-class paper was one of the biggest influences on the popularization of socialism and political issues, due to the paper's accessibility. (The *Clarion* was also the first radical newspaper since the Chartist *Northern Star* to pay its way.)

The *Clarion* was eagerly awaited every week in working-class homes, and around it and editor Blatchford's writings there were a host of other activities, such as the Clarion Cycle Club. The paper carried adverts for cycles – a sport that appealed to women as well as men. In fact cycling was considered a daring liberation at the time, and was associated with women's rights as being equally radical. Coverage of cycling issues in *The Daily Mail*, as mentioned in Chapter 3, was extensive, as cycling was a favourite hobby of Harmsworth and his wife.

Another idea that impinged more directly on citizenship was conceived by the paper's women's editor Julia Dawson in her 'Women's Letter', early in 1896. 'The Van' – a caravan staffed by women readers – took the socialist message to small market towns and country districts. The paper published the names of the 'vanners' and their route – the majority were women. The project gave them valuable experience in open-air public speaking. It was supported by Radical suffragists campaigning for socialism as well as the vote for women who aimed to influence Labour at grass roots level.[1]

Solidarity and public communications

Indeed, Labour politicians needed to be convinced that working women would qualify for the vote and that it would lead to further reforms in their interests (especially that improved conditions would mean that women would no longer undercut the industrial wages of men). The trade union movement was split over the issue of the vote and the new Labour Party, formed out of the Labour Representative Committee, was divided over the principle of adult versus women's suffrage. Yet despite agitation and promotion by the *Women's Trade Union Review*, women did not have representation on the important TUC Parliamentary Committee and still had to struggle for recognition from other trade unionists.

Mrs. Pankhurst and her daughters, who proved to be outstanding self-publicists, dismissed earlier efforts prior to 1906 (when they moved their organization from Manchester to London and started to escalate militancy) as 'a dreary record of disappointed hopes and trust betrayed' (Pethwick-Lawrence and Edwards, 1907: 152). Admittedly many of the battles were actually aimed at persuading the new Labour Party to adopt women's suffrage, but in her carefully researched history, *The Suffrage Movement*, published 13 years after the victory of the vote, Sylvia virtually ignores the impact of earlier campaigns led by working women outside the Women's Social and Political Union. To do this is also to ignore issues of class and their relationship to gender – itself the subject of scholarship since that time. In fact, authors such as Marian Ramelson (1976) have used media sources such as a 1902 pamphlet entitled *Working Women on Women's Suffrage* and an essay by Esther Roper in the same year, 'The Cotton Trade Unions and the Enfranchisement of Women' as evidence of working women's campaigns for the vote.

By the 1890s more than 1.25 million women were in service with working conditions not covered by trade boards, yet skilled men, organized into strong craft unions as a kind of aristocracy of labour, traditionally tended to believe that married women should not go out to work. By the end of the century, as trade unionism broadened its appeal and consequently grew stronger among women workers, attitudes changed within the movement itself. By then the Women's Protective and Provident League (est. 1874) was organizing and coordinating small unions of women throughout Britain.

Such activities provided an introduction to citizenship for thousands of ordinary women, so sensitively described by D.H. Lawrence: 'When the children were old enough to be left, Mrs. Morel joined the Women's Guild. It was a little club of women attached to the Cooperative Wholesale Society, which met on Monday night in the long room over the grocery shop of the Bestwood "Co-op". The women were supposed to discuss the benefits to be derived from cooperation, and other social questions. Sometimes Mrs. Morel read a paper. It seemed queer to the children to see their mother, who was always busy about the house, sitting writing in her rapid fashion, thinking, referring to books, and writing again. They felt on such occasions the deepest respect' (Lawrence, 1977: 68).

The Women's Labour News, a suffrage quarterly, led the way, and during the 1890s the Women's *Trade Union League Review* similarly campaigned to create solidarity through its pages on the issue of work conditions. In the cotton towns women were gaining valuable trade union experience (despite inherent conservatism among many male Liberal weavers and Tory spinners in Lancashire) that provided a grounding for later suffrage campaigns. Through the labour movement press they gained a sense of unity around collective actions: while they were protesting in their own town, so too were others elsewhere. In short, the labour movement carried news of solidarity through its reporting, and thereby also created and strengthened solidarity.

Traditions of working class self-help education aided female citizenship. Women often joined the Co-op library and were encouraged by the *Clarion* when the paper serialized Blatchford's own *Merry England*, later published as a shilling booklet – with sales of over 700,000 in a few months. It was said that for every convert made by *Das Kapital*, there were 100 made by *Merry England* (Liddington and Norris, 1978: 120). Later, Blatchford's *God and My Neighbour* was regularly read and discussed. Yet Robert Blatchford was no feminist. He had become converted to socialism after writing a series of articles on conditions in the slums of Manchester for the *Sunday Chronicle*.

The upsurge in working class agitation in the late 1880s was sparked by the famous match-girls strike, itself prompted by an article in the socialist paper *The Link*, edited by Annie Besant, who helped them to win some improvements. In 1888 Besant revealed the shocking working conditions of girls and women in an article entitled 'White Slavery in London' and published the details of the industrial conditions of the sweated labour at the Bryant and May Match Company, encouraging a strike by the match girls. Three girls were sacked for giving information to *The Link*, but Besant then encouraged them to establish a trade union, while other newspapers also exposed the facts, eventually forcing the firm to improve conditions.

That same year and the following year there were a number of different strikes by female textile workers, followed by the London Dock Strike when very poor workers took action for a month to gain a rate of 6d per hour. Once more, the power of newspaper publicity was evident. Industrial campaigning led on to political campaigning for longer term reforms as some strike leaders joined the Marxist Social Democratic Federation (including Eleanor Marx and Annie Besant), although the founder H.M. Hyndman and many other members were not sympathetic to feminism.

For activist women, social events were linked with politics. So too were friendships and marriages. In 1902 the *Women's Trade Union Review* reported on Helen Silcock's marriage to a fellow activist by listing the labour organizations that were represented at the wedding (July 1902). In towns like Bolton and Oldham it was almost taken for granted that a working-class girl would go to the mill when she left school, although the majority left the mill when their first child became due or when they married. Working-class women were influenced by the Independent Labour Party, led by Keir Hardie, and in local branches worked with more educated middle-class women, becoming itinerant lecturers for the causes of socialism and feminism. Such women also wrote in the movement's newspapers. For example, Enid Stacey wrote in 1894 in the *Labour Prophet* (the monthly of Labour churches) a dialogue between two male socialists against male prejudice in the *Clarion*, It sympathized strongly with women who were left at home to carry out domestic affairs while their husbands were out and about participating in politics.

During the period 1900 to 1901 women employed in the textile industry organized a mass petition through their union branches and workplaces. Their organization of canvassing for signatures was described in papers such as the *Englishwoman's Review*. From such coverage (but not from the mass circulation press), it is possible to gauge the *scale* of peaceful campaigning strength on the ground: 'canvassers in fifty places – one, two, three, four in each, according to the numbers of the factory population – were soon at work. The method of canvassing has been chiefly that of going to the homes of the workers in the evening, after factory hours . . . Some employers allowed petition sheets in the mills, and others allowed canvassers to stand in the mill yards with sheets spread on tables so that the signatures could be got as the women were leaving or returning to work (15 April, 1902).

By 1901 the textile women had collected 29,359 signatures and 15 of them took the enormous petition down from Lancashire to Westminster, again reported in the *Englishwoman's Review* ('it looked like a garden roller in dimensions'). The women who spoke when the petition was presented, explained how unjust they felt it was that 5 million working women in Britain were denied the right to assist in making the laws that they were obliged to obey (Liddington and Norris, 1978: 148).

Labour organizations such as the Guild and the local Women's Trades Councils provided a vehicle for women to express their ideas, campaign, and adopt organizational and leadership roles, although most of the latter was provided at national level by middle-class women. However the paid organizer jobs for the Women's Trade Union League, with wages provided by trade union fees, offered a more permanent structure for gaining experience of organizing solidarity. Many of these people became radical suffragists.

In general, it seemed that the radical suffragists received support locally in Lancashire and within the Labour Representative Committee (LRC – established in 1900 as the precursor to the formation of the Labour Party), but lacked support in London and elsewhere in the country. Yet no other group of women could match the cotton workers' power. Lancashire cotton was the pre-World War I industry where women worked in large numbers, were adequately paid (comparatively) and were stronger in terms of industrial organization than any other group of working women. Keir Hardy gave them support in *Labour Leader*, but 'they kept on finding that their campaign did not travel well outside Lancashire' (Liddington and Norris, 1978: 42, 162).

Whereas the radical suffragists aimed to influence Labour at grass roots level, the WSPU initially wanted a national campaign to pressurize the Independent Labour Party (ILP) to support legislation and thereby influence the rest of the labour movement. There were also divisions over tactics and the relative importance of local versus national campaigning. Emmeline Pankhurst joined the Independent Labour Party in 1894; she and her husband had originally been active in the Liberal Party, but became disillusioned after the 1884 Reform Act precluded women, leaving in disgust with the feeling that Gladstone had let women down. The widow Pankhurst and her daughters had gradually become more left wing, believing that civil insurgence was the best model to follow, as it had been a factor in the passing of the 1832 and 1867 Reform Acts.

Labour issues as public discourse on citizenship

In fact both pro- and anti-suffrage supporters more generally referred to a discernible feature of previous extensions to the (male) franchise in 1832 and in 1867, 'in which after a prolonged period of education and propaganda followed by a more concentrated phase of agitation, parliament would accept that the issue had become too urgent to be ignored any longer' (Pugh, 2000: 124). In 1906 the *Daily News* (25 October) exclaimed 'No class has ever got the vote except at the risk of something like revolution' and the *Daily Mirror* (23 October) seemed to agree.

Discussions on points such as these took place within feminist groups and political parties and their newspapers, but also featured in the national political press, for instance, between adult suffragists and women suffragists. Both the WSPU and the ILP were based initially in Manchester and organized parallel activities. By this time, larger papers such as the *Manchester Guardian* and the *Daily News* carried letters and reports, while papers of the movement such as *Labour Leader*, the *Clarion*, and the *Women's Trade Union Review*. Local newspapers where activities were organized also carried discourses on differences in policy and principles.

During this early period much of the suffragette efforts were concentrated on converting the Labour Party, as increasing numbers of Labour candidates were presenting themselves at elections. Mrs. Pankhurst put great faith in converting members of the Labour Representative Committee, via the Independent Labour Party (ILP) left-wing element within it. To this end she organized a parallel Women's Labour Representative Committee (LRC) to agitate for votes for women, while the radical suffragists formed a local Lancashire Women Textile Workers Representative Committee.

In 1902 a bi-election took place in the traditionally Liberal seat of Clitheroe (that included Nelson and Colne). A campaign issue that arose for the Labour candidate was one of trade union sponsorship for his salary, when so many of those union members who contributed were women, and had no representation in return. David Shackleton, a former secretary of the Darwin weavers, and candidate, came out in favour of the vote for women, and a letter from Eva Gore Booth in the *Manchester Guardian* pointed out that 60 per cent of members of the Clitheroe Weavers Union were women and children. The *Clarion* also referred to her letter and noted this unfairness, with the paper's women's column referring to the issue as 'taxation with representation' (17 July 1902).

One issue that raised the profile of debate on women's condition was whether or not legislation should be used to control working hours for women in certain trades governed by the Factory and Workshop Act, or whether married women's right to work should be completely prohibited. In 1907 and 1908 proposals were launched to widen the parameters to include barmaids, for instance, by restricting women's right to work after 8 p.m. Radical suffragists opposed any limitation on women's right to work, whereas certain sectors of the labour movement were strongly pro-temperance. This participatory discourse was relatively complex, as the British Women's Temperance Association was one of the most influential suffrage supporters. The Countess Markievitz, sister of leading campaigner Eva Gore-Booth demonstrated some promotional flair in support of the barmaids when she drove a coach and four white horses though Manchester, but when liberal Winston Churchill lost the election over the issue, the equally pro-liberal *Manchester Guardian* blamed it on the brewer's lobby (22 April 1908). Although the idea that public lobbying could influence an electoral outcome was by no means new – the legacy of the Anti Corn Law League was a strong one – nevertheless the newspaper's comments indicate the significance of public discourse involving women in issues of citizenship, with communications crossover between temperance, employment rights and suffrage.

Although contemporaries in the labour movement complained that peaceful campaigning was not considered newsworthy, a strong exposé could be very influential. Conditions of female work in sweated industries were revealed to the public by the *Daily News* exhibition of 1906 (Liddington and Norris, 1978: 16, 36). This publicity prompted the inauguration of trade boards in 1909 to fix minimum wages in work areas such as tailoring and chain-making. The lessons from this episode were transferrable to suffrage.

Suffrage, parliamentary politics and public opinion

Unfortunately the radical suffragettes who campaigned within the labour movement were not as publicity conscious as other suffrage groups. The latter – especially the WSPU – ensured that their daily activities were recorded and discussed within the pages of newspapers such as the monthly *Votes for Women*. However, suffragists overestimated the power of the press to help their cause, although it is feasible that more 'public' press coverage at an early stage could have helped to influence the Liberal manifesto. If women's suffrage had been included in the 1906 Liberal edition as a policy commitment, when the party faction in support was relatively large, it could have been passed before Asquith took over as leader. Thereafter he posed a demand that seems in retrospect to be a 'mission impossible' (without the precedent of a referendum): he wanted to be convinced by substantial proof that the women of Britain supported having the vote *before* he would even entertain parliamentary legislation.

Later on Asquith actually proposed a referendum – in fact he was the first high-level politician to do so (Nessheim, 1991: 226). He then hastily withdrew the suggestion, presumably because the Liberal Party may not have benefited from the exercise. A referendum would only have gauged opinions of male voters, of course. As long as the government demanded 'proof' that large numbers of women desired the vote, with what the *Morning Post* called 'a powerful fulcrum of public opinion' (15 June 1908), practical politics had to consist of a range of activities that would be communicated within the public sphere, and suffrage propaganda was focused on this aim.

Politicians wanted to be assured that the views of activists really *did* represent those of the general public as well, but in the absence of polls and surveys they were handicapped in their assessment of what the public really wanted. Contemporaries were divided over the extent of support among women. Each side conducted their own research, coming up with findings that confirmed their own views (Searle, 2004: 460). Thus, the onus was on women's suffrage supporters to demonstrate that change was necessary, rather than on people who wanted to maintain the status quo to defend that stance (although later, as views polarized, both sides waged justifications in public). The two-party system had become stronger since the extension of the franchise to working men in 1867, but neither Conservative nor Liberal parties were willing to adopt the female vote as a leading cause. The Conservative leadership was sympathetic but its rank and file was not, while the Liberals were generally in support but their leadership was strongly against – especially Asquith who succeeded Campbell Bannerman as Prime Minister in 1908.

Contemporary understanding of 'public opinion' at the time was complicated by the fact that public opinion in support of the vote for women was not homogenous, consisting (as it always has) of a range of special interest and pressure groups, political activists and other sections of society, refracted in the press. The press provided an indication of change in attitudes, and pro- and anti-suffrage supporters accepted that public opinion was likely to be decisive in the timing of this factor. Thus, media were central to the engagement of early women's movements with the wider public. In a perverse sort of way, Asquith's 'mission impossible' demand for proof actually had the effect of focusing suffrage supporters on the development of an identity in the 'public' press – one of the defining features of cultural citizenship.

However, the battle for the attention of what suffrage supporters called the 'public press' was made more difficult by the fact that the vote as a parliamentary priority was overtaken by problems such as the Boer War (1899–1902) and other imperial issues. It seemed that national newspapers tended to be more interested in the affairs of Empire and foreign territories than in the state of society on their doorstep. There was also the crucial Home Rule crisis (with the Irish nationalists later holding the balance in votes), the struggle for power between the Commons and the Lords over Lloyd George's 'People's Budget' and the subsequent Parliament Act, industrial disputes, licensing laws and tariff reform.

Between 1908 and 1911 three women's suffrage bills and two conciliation bills passed second readings, only to face Government delay. In this highly charged public arena the demonstration became a major communicative weapon: suffrage supporters considered that mainstream newspapers could not be silent when faced with a two-mile-long procession of women in central London. Furthermore large crowds watched such events, lining the route of the march and attending the rally with speeches as the culmination, and they would also read about it in the newspapers.

The battle did not end there: obtaining press coverage did not necessarily mean that newspapers were converted to the cause. Newspaper reporting was inflected by personal opinions, political allegiances and other vested interests. The mass demonstration also had to be a political lever that made an impact on spectators as well as supporters and the press. People who watched needed to appear sympathetic and engaged by the event: national newspapers needed to pass a verdict on the demeanour of onlookers as a barometer on change. Applause or heckling were good indicators!

The vote and newspaper commercialism

It would be fair to say that the mainstream press held a definite (but not exclusive) 'monopoly on the commodity of propaganda'. In an informational climate where pamphleteering and speeches were ceding ground to newspapers as the main influence on the public, Fleet Street remained: 'the best available index to popular opinion as well as the single most convenient mechanism for guiding it' (Koss, 1981: 2, 9). However, analysis of this is confused by the impact of commercialism. Northcliffe owned the leading newspaper opponent of women's suffrage – *The Times* – and another leading opponent – *The Observer*. It was Northcliffe who had first propagated the idea that, as far as newspapers were concerned, public support should be measured by profitability. If a newspaper sold well, then its views must reflect a sizeable proportion of the population.

It may well have been this view, later echoed by others, that prompted J.D. Symon in 1914 to refute the idea that the press could 'guide' or even 'form' public opinion: rather newspapers were a *reflection* of public opinion.

Hampton, citing this contemporary interpretation comments: 'If newspapers reflected rather than guided or influenced public opinion, then they were well positioned to represent the people to an extent unmatched by Parliament' (2004: 109). However, the question of whether the press led or followed public opinion was a thorny one, even to contemporaries such as Asquith who admitted that: 'How far the Press (sic) actually operates as a dominant force in the formation of public opinion is not quite such a simple question as some people imagine' (Hardman, 1909: 65). Furthermore, Hampton's assumption misses the point that the introduction of the profit motive into the equation had led to journalistic evaluation of what was likely to sell, followed by the development of a concomitant culture to achieve this, referred to these days as 'news values'.

In other words, commercialism entered the equation and this in turn came to involve a certain kind of framing of women's suffrage as news. To achieve the aim of high sales, newspapers needed to provide a broad range of information, but they were also obliged to streamline news coverage in order to appeal to the largest possible number of readers in an attention-grabbing way – and in turn deliver a readership to advertisers. The perception was that to reach the maximum readership, bad news would sell – and unrest or violence over the vote constituted bad news, so was worthy of headlines. Good news, such as patient discussion of policy at meetings, was not news.

In January 1906 *The Daily Mail* started to use the word 'suffragette' in its pages for the first time – referring to protesters who resorted to direct action. Activists themselves accepted that such a public label distinguished them from 'suffragists' who sought lobbying and peaceful persuasion. Two months later *The Daily Mirror* – the first 'picture paper'[2] – devoted its entire front page to such publicity-seeking women. Thereafter the development of a promotional tactic of suffragist spectacle (such as demonstrations with banners and other photo opportunities) went hand in hand with the rise of halftone photography as a visual tool for the popular national press and periodicals.

Early militancy

It was militancy that really attracted the attention of the press, and this was propagated by the WSPU (motto 'deeds not words'). They believed that constant public pressure was needed in order to keep the subject of the vote perpetually in the press, parliament and the public's minds. The Union led the way in courting the attention of the popular press with striking photographs and sensational actions to provide a headline; they also used the traditional press effectively by setting the pace in political and moral discourses with a constant supply of reader letters and content for articles.

The first militant act took place in October 1905 when Christabel Pankhurst and Annie Kenney disrupted an election meeting at the Manchester Free Trade Hall by heckling and attempting to speak. They were arrested, refused to pay the fine and were imprisoned, as preplanned by Christabel (who had announced in advance that she would be spending the night in jail, and correctly calculated that militancy was news worthy). The *Manchester Guardian* was so interested that it published a transcript of the trial and a lengthy explanation of WSPU policy by Teresa Billington. Even *The Times* eventually came round to publishing the story. Although Christabel's tactics of deliberate arrest were heavily criticized, a repeatable strategy was established: premeditated militancy led to imprisonment and thus 'martyrdom', providing press coverage that in turn prompted extra funding and new membership.

After the end of 1905 and the resignation of Balfour as Prime Minister, the WSPU adopted mixed tactics until 1907. At this point heckling was the most popular form of direct protest: people attending meetings tended to view heckling as a form of entertainment, and therefore were strongly opposed to any violence by stewards in ejecting suffragettes (*Daily Chronicle*, 12 November 1907). This view was shared by some supporters within the Liberal party, despite any embarrassment that suffragette methods caused (Pugh, 2000: 189). A small-scale march on Parliament in February 1906 attracted the attention of the *Manchester*

Guardian, Daily News and *Evening News,* with a photograph of women carrying a large 'Votes for Women' banner featured in *The Daily Mirror* (20 February). It was activities such as these, and attempts to enter the House of Commons (with the imprisonment of ten women for noisy demonstration in the Lobby) that obtained more sympathetic head-lines, funds and members than ever before.

The idea that suffragettes were introducing into the polity new forms of agitation was erroneous. Most tactics, such as laying claim to public space and verbally assaulting politicians, had been long used by male agitators, but the sight of women doing it provoked equally vigorous protest from male crowds. The fact was that women were claiming their rights in ways that challenged accepted codes of behaviour for their sex (Searle, 2004: 458, 470).

Peaceful tactics

In the period 1907 to 1908 the WSPU also held 3,000 public meetings, sold 80,000 publications and contested eight bi-elections (Tickner, 1987: 8), yet the scale of peaceful suffrage campaigning was often overlooked by the 'public press' – although competitor groups were prompted to greater vitality by the WSPU's great energy. The NUSWSS did not hold any public open-air demonstrations until 1906, but there-after adopted, with gusto, public campaigning such as processions and election campaigning for its constitutional cause. The point of this new public energy was to indicate that peaceful methods could be conducted with just as much dedication and inspiration as that of the WSPU for increasingly violent activities.

Protest (both constitutional and direct action) required eye-catch-ing promotion, so considerable promotional effort was expended by the main organizations and their newspapers on visual creation. These consisted of illustrations for their press, pictorial supplements also reproduced as postcards and posters, and banners for meetings, processions and protests. Visual information was an essential part of suffragette propaganda for every printing opportunity that arose. In fact, suffrage organizations' larger demonstrations were professionally filmed and prints were sold commercially (Fawcett Archives, 1912). Emily Wilding Davison's death on the Derby racecourse was captured on newsreel. Her funeral as a martyr for the cause was a grand occa-sion of suffragette pomp and ceremony, attended by a large number of organizations, including trades unions. Onlookers were mainly silent and respectful, and the scene was described as 'both mournful and picturesque', although press reports of continuing suffragette outrage were juxtaposed on the same page as reports of the funeral (*Daily Chronicle*, 15 June 1913).

The NUWSS's first big demonstration in 1907 was referred to as the 'Mud March' because of the bad weather. The event marked a move for the constitutionalists from the confines of what the *Manchester Guardian* described as the 'regional debating society' to the realm of 'practical politics' (11 February 1907). The demonstration established a precedent for advance press publicity, and a format for processions that both press and public were later to become accustomed to – a well ordered event with banners, bands and the colours of participating societies. Over 40 organizations participated, prompting even *The Times* to concede the 'representative character' and to comment on the size (11 February 1907).

Compared to later, more confident shows of strength, some participants at this first major mass public protest seemed a little diffident about being 'out in the open'. An account by one of the demonstrators in the *Manchester Guardian* (11 February 1907) discusses her problems in coming to terms with this new experience while also assessing its political validity. Women's discomfort about public display was worsened by the disdain of (male) onlookers, described by the *Morning Post* as 'scoffs and jeers of enfranchised males who had posted themselves along the line of the route, and appeared to regard the occasion as suitable for the display of crude and vulgar jests' (13 February 1907).

Previous associations between women and the streets had been degrading ones, so in the early days of suffrage processions, abuse from the public was common. For middle- and upper-class women in particular, it was a new and uncomfortable experience to have to face insults from strangers out 'in the open'. The discomfort of abuse from the general public is confirmed by Helen Swanwick in her memoirs (1935). In 1908 she addressed 150 meetings all over England and Scotland, attended by an average of 600 people, and describes the stress and strains, not to mention the basic hard work, that public communication entailed. This may have been part of the course, but it was not a performative role that came easily to many women, even those as articulate, talented and motivated as Swanwick.

By 1908 the suffrage campaign was reaching its first peak, and so far, publicity was not all bad. On 13 June 1908 *The Times* published Mrs. Fawcett's entire, lengthy account of preparations for the NUWSS march that day. The volume of publicity for the 13 June 1908 demonstration was undeniable: in fact many newspapers gave the event several reports, and/or an opinion column. The editor of the *Daily Chronicle* spoke for many others when he stated in correspondence to Maud Arncliffe-Sennett that he had not published her letter because his newspaper 'like other journals has latterly contained little else than Suffragist information' (15 June 1908).

The NUWSS astutely used this press invasion as ammunition for further political discourse and parliamentary lobbying. Favourable coverage provided an opportunity for their own papers and leaflets to carry quotes from the 'public press' as a badge of endorsement. They published leaflets for circulation to MPs with newspaper extracts quoted in support of their arguments. As *Women's Franchise* commented: 'The importance and variety of the papers quoted from will greatly add to the value of their testimony; they will also be useful in controverting (sic) the argument often advanced that processions do no good, as no one is convinced by them' (25 June, 1908: 615).

Even national papers that were hostile to female suffrage were nevertheless impressed by the next procession – the 21 June 1908 WSPU demonstration. The press commented in particular on its organization, demeanour, pageantry, spectacle and the women's bravery. Although *The Times* (25 June 1908) admired the spectacle of the women's colours, music and banners, the paper was grudging about the level of onlooker support and in its assessment of the number of participants. Suffragists had not proved the political argument had been won: 'it cannot be regarded as an unqualified success'. In other words, suffrage spectacle was not enough.

Lobbying and emulating the mainstream press

In 1910 *The Times* reported 21 suffrage organizations where there had only been three previously, the third main suffrage paper (in addition to *Common Cause* and *Votes for Women*) being the *Vote*, the journal of a militant but non-violent society (with tactics such as picketing and tax resistance), entitled the Women's Freedom League. This organization had been set up following a split in the WSPU in 1907. In fact, the task of the press in giving coverage, comment and interpretation to the suffrage movement was greatly enhanced by the fact that there was not one movement, but several differing strands that provided a regular flow of arguments. In addition there were other papers produced by some of the hundreds of groups that were formed along religious, social, political, local or professional lines, some denominational suffrage journals, others were militant or non-militant and there were also those that were politically partisan.

As most activists aimed to influence mainstream papers, the scale of suffrage activity devoted to achieving this should not be underestimated. Press lobbying was relatively sophisticated: in 1912 the London Society for Women's Suffrage had 33 press secretaries working in 61 constituencies (Fawcett, 1912–13). 'Press work' and 'press departments' were a regular feature of women's organizations: favourable coverage was seen as an indication of progress in changing public attitudes more generally.

Women's papers increasingly emulated the commercial approach of the Fleet Street style of New Journalism, with human-interest features, catchy headlines, illustrations and photos – and also advertising as a means of achieving financial viability and legitimacy. Within the cut throat world of newspapers advertising the WSPU's *Votes for Women* managed to achieve a balance that had often proved to be an impossible challenge for many – namely the maintenance of a highly political stance while simultaneously exploiting the market system with advertising and merchandizing, and thereby extending their message.

Scholars are divided on how contradictory it was to have fashion advertisements next to politically progressive editorial. DiCenzo (2000: 123) supports Kaplan and Stowell (1994: 153–5) in arguing consistency ('dressing fashionably became a political act') whereas Harrison (1982: 282), supported by Beetham (1996: 176–7) and by Nuttall (Chapman and Nuttall, 2011: 253) perceive inconsistencies. From a contemporary perspective, feminists needed to show that they were 'womanly' in order to dispel negative press propagation of the 'shrieking sister' image. Respectability of the sex was the key concept. Women felt they needed to prove that they had a sense of responsibility, and for middle- and upper-class women, dress was the main indicator in public. Respectability (in dress) was one indication of capacity to govern. Anna Yeatman explains the logic from a feminist perspective: 'Nineteenth century feminists had to refuse patriarchal models of independence and self-government, but they did not, and given the terms of political discourse of the time, could not, refuse the association of citizenship with an individualized capacity for self-government . . . a feminist deployment of the classical democratic rhetoric of self-government maintains patrimonialism but gives it a distinctive feminine and maternalistic cast' (Yeatman, 2001: 143).

Of course, purchasing power, a prerequisite for smart dress, was a middle-class phenomenon. In working-class homes, wives tended to adopt the role of domestic Chancellor of the Exchequer: husbands and working children would give the mother/wife their wages at the end of the week for food, lodgings and household necessities, and she would give them in return some pocket money. Few wives were left with enough to spend on themselves. According to Liddington and Norris, working-class women's priority was 'to hold the family together, even though in the process their own health and needs were the first to go by the board' (1978: 32). Despite earlier labour movement roots, the WSPU decided in 1905–06 to appeal directly to more affluent, educated women rather than the working class – one reason Sylvia Pankhurst defected to work with the East End Federation of Suffragettes (organized by local, professional, social and political affiliation). Her allegiance to working people was not shared by the other Pankhursts.

As the suffrage issue increased its newsworthiness, mainstream 'quality' dailies started to supply more information about the changes in the various organizations. Before the advent of direct action (see Chapter 6) this had not been perceived as topical background. Suffrage organizations, however, were as concerned with what the 'public press' did *not* include within its columns as they were with the tenor and content of what was reported (DiCenzo, 2000: 117). More positively, a diversity of views in the press helped to focus support and arguments both for and against. Each side had to react to, and in some ways was encouraged by, the increased polarization of public stances on the suffrage issue.

According to Tickner, 'Most of the central arguments had been repeated *ad nauseam* by the Edwardian period, but this did not prevent their zestful elaboration on both sides' (1987: 153). It was in the interests of opponents such as *The Times* that issues should continue to be raised because they had not yet been adequately answered, and to this extent Asquith's intransigence along the very same lines was manna to the journalist's job of providing regular copy. 'The arguments as yet put forward by the association (NUWSS) have already been denounced by some of the suffragist women as "the old arguments". So they are; they are the old arguments, and they have never been refuted' (*The Times*, 12 June 1908). In the case of the 'antis', their arguments were usually first launched in the letters page of *The Times* in addition to *The Anti Suffrage Review*, analyzed in the next chapter.

Conclusions

Early suffrage promotional efforts demonstrated that it was possible to gain access to the public sphere, and in doing so, women were claiming for their sex a space that had become – especially since industrialization – a male-dominated domain. Public display of protest was one legacy from the trade unions, and by public display, women were manifesting their own cause.

Success in gaining publicity was cumulative from the late 1860s onwards, but escalated after 1906. By the end of the first decade of the twentieth century, public protest was well developed as a promotional tool. By coming 'out in the open' women were managing to communicate their ideas to a wider audience among the general public. This very act of mass spectacle in the streets and large public venues provided ongoing newspaper stories. As Carrie Chapman Catt of the International Women's Suffrage Alliance said to British women in 1909 at the organization's convention held at the Albert Hall: 'You are an argument'.

Advance publicity about marches and rallies played a critical role while the suffrage press itself was still in its infancy. At this time the movement was more dependent on other newspapers than their own: the curiosity of the local and national press needed to be stimulated by the promise of a unique event. From 1905 onwards militancy began to interest Fleet Street, but there is controversy about the effectiveness of suffrage tactics to court such publicity. The next chapter analyzes this more fully in relation to the period 1910 to 1918.

In general national newspaper interest in suffrage from 1906 onwards, when compared to neglect of women's issues for so many years previously, must be seen as a positive influence on the movement's drive for the vote. According to G.R. Searle, the intellectual argument over the vote had largely been won by 1906: it was the fact that franchise bills before 1914 were limited in scope, causing objections that accounts for delay. Newspaper discourses after 1906 do not entirely support the contention that intellectual argument was over. One facet of cultural citizenship that was beginning to emerge was recognition by female activists that their messages needed to be constantly repeated and reinforced with the evolution of events. Continuing public discourse was both necessary and desirable if changes in legislation were to be achieved in the face of ongoing opposition.

The next chapter analyzes newspaper rhetoric prompted by the launch of an organized 'anti' campaign. This revived and focused press discourse on both sides. The early publicity successes for militancy became a double-edged sword, for they created a precedent. As success led to further promotional efforts in the face of parliamentary intransigence, it then became more difficult to abandon such tactics. However, as women activists experienced the treadmill of public persuasion using newspapers, they ran a risk: suffrage supporters could become prisoners of their own attention seeking 'public press' promotion. This process, examined in more detail in the next chapter, became part of the various manifestations of their developing cultural citizenship, increasingly characterized by repetitive performance.

Part IV
Cultural Citizenship and Direct Action

6
Britain

Apocalypse and Press as a Double-edged Sword

As the last chapter established, pro-suffrage women had begun to begin a new phase in the struggle, even if many issues concerning the nature of female relationships with the media and how they were manifested had yet to be resolved. This was part of the mobile process of cultural citizenship, although definitions of the concept were still opaque and the tensions first identified in the 1860s in France, in relation to the potential clash between 'conservative feminization' and emerging female citizenship of a more political nature, were still present. Despite, or maybe because of this, women's public profile as mediated by mainstream newspapers, influenced in turn by the movement's own press, was taking a giant step forward with the campaign in Britain for the vote.

The British suffrage movement, through this public challenge to behavioural norms, through its long, creative and vigorous campaigns, highlight cultural citizenship to such an extent that no other country or activity hitherto can be said to have effected the same intensity. However, notoriety in the press, when acquired through discourse prompted by direct action, came at a cost to the suffrage movement. This chapter examines the precise dilemmas involved in increasingly violent publicity campaigns with attention-grabbing tactics.

The anti campaign

On 25 June 1908 in *Votes for Women* Christabel Pankhurst announced the resumption of militancy, and Emmeline Pethwick-Lawrence stated that 'We have touched the limit of public demonstration . . . Nothing but militant action is left now'. By this time the WSPU in particular had become very astute at publicity, but this proved to be a double-edged sword, prompting others to react. On 12 June in that same year, *The Times*, for years consistently anti-suffrage, reported on the launch of a (much smaller) counter movement 'of considerable force'.

The *Morning Post* and *The Times* were the two hard-liners against suffrage. Although the launch of The Women's National Anti-Suffrage League (WNASL) brought further polarization of sides, the suffrage movement was spurred on by the new organization of the antis. Henceforth suffrage comment in their own papers and also the mainstream press was spread across a range of activities: reacting to the antis; defence of their own tactics (whether constitutional or militant); providing evidence of their public support; and dealing with government policy.

The 'anti' campaign also raised contradictions – not least that women used politics to refute politics, that is, they had to mobilize politically in the same way as the suffragists with leaflets, posters, branches and public meetings, to prove that they *did not* want politics, symbolized by the vote! Unlike the suffrage movement, the 'anti' organization never took to the streets. As *The Times* explained in their defence: 'the women who are opposed to the extension of the suffrage are by tradition and temperament particularly disinclined to make themselves prominent in a political cause' (22 July, 1908: 13). In fact, the 'anti' side included highly-educated women, including a considerable number of female intellectuals and/or reformers[1] –Beatrice Webb, Mary Ward, Octavia Hill, Gertrude Bell and others, who were hardly hiding their lights under a bushel.

Nevertheless, it is likely that at first, both sides benefited from increased media coverage generated by the escalation of militancy, and there were lively bi-partisan exchanges in the letters page of *The Times*. From July to October 1908 debates for and against Mary Ward's advocacy of the American anti-suffrage experience as a learning point for Britain proved to be especially provocative. An early leaflet produced by the group effectively summarizes the overall impression that had been created in public minds up to this date by mainstream media coverage: it acts as a description of how press information had been received by the newly formed organization. 'When a Women's Enfranchisement Bill has passed its second reading in the House of Commons by a large majority; when we have a militant Society (sic), amply supplied with money, and served by women who seem to give their whole time to its promotion; when we have before us the spectacle of marchings (sic) and counter-marchings, alarums and excursions, on behalf of the Suffrage cause, in all parts of England; when Ministers' houses are attacked and political meetings broken up; when besides the pennyworth of argument, added to an intolerable deal of noise, with which the Women's Social and Political Union provide us, we have the serious and impressive sight of Mrs. Fawcett's procession of a month ago – then, indeed, it seems to be time . . . that they (women who feel strongly against this) should bestir themselves' (Museum of London, nd).

The *Anti Suffrage Review* reserved its strongest criticism for the WSPU. To further rub salt into their wound, when Mrs. Pankhurst, Christabel and Mrs. Drummond went on trial for circulating a handbill urging supporters to storm the House of Commons, they conducted their own defence (led by Christabel who had a law degree). She subpoenaed Home Secretary Herbert Gladstone and also Lloyd George. It proved to be a particularly effective stroke of publicity, with photographs dominating the front pages of the *Daily Mirror* and the *Daily Graphic*, and many columns of text in *The Times* and the *Manchester Guardian*, as well as other dailies (22–26 October 1908). Such prodigious talent did not go unnoticed: it was Gandhi who is said to have later commented (off the record): 'it is no wonder that a people which produces such daughters and mothers should hold the sceptre' (quoted by Burton, 1994: 207).

By 1910 this rich and influential group of antis had become the National League for Opposing Women's Suffrage (NLOWS). *The Times* carried 43 editorial columns between June 1910 and June 1914, with headlines such as 'Anarchy in Politics' designed to generate fear and anxiety about what would happen if women obtained the vote. Use of the word 'revolution' became a feature of a literary devise that spelt out doom for the Empire, disaster for family life, the disqualifying effects of physical and mental female sex distinction, and the absence of a clear mandate for giving women the vote (Nessheim, 1991: 88). Even a limited franchise would mean a slippery slope to further concessions to militants who were hooligans, a dangerous minority seeking notoriety, as opposed to the silent, respectable majority who were against any change to the franchise (1909, November: 1; 1909, March: 1).

For the antis, good government was dependent on property and education (*Morning Post*, 5 May 1913). The counter argument was that the vote for women was long overdue in a progressive country, and that opponents were badly informed, reactionary and prejudiced. Ironically, although the antis clearly had the unequivocal support of *The Times*, they still believed that pro-suffrage activists were better at publicity (Harrison, 1982: 289). Ultimately, theirs was a different sort of contribution: the ideas of the anti-suffrage movement (with significant male input and a men's section) were developed within existing informal frameworks, such as London's club-land – an arena that was hardly accessible at all to suffrage supporters. Harrison points to a: 'formidable anti suffrage press network' (1978: 104). The political significance of such informal networking is difficult to substantiate, although histories of individual clubs point to widespread support from establishment figures. By and large, this was a closed but intimate public sphere from which women were excluded. The suffragette politics of apocalypse, highlighted by the press, lacked any comfort factor for people who frequented these worlds, making influence less achievable, not more. Unlike the suffragettes, who had to be constantly ingenious to gain publicity, the antis press support required little effort, for they could rely on inherent conservatism.

The *Manchester Guardian*

Not all national newspapers were hostile: the *Daily Herald* even printed the *Suffragette* newspaper when its own presses were raided. The strongest press supporters of the vote were the *Daily News* (48 editorials between June 1910 and June 1914) and the *Manchester Guardian* (46 editorials). The *Manchester Guardian* was the most energetic champion of feminism, democracy and left Liberalism, supporting any compromise bill that would be a step towards franchise. During 1910 its arguments in favour of the Conciliation Bill (presumably aimed at Liberal MPs who had not yet committed their vote) dominated the paper's editorial columns, and persisted in 1911 and 1912 when such legislation was still on the cards. Even after the defeat of the third Conciliation Bill in 1912, editor C.P. Scott warned Liberal MPs that their credibility was at stake, and the paper's columns still persisted with strong arguments that identified women's rights with human rights, in support of a democratic suffrage measure. The paper continued to exude a genuine and heartfelt optimistic hope that a majority in parliament and in the country at large actually wanted women to be enfranchised (Nessheim, 1991: 214).

Yet the *Manchester Guardian*, like all the mainstream papers, or 'public press' as contemporaries referred to them, drew the line at militancy, reminding readers that constitutionalists represented the majority (11 and 13 July 1910). Unlike the other two Liberal papers (the *Daily News* and the *Westminster Gazette*), the *Manchester Guardian* seemed to believe that the inalienable human rights of women seemed to override the practicalities of day-to-day politics – namely the precarious position of the Liberal Party in parliament – a factor that the majority of Liberals actually put first. In fact, the voting record for the final Conciliation Bill would indicate that once militancy began to play into the hands of the antis, pro-suffrage papers lost any initiative that they may have had in the earlier years of the campaign, and from 1911–12 they did not have any discernible influence on Liberal MPs.

In fact if one compares C.P. Scott's diary entries on meetings with Lloyd George with the actions and initiatives of the latter, it would seem that this particular rising star of the Liberal Party ignored his newspaper editor's suggestions. Scott was also in regular contact with Mrs. Fawcett and the NUWSS, and corresponded with Mrs. Pankhurst and other leading militants: through his editorial influence he wanted to be in a position to 'encourage, to be consulted and to "warn"' (Wilson, 1970: 23–4).

Positive coverage for the vote

By 1911 the NUWSS and the WSPU were working together again in unity, and cooperation was rewarded by positive coverage for 'The Women's Coronation' of 17 June. This event proved to be the jewel in the crown of image conscious pageantry. The date was significant as this was Coronation year and 17 June was the beginning of a week of national festivity and holiday, with two royal processions. London was full of visitors. The women's event was the most spectacular of all the pre-War marches and rallies, and the only one in which all the suffrage groups participated, attended by 40,000 women from at least 28 suffrage organizations. The gala of floats, banners, historical costume and music – said to be seven miles long – rivalled the official Coronation procession in terms of scale and spectacle.

As *Votes for Women* (28 April) announced, this event was designed as a series of 'pageant' displays that were intended to be national (every suffrage society in Britain was invited to participate), imperial (a pageant of empire) and international (with overseas suffragists and other national flags) with 'an accumulated language of symbolic identities' (Tickner, 1987: 124, 126). This included a prisoners' pageant (700 or their proxies, dressed in white, with pennions fluttering from glittering lances), 'a stroke of genius' according to *The Daily Mail*, (19 June 1911). *The Spectator* praised the Empire pageant as a 'thing of beauty . . . far surpassing the crude symbolism of the Lord Mayor's show' (quoted in *Votes for Women* 30 June 1911). The WFL section with a banner 'Six Million Women Workers Need the Vote' received great applause from onlookers.

Press coverage from both pro- and anti-suffrage newspapers was the best ever received – exuding enthusiasm for the public spectacle. All sides were hypnotized by the scenes: the richness of the pageantry, brilliant organization, courage and diversity of participants, size and response of crowds. There was no hostility at all, and even the *Anti Suffrage Review* referred to the 'charming spectacle, well stage-managed' (July 1911). Their League had hired 'half a dozen sandwichmen to parade with boards proclaiming "Women Do Not Want the Vote"', (Tickner 1987: 130). The whole event showed a spirit of optimism and cooperation, as described in the *Daily Sketch*, *The Spectator*, *The Times*, *The Star*, the *Manchester Guardian* and many other papers (19 and 22 June).

The changing barometer

Good publicity and plenty of national coverage did not necessarily equate to influence, however. Emily Davis (see later) made a differentiation between notoriety and influence: arguably women's engagement with the mainstream media on the suffrage issue gained them notoriety rather than influence. This analysis of the effectiveness of press promotion permits some conclusions on the evolving contribution to 'cultural citizenship'. It appears that around 1911, the barometer of suffrage and suffragette impact on the press and politicians more generally shifted from influence to notoriety and that it was only World War I that shifted the focus back again.

As the Women's Coronation – the most elaborate and theatrical pageant and public demonstration of the WSPU – had underlined, both sides could, and frequently did, evoke empire. The 'antis' repeatedly spelled out doom and gloom (woman suffrage would bring 'ruin on our Empire') (*The Times*, 15 July 1910: 9). Indeed, the successful running of the Empire was seen as a form of virility – the state was a virile one, and secured by virility. Among the anti-arguments, as presented in *The Times*, was the point that in matters of state, physical strength (violence) had to be adopted as a last resort (15 June 1908). To the 'pros', the civilizing mission was more important, for the vote would demonstrate their fitness as participants in the imperial nation-state. As Burton (1994: 208) reminds us: 'Saving Indian women was as much a part of the civilizing mission for feminists as it had been for generations of colonial policymakers', although World War I and the contribution to the war effort of Indian women caused many of these attitudes to change (see Chapter 7 for post-World War I colonial attitudes to women). Militancy may have been a contributory factor in winning the vote in the early days, but it is more likely that, in terms of the impact on the 'public' press from 1911 onwards, it actually hindered progress (Pugh, 2000: 212). One of the reasons behind anti-press complaints was the fact that suffrage supporters did not recognize news values as representing a specific professional culture of framing events in the way that we do today, with the result that they were quite insulted by the different Fleet Street sense of priorities. 'Far more notice has been extended by the newspapers of today to the trial of some contemptible murderer than to all the public demonstrations for Reform that our streets during this century have known', *Common Cause* complained in 1912 (18 April: 21). For the new mass circulation dailies such as *The Daily Mail*, *Daily News* and *Daily Mirror* peaceful tactics did not make good copy – direct action such as hitting a policeman, or suffragettes being ejected from a public place made far more dramatic news, even if the publicity was not necessarily beneficial to the cause. Fleet Street had its own constraints as well, and the main one being the imperative to deliver readers to advertisers through mass sales. Harrison recognizes this business reality when he criticizes approaches that underestimate the extent of 'the press freedom that is feasible under competitive proprietorship at any time' (1982: 261).

Press fluctuations

In fact, looking at year on year variations and how they related to other competitor issues, it would be more accurate to say that coverage fluctuated. In 1906 the election had been dominated by free trade and tariff reform, so that afterwards women's activities provided a refreshing novelty value, but by 1909 this news value was overtaken by the budget and the House of Lords crisis. When the suffragettes broke the 'truce' by boycotting the census, the so-called press silence was broken. When there was a truce on violence, it fell, but when militancy was resumed, it increased.

By 1911 Lady Constance Lytton was justifying militant tactics in *The Times* on the grounds that the press was closing down on non-militant suffragism (15 March). In fact, by 1909 the WSPU campaign was already beginning to lose impact: *Votes for Women* used the failings of the national press as an argument to persuade readers to support their organ instead: 'At the present time when ordinary National Press (sic) is closing down its columns more and more against suffrage news, boycotting peaceful propaganda and distorting militant action, no one can understand aright (sic) what is going on who is not a regular reader of our paper' (WSPU, 1910). It was not entirely accurate to claim that national newspapers did not provide adequate information on the activities of the movement. The *Manchester Guardian* remained constant, and in 1911 the *Standard* advertised in *Votes for Women* that its women's section would break the 'conspiracy of silence' and the boycott that suffragettes were complaining about (27 October: 59).

Yet it is true that in many ways exaggeration of militancy led to misrepresentation. For example, Millicent Fawcett took pains to disassociate the NUWSS from such tactics – crucial given her claim that antis were trying to discredit suffragists by association with the WSPU. *The Times* did not include these comments in the space allocated to her (9 March 1912). By the summer of 1910 most papers had made up their minds on the issue, and thereafter there was a closing of ranks: the tone of articles gradually became more acerbic as militancy escalated. Newspapers now seemed more aware of one another and quoted each other more frequently between 1911 and 1914. Thus both the *Morning Post* and *The Times* (29 March and 9 April 1912) attributed the entire suffrage movement to the discontent of unmarried, surplus women, recalling the suggestion by the *Pall Mall Gazette* two years previously that economic reform was the solution – the *Morning Post* advocated state-aided emigration to parts of the Empire where wives were in demand (Nessheim, 1991: 225). In 1913 Northcliffe wrote to his editor of the *Daily Mirror* that he wanted 'no more of the suffragettes' (British Library: 62234).

Yet what happened in practice did not amount to a blanket ban. The indefatigable C.P. Scott continued undeterred, although (like other Liberal editors) he resisted any criticism of Asquith for the sake of Party unity and appeared to be inordinately flattering to Lloyd George – despite the Chancellor's outspoken criticism of the Conciliation measure outside Parliament. Even *The Times* published philosophical arguments and debates on ideas in editorials during the 'truce' – although the emphasis was usually on the 'anti' arguments as an agenda. Pugh points out that the ratio of pro versus anti letters that were published was clearly in the antis favour, but suggests that this was probably a statistical reflection of *The Times* readers' views (2000: 229).

Hardening of attitudes

As WSPU extreme tactics escalated, so did defence of these developments in their own press. *Votes for Women* quoted Frederick Pethwick-Lawrence's letter to Marion Wallace Dunlop: 'Nothing has moved me so much – stirred me to the depths of my being – as your heroic action' (16 July 1908). This had consisted of stencilling an extract of the 1689 Bill of Rights onto the wall of St Stephens Hall in the House of Commons, refusing a fine, being imprisoned for a month and then released as a result of a 91-hour hunger strike. In fact a deputation to Parliament had ended with 122 arrests and an evening of window breaking around Westminster, with 13 stone-throwers also becoming hunger strikers in jail.

In 1908 the *Daily News* summed up the tactic of drama attached to mass hunger strikes and arrests: 'Those who dominate the movement have a sense of the dramatic. They know that whereas the sight of one woman struggling with policemen is either comic or miserably pathetic, the imprisonment of dozens is a splendid advertisement' (22 June). Achievement of the newspaper 'advertisement' became a well-developed aim: hunger strikes were standard WSPU practice by 1910. Force-feeding was introduced in August that year, and was referenced extensively in WSPU posters and postcards. H.N. Brailsford and Henry Nevinson, both suffrage supporters and well-known journalists, announced their resignation from their positions on the paper by explaining in a letter to *The Times* 'We cannot denounce torture in Russia and support it in England, nor can we advocate democratic principles in the name of a Party which confines them to a single sex' (5 October 1909). They considered that the government had other options –Home Secretary Herbert Gladstone could release the prisoners after 5 or 6 days of starvation. In addition, 116 surgeons had already signed a petition against it that was presented to the Prime Minister; in addition, Keir Hardie and others protested in parliament.

A letter to *The Times* by Mrs. Pankhurst, Christabel, Emmeline Pethwick-Lawrence and Mabel Tuke, all as recipients, described their bodies having been 'violated'. Although hunger strikes and forced feeding had the effect of increasing tensions between constitutional and militant wings of the movement, on the WSPU led 'From Prison to Citizenship' march of 18 June 1910, onlookers cheered the prisoners' sections, and, according to the 20 June's *Daily Mail*, hundreds of men, leaning from windows of the Lifeguards' Barracks in Knightsbridge, cheered. *The Times* on the same date could only bring itself to admit that the crowds were well behaved.

Bias

Women's organizations provided a critique of the mainstream press that helps to illuminate the changing expectations of newspapers during the Edwardian epoch. Christabel Pankhurst deplored the fact that WSPU 'constitutional' work was ignored by the papers, and militancy was 'misrepresented' and 'distorted' (Women's Library, 1911). Her complaints were prompted by the fact that the 'truce' on militancy designed to promote the Conciliation Bill did not produce much copy, but within her ranks there was a diversity of viewpoint. Some suffragettes deplored the press publicity of direct action and the emphasis on the Pankhursts to the detriment of agitation for peaceful reforms and the cause of women more generally. The vote, they argued, was part of a much wider political campaign (Liddington and Norris, 1978: 17).

Militancy certainly diverted attention towards methods rather than arguments, meaning that underlying intellectual ideas such as the belief in freedom were lost. Bolt lists other symbolic concepts that were sacrificed to this obsession with tactics: 'the repudiation of submissiveness and the double moral standard; [with] the belief that women's special qualities and concerns entitled them to citizenship, which would in turn benefit men, women and the state; [with] a conviction that economic and political enfranchisement went hand in hand' (Bolt, 1999: 45). To this extent , the public focus on militancy that had been successfully engineered by the WSPU had a downside in terms of the ways that it narrowed discourses on varying aspects of citizenship.

WSPU strategy was indeed high-risk 'make or break', with no respite: this would inevitably and intentionally provoke a reaction on the part of both press and public. Suffrage papers such as *Votes for Women* were distributed free of charge to MPs and to Fleet Street editors, who could then see only too well for themselves that suffrage supporters were encouraged in the pages of such publications to engage in protests involving clashes with the police and destruction of property. Suffragettes were attempting to create a romantic newspaper image of activists as 'freedom fighters'. The negative reaction of the more conservative mainstream nationals was thus fairly predictable.

The suffrage movement complained of press 'boycotts' in 1907, 1909 and 1911 (Pugh, 2000: 228): Frederick Pethwick-Lawrence complained that proprietors and editors deliberately wanted to 'check the advance of the Woman Suffrage Movement' (*Votes for Women*, 25 June, 1909: 841) while Helen Swanwick later wrote: 'The censorship was extreme and grotesque' (1935: 221). It was suffrage activities involving day-to-day persuasion that were the victims of newspaper neglect. Silence over peaceful activities was probably more damaging to the cause than hostile coverage, as the suffrage movement was hugely dependent on publicity. It is true that the national press tended to ignore local activities, and could be patronizing, but editors were more respectful of international gatherings.[2] International suffrage events and news attracted more newspaper interest: the International Women's Suffrage Alliance Quinquennial Congress in London that was held simultaneously attracted attendance from the press of 27 countries, according to the *Morning Leader* (6 May 1909).

Most national press reports on the 29 April 1909 Pageant of Women's Trades and Professions were favourable, but short. In the past, on the day of the big NUWSS march in 1908 for instance, *The Times* had published an entire account by Mrs. Fawcett: now this facility was put at the disposal of the antis. In March 1909 the entire, full-length speeches of both Mary Ward and Lord Cromer at a League rally (27 March) were published and the following year Mrs. Moberly Bell (wife of *The Times* manager) was prompted to write to Lord Cromer: '*The Times* has done more for the anti-suffrage cause than any other paper' – certainly the paper had already become the regular and reliable chronicler of all events and opinions connected with the 'anti' organization and the main publicity outlet for the antis. In 1910, for example, 'The Thunderer' published not only detailed information on an 'Anti Woman Suffrage Appeal' but also salutatory editorial and a full list of signatories (21 and 22 July).

Another damaging campaign by the antis, elaborated in letters to *The Times* involved the perceived sexual threat that feminist teachers were seen to pose to young women: suffragist's 'nauseous publications' (sic) were condemned as being linked to feminist sex education in schools (12 and 18 April 1912). In fact, Northcliffe himself told Lord Curzon in February 1912: 'My papers are going to do anything they can for the anti-Suffrage party' (1978: 153). On 28 March 1912, just when the Conciliation Bill was due for decision, *The Times* promoted the 'scientific' case for female hysteria (i.e. madness) associated with suffragettes, propagated by Sir Almroth Wright who argued that sexless women needed marriage rather than the vote. These views were referred to in the *Pall Mall Gazette* editorial title that same day as 'Science and Suffragitis'. In 1913 an expanded version of Wright's contribution was republished as *The Unexpurgated Case against Woman Suffrage* (Wright, 1913; Mulvey and Mizuta, 1995). Theories like these would not have been taken so seriously by the press, but for their presentation in the wake of some suffragette outrages. Although Wright's extreme 'medical' views had the effect of disrupting the anti-suffrage camp (Bush, 2007: 230), the point to be stressed here, however, is that biased publication on the part of *The Times* was tactical and therefore potentially damaging.

Letters to the paper repudiating Almroth's views appeared too late to influence the decision on the third Conciliation Bill. In the run up to the final debate (March 1912) the paper's anti-suffrage stance was strengthened by reports on the Pankhurst conspiracy trial that also proved to be manna to the antis (Nessheim, 1991: 360). Although in total *The Times* published more letters from suffrage supporters than any other paper, the importance of the March deluge of anti-suffrage attention lies in its timing. The intervention of *The Times* provided a salutary reminder of its traditional support for government and establishment, as articulated by Asquith when he stated that the 'Press is the most potent, the most flexible, the most trustworthy auxiliary' (Hardman, 1909: 65).

The 'pilgrimage'

Publicity had clearly had a dual effect of encouraging the public to become accustomed to suffragist pageantry and marches as a form of weekend spectacle, but of not convincing parliamentarians sufficiently of widespread desire for the female vote. Within this context, the NUWSS deemed that a different approach – the Women's Pilgrimage – was necessary. From the start, the suffrage movement had been criticized for not having a sufficiently popular mandate: with extensive press coverage of violence, the NUWSS's hope of converting the public through reasoned argument had been sacrificed, so their 'Pilgrimage' was an attempt to restore the potential of debate and peaceful persuasion – that spectacles had failed to achieve. The event aimed to raise discussion with lots of small groups of population, even in remote areas.

The current gloom of suffrage supporters was analyzed by *Common Cause* on 1 August: 'It is to be borne in mind that the Pilgrimage was organized when there might have been expected to be a setback in Suffrage enthusiasm. The Franchise Bill had been withdrawn, the Dickinson Bill defeated. For the first time for several years, Suffragists had no Bill in being to work for; no immediate and urgent incentive; no feeling that *one* ounce of energy might win the day . . . [the NUWSS] had to appeal generally for support, and general appeals are not usually interesting.'

The plan involved members located along different routes converging on London – not altogether, but over the course of a month, having made contact with people in towns and villages. This meant sustained publicity over a longer period as they travelled on foot (with some on bikes and horses, or in cars lent by wealthy sympathizers), holding meetings, gathering petitions, and selling the *Common Cause*, plus other literature and support accessories such as banners, megaphones. *Common Cause* provided weekly reports on progress. When the pilgrims converged on London for a final rally in Hyde Park, the paper – with a special souvenir programme – was sold en route and at the 30 meetings. Pirated twopenny versions went on sale in the streets (Tickner, 1987: 146) – proof of the paper's popularity, and also evidence that purchasers saw this as an historic event that merited collectable paraphernalia.

Arguably the 'pilgrimage' had been the most impressive of all pre-World War I demonstrations. Both *Common Cause* and the *Manchester Guardian* (1 August 1913) commented on the success. The exercise had 'provided an opportunity for the great mass of suffragists to dedicate themselves anew to the service of their cause', and they had reached thousands of people in their own streets and homes and been able to show them why women wanted the vote.

The frustration of notoriety

It seems that a majority obtained for women's vote by the Conciliation Bill in May 1911 gave out the impression to the press of the inevitability of women's suffrage, thereby focusing editorial attitudes, although both MPs and national press were still side-tracked by other parliamentary issues. The WSPU's 1912 'argument of the stone' and mass window smashing in London's West End was followed in 1913–14 by a phase of arson attacks that seemed to ignore the likely public response to a campaign 'waged by a relatively small group of middle class women' (Rosen, 1974: 145). What Mrs. Fawcett considered to be sensational posturing and millenarian language (Searle, 2004: 458)[3] was accompanied by further tactical shortcomings that appear to substantiate a comment made by *New Age* back in 1908 towards the vote – that militants 'were determined to have it whether it inconvenienced anyone or not' (27 June: 168).

A new tactic, as yet untried by Irish nationalists, was the hunger strike. These were usually followed by force feeding and have been described by Rosen as an over-dependence on apocalyptic politics, based on a calculation that self-imposed martyrdom would be persuasive, but 'the comfortable and the secure are not always deeply moved by the suffering of the oppressed, particularly if the oppressed can be portrayed as in some sense having brought their own fate upon themselves through their own disagreeableness' (1974: 244). It is likely that newspaper coverage encouraged this standpoint, but from the WSPU standpoint, these were martyrs to the cause, attracting new members and further financial donations. Although Annie Kenney had to be carried on to the stage of a public meeting on a stretcher (Rosen 1974: 220), despite such clear damage to health, the Asquith government still appeared to be saving lives. The Evening Standard (8 June 1912) reported that 100 MPs, not to mention Jean Jaures, Upton Sinclair, Victor Adler, Romain

Rolland, Madame Curie, Edward Bernstein and other intellectual luminaries signed an appeal to Asquith, requesting he support the suffragette claim, but not everyone appreciated the significance of suffragette demands for political prisoner status for prison hunger strikers.

Sylvia Pankhurst took the view that rather than the extreme suffering of a few through force-feeding, the WSPU should prioritize a stronger appeal to the masses (Pankhurst, 1913: 316). Nevertheless, she spoke in support of hunger strikers, although by 1912 her appeal at a WSPU public meeting in Hyde Park 'for women who are dying of tortures' and facing death was greeted with howls of derision according to an Evening Standard report (15 April). Meanwhile, reader letters in the 'anti' press suggested that hunger striking to death 'would serve the Suffragettes right' (Nessheim, 1991: 247).

During 1913 to 1914 there were anti-suffrage riots in the country at large in which university and medical students participated, indicative of widespread anti-suffrage feeling (Harrison, 1978: 188). Already by 1912 it was becoming difficult for the WSPU to hold outdoor meetings. One response was to avoid ground operations by taking to the air: Two well-known aviators also dropped suffrage leaflets over North West London from their aeroplanes, while a mob of 200 men had wrecked a WSPU shop in Glasgow, and two supporters in Wales who heckled a Lloyd George speech were assaulted by the crowd and had their clothes torn off and cut into shreds as souvenirs of the occasion (Rosen, 1974: 171). This had led to some rather lurid publicity with an entire front-page photo in *The Daily Mirror* and similar photographs of the attack in the *Illustrated London News*. Later Sylvia revealed the extent to which WSPU leadership was image conscious – dubbed by Green (1997) as 'performative activism'. She wrote that some activists at HQ objected to the lack of 'womanly distress' displayed by the girls who were attacked. 'Quietly they were replaced by a more orthodox type of young woman' (1931: 392).

In 1912 a Reform Bill was introduced that displaced the Conciliation Bill (for which suffragist lobbying had come the nearest ever to victory). The new bill threatened to give no votes to women, but more to men. Temporary unity between the suffrage organizations had been terminated by the resumption of WSPU militancy at the end of 1911. During the ensuing year militancy reached a new high of activity: the main aspect of suffrage politics that received much discussion in the national press, led by (but not confined to) *The Times* that 'the window-smashing outrages have given such a setback to the cause of women's suffrage as none of its opponents could have hoped for under normal circumstances' (2, 7, 11, 18, 22, 25 March). This was generally referred to as 'the argument of the broken pane'. Militancy acted as a catalyst for further alienation of politicians, press and public away from the cause, especially when the nature of tactics changed between 1912 and 1914 from the original intention of acting as an attack on the government, into what appeared to be an indiscriminate campaign against members of the public (Pugh, 2000: 188). The issue for newspaper mediation of such activities centred on how far violent direct action such as window smashing was destroying the credibility and the chances of success of constitutional reform.

'One woman breaking a window could make all England ring. This was the militant discovery, and they did not mind if the publicity was unfavourable so long as there was noise' (Tickner, 1987: 59). As windows at the offices of *The Daily Mail* and the *Daily News* were among the targets, according to *Daily Express* coverage on 22 November 1911, the tactic could well be construed as an 'own goal'. By the following year, as the plate glass offensive escalated, most of Fleet Street and the *Manchester Guardian* were construing it as a deliberate WSPU attack on NUWSS (peaceful) effectiveness. *The Times* bluntly stated: 'None of its previous follies has been so thoroughly calculated to discredit the suffragist cause' and the former referring to the 'madness of militants'. Even the *Manchester Guardian* subscribed to the view that extremists were deranged: an editorial on 2 March 1912 was entitled 'The Madness of the Militants'. The *Morning Post* drew the conclusion that such people could not be trusted with political power, the *Daily Chronicle* concluded franchise legislation was impossible under the present conditions, while the *Pall Mall Gazette*'s reaction to the central London window destruction was: 'Somewhere deep in the councils of the suffrage movement there surely lurks a persuasive "Anti" in disguise, who is sworn to the prompting of just such self-defeating raids as yesterday's' (2 March 1912).

By 1912, in the context of industrial unrest and a danger of civil war in Ireland, the WSPU's new campaign of violence 'stopped short only at the risk to human life' (Tickner, 1987: 134). The Irish, the women and the workers were all espousing aspects of emancipation and all adopted militant methods to further their causes. The 'great labour unrest' of 1911–12 was characterized by a small number of very big strikes (Searle, 2004: 441) – all competitors in the news stakes. Extra-parliamentary action was also used by those who wished to maintain the status quo, so suffragettes were operating within a context of serious instability, first analyzed in detail by Dangerfield, who points out (1971: 119) that in Ireland, Sinn Fein was becoming an influence to contend with.

Paintings such as the Rokeby Venus were damaged, pillar boxes set on fire, empty buildings burned, golf courses treated with acid and telegraph wires cut. Extensive amounts of property were destroyed or damaged, despite the fact that the NUWSS asked for a truce during the passage of the Reform Bill. The Pethwick-Lawrences, believing that there was still mileage to be gained in mass demonstrations, left the WSPU in dispute over the new militancy policy (October 1912) while H.M. Richardson stated on 20 August 1912 in the *Manchester Guardian*: 'Had the violence of the WSPU possessed the essential virtue of popularity it would by now have won women the vote'. Harrison goes even further in his scepticism by arguing that the publicity generated by suffrage papers such as the *Suffragette* ultimately had no political influence (1978: 290).

When the Reform Bill was withdrawn, it became clear that there would be no further opportunity for a parliamentary measure until after the election (due to take place in 1915). The WSPU's reaction was to start a further round of arson, with Mrs. Pankhurst, who was indifferent to public opinion, now referring to her militants as 'guerrillists' (*The Globe*, 28 January 1913). Meanwhile the next public spectacle was a martyr's funeral for Emily Davison. The *Morning Post* reported on 21 March 1913 a police raid on a suffragette studio where they found firelighters, wire cutters, corrosive fluid and ribbons with slogans 'No votes – no telegraphic connection' and 'No security by post or wire until justice be done for women'. The Cabinet's next move was to introduce what became known as the 'Cat and Mouse Act' that authorized the re-arrest of prisoners who had been released due to ill health (i.e. hunger strikes). The voting record in parliament for this measure points to widespread support: 'eloquent of the hostility that militancy had aroused' (Harrison, 1978: 179). A climate of government oppression, with raids of WSPU offices, prohibitions on open air meetings and attempts to ban *The Suffragette* all point to a change in the performance of politics, 'a radical transformation in feminist spectacle and a repositioning of the street as a space of surveillance – an extension of the prison itself' (Green, 1997: 106).

The fact that women came so close on so many occasions to winning the vote in parliament obviously led to huge frustrations: in one incident a suffragette clutched Asquith by the lapels of his suit and shook him (Rosen, 1974: 171). Even after the 1913 NUWSS 'pilgrimage' that had spent 6 weeks with marches to the far reaches of Britain and had culminated in an end rally attended by 50,000 spectators, addressed by 80 to 90 speakers on 19 platforms – government ministers with whom they met *still* raised the same old arguments against them. This was despite the fact that constitutionalists had aimed to neutralize the effect of violence by converting the public to their cause, but neither constitutionalists nor militants had been able to totally overcome objections by some other organizations and politicians. Conservatives wanted to be sure that educated women's vote would offset to their advantage any losses conceded by the franchise acts of 1867 and 1884. The Liberal government did not seem convinced that even a limited female franchise would work to their advantage either.

The unorthodox tactics advocated by Christabel may have caught the headlines, but according to Rosen her political Achilles heel was that she consistently exaggerated the political effectiveness of the policies she propagated (1974: 121). By this time even passionate suffrage supporters like C.P. Scott were speculating about the sanity of militants: his diaries relate a conversation with Lloyd George where they both likened Christabel Pankhurst's attitude to a man in a mental asylum with a God delusion (Wilson, 1970: 58). Furthermore it was clear that the press was now less enthusiastic than in earlier years. *The Daily Mail* reflected Northcilffe's scepticism when it took the view that women would have greater impact if they concentrated on other grievances rather than the vote (20 January 1913; 28 July 1913). Equally the *Daily Chronicle*, a loyal Asquith supporter, failed to support NUWSS peaceful tactics in 1911 to 1913 because it was alienated by suffragette violence (5 May 1911: 1, 6; 27 July 1913); during 1911 *The Standard* had given a daily page to suffrage activities, but by 1913 was driven to condemn Mary Richardson's six-month sentence for slashing the Rokeby Venus as 'absurdly lenient' (13 March 1913, quoted in Pugh, 2000: 231).

Extremism on both sides – police and WSPU – seemed to be self-defeating, as the press had pointed out. From 1911 onwards, newspaper correspondence columns were full of letters from members of the public whose letters had been burned in post boxes and whose shop windows had been smashed, with numerous conversions to the anti side (Nessheim, 1991: 231). Pro-suffrage papers tried to persuade MPs that violence was the work of a small minority, in order not to jeopardize the third Conciliation Bill and tended to point to militancy in accounting for suffrage setbacks (rather than the Irish nationalists holding the balance in the second 1910 parliament, for instance); the escalation of violence serves to explain the reluctant acceptance of the *Manchester Guardian* and the *Daily News* of the 'Cat and Mouse Act' in 1913. From the spring of that year, militancy dominated political editorials. As coverage of militancy increased, so the fortunes of the Anti-Suffrage League also seemed to be enhanced.

More and more extreme forms of militancy such as increased arson attacks and the bombing of Lloyd George's house inevitably led to press hostility as they claimed that more and more people were being forced to support the 'antis'. *The Observer* referred to the 'crab-like progress which has for a long time been carrying it [the women's cause] away from the vote' (23 February 1913). That same day suffragettes at a meeting on Wimbledon Common were attacked by a mob. The *Morning Post* referred to women's 'dangerous and wicked violence' and the *Sheffield Daily Telegraph* of 'criminals': other newspapers responded similarly (20 February 1913). The WSPU reaction was to form a strong-arm bodyguard group of women to protect leaders such as Mrs. Pankhurst, who were physically weakened by regular hunger strikes. Although the police were pretty ineffective in stopping arson, they compensated in numbers by sending 50 officers to arrest Mrs. Pankhurst in July 1913. Yet the WSPU continued to display a surprising ability to raise funds from big individual donors (Rosen, 1974: 228).

During 1914 up until the outbreak of war, militants continued guerrilla activities, constitutionalists continued to campaign peacefully and the *Daily Mirror* continued to represent suffragettes as a stereotype in a special feature entitled 'The Suffrage Face: New Type Evolved by Militancy', in its use of photos with sarcastic captions for a whole page visual spread, and an accompanying article on 25 May 1914: 'There is no longer any need for the militants to wear their colours or their badges. Fanaticism has set its seal upon their faces and left a peculiar expression which cannot by mistaken. Nowadays, indeed, any observant person can pick out a suffragette in a crowd of other women. They have nursed a grievance for so long that they seem resentful of anyone who is happy and contented and appear to be exceptionally bitter against the members of their own sex who do not support their policy of outrage.' The government itself seemed to take the view that a press boycott would stop the tactic better than anything the state could do, with Home Secretary Reginald McKenna pointing out: 'I am sure that the immediate effect of the denial of all advertisement of militancy would do more to stop their actions than anything the Government can do' (House of Commons debate, 11 June 1914, c.522).

Watershed

The existence of a National government during World War I removed suffrage politics from inter-party rivalries. With some prescience, *The Times* predicted in 1913 that the vote for women would be influenced by wider political considerations rather than on the merits of the issue itself – when 'a genuine and incontestable majority of the British people' decided that it should be granted (21 January 1913). World War I redrew all previous definitions, policies and organizational boundaries. As the majority of war workers were women, it seemed natural to include them in the electoral reform package for voteless servicemen on their return from the war, for it was the need to revise the register and include servicemen on it that caused the issue of potential women voters to be raised again – not suffrage agitation, or even the need to reward women's participation in the war effort. Expediency was the order of the day; the vote could now be introduced with a minimum of fuss.

Some newspaper proprietors, such as Northcliffe and J.L. Garvin of the *Observer* (also a long time opponent from the Northcliffe stable) were not convinced of the inevitability of the franchise until 1916 – in Northcliffe's case he first showed signs of conversion in 1915 by announcing that he intended to put his papers at the disposal of the suffrage movement after the end of the war (Harrison, 1978: 205). Northcliffe is much quoted as being surprised – even frustrated – that there was no suffrage agitation to report on in 1916: 'Try and get a public meeting . . . and I will support it', he wrote to Lady Betty Balfour in December that year (Fawcett Archives, 1916, 22 December). By 20 June 1917, *The Times* was stating: 'Public opinion, manifesting itself in a hundred ways, has set more strongly than ever during the last few months to the side of the suffragists.'

The paper was unapologetic about its conversion: 'we have always regarded Woman Suffrage as one of the changes which are inherent in the circumstances of the war, though these circumstances are far too seldom understood or expressed' (1 February 1917). Women's work was now recognized as central to the war effort. The argument in support of women's wartime service also provided Asquith and many former 'antis' with a means of escape from the corner that they too had driven themselves into during the pre-World War I period. Only the *Morning Post* remained anti-suffrage, but then this paper had predicted that women would not be enfranchised in a hundred years (15 January 1912).

With the onset of World War I, 60,000 members of the Weaver's Association were thrown out of work (Liddington and Norris, 1978: 254) – this was symptomatic of the beginnings of the decline of the Lancashire cotton industry. In 1917 the government allowed India to increase its cotton imports duty from 3.5 per cent to 7.5 per cent. Many women moved from the mills to new openings in munitions, nursing and office work. Some suffragists such as Ellen Wilkinson and Helena Swanwick were still active and Ada Nield Chew continued to write in the *Common Cause* and the *Cotton Factory Times* in support of women's working conditions. The radical suffragists were pacifists, and rejected the war, as much as they had also rejected the Pankhurst's militancy (Liddington and Norris, 1978: 257).

Women had suspended suffrage activity, yet they were included in the bill for extension of the vote (over 30). The age bar was because it was feared women would dominate the electorate, and their political allegiances were considered fickle and unstable. During the war the labour movement was hopelessly divided: the ILP was the only group that was openly pacifist, but with some dissentions. Blatchford and Hyndman of the *Clarion* and the *Labour Leader* respectively were both keen war supporters who put patriotism before internationalism. As for Keir Hardie, before he died, his hopes for international working class solidarity to stop the war had been dashed and his hopes for women's suffrage postponed, first by the Liberal government and then by the war (Liddington and Norris, 1978: 256).

Similarly, the war brought to the surface the political divisions in women's public culture. When the war broke out, Mrs. Fawcett urged NUWSS members to support the government by showing they were worthy of citizenship, but the organization was split. In 1915 half the executive committee and all the national officers resigned (including Helen Swanwick who had so ably edited the *Common Cause*), leaving only Mrs. Fawcett and the treasurer. The breakaway group formed the Women's International League for Peace and Freedom, which set up the Women's Peace Conference at The Hague. The radical suffragists also became pacifists, as did Sylvia Pankhurst and the East London Federation, becoming the Workers' Federation. Its paper – the *Women's Dreadnought* – became the *Workers' Dreadnought*, along with *Jus Suffragii*, publishing internationalist and pacifist propaganda. Now the female activist was portrayed as a world citizen.

For the WSPU, the larger conflict now took precedence, and they suspended all normal activities. When Christabel Pankhurst proclaimed on 8 September 1914 (according to the *Manchester Guardian*) at a public meeting 'I agree with the Prime Minister that we cannot stand by and see brutality triumph over freedom' her followers were startled into laughter. She and her mother committed their organization to actively campaigning for recruitment, conscription and in support of internment.

Meanwhile suffragette prisoners were released, as the militant movement ground to a halt. In effect Mrs. Pankhurst and Christabel became part of the government that they had previously opposed so vehemently in their actions, speeches and newspaper communications. Their new-found chauvinism came increasingly to the fore, a comparable one to the message embedded in the Women's Coronation' pageant, with colourful patriotic displays of support for Empire, resplendent appeals to heritage and to the traditions of British royalty and establishment. Similarly, the role of the press – all branches – in this new scenario was now a very different one. National newspapers faced financial uncertainly because of wartime restrictions on advertising, the rising cost of newsprint and supplies and labour shortages among journalists and printers who had been called up. World War I created a hiatus in the development of careers for most women journalists (Chambers, Steiner and Fleming, 2004: 27–8). Frequently, newspapers and magazines published fewer pages or ended production altogether. Faced with a climate of censorship and unable to report on the conflict from the front itself, women's writing efforts emerged through books, diaries, essays and letters, many of which describe human suffering and the impact of World War I on civilian populations.

Nevertheless, there was widespread support for the war among the public. In fact readers seemed to want newspapers with stories about heroes, patriotism and national service, evidenced by Northcliffe's enthusiastic pre-war nationalism that boosted his circulations considerably. Mrs. Pankhurst, Christabel and other militants quickly realigned themselves with the male sex[4] as their paper *Suffragette* became a jingoistic and patriotic organ entitled *Britannia*. It was probably more in tune with public opinion than ever before in its support for the war and the efforts of the state. This time propaganda campaigns in the leading women's own newspapers were in line with Fleet Street in the way they explained how women could help win the war.

It is possible to view female participation in the war effort either as a sell-out or as a further break through for citizenship, and a re-negotiation of the boundaries of a previously masculine-biased definition of the concept (Gullace, 2002: 9–10). Certainly there were new and different sorts of opportunities for women in the public sphere. Searle (2004: 791) argues that the debate on suffrage was essentially over by the 1890s and that the intellectual argument had been won by 1908, but public opinion as manifested in the national press needed to be influenced and constantly reminded of the urgency of the need for women's enfranchisement. The process of public persuasion needed to be a repetitive one, until victory was achieved.

Conclusions

The evidence points to forms of identity developed through the agency of the public press that can be characterized as both discursive and performance oriented. As a practice of signification characterized by a socially constructed agency of performance, elements of women's identity were constantly being reinforced through the relentlessly repetitive and rhetorical processes of newspaper communication. The process finds theoretical resonances in the work of Judith Butler (1990, 1987, 1983), for whom the notion of a subject is formed through repetition and of Erving Goffman (1979) as mentioned in Chapter 1. The fact was that newspapers, right up to the disruption of World War I, continued to provide a forum for lively rhetoric and performance-influenced discourse on gender and the vote. The arguments may well have been constantly recycled, but the process of repetition constantly re-energized the polity, because the symbolic interaction of gender necessitated on a daily basis an obligation to re-stage the performance. This can be partly attributed to the routine consumption of newspapers in their millions that reached an apex in the pre-war years, and partly to delays by Parliament in introducing franchise legislation. A series of near-misses in achieving their goals served to position the suffrage movement on a treadmill that was destined to result in the evolution, reinforcement and focusing of identities – both positive and negative – of aspects of the process of cultural citizenship. These conform to the symbolic interactionism of 'doing gender' as articulated by Erving Goffman (1979), who also argues that events and thinking only become meaningful experience when integrated into an interpretative, cognitive framework (1974), and in this case it was a fluid, changing one.

Kate Millett points out that some militant tactics such as the hunger strike led the way for later campaigns such as those led by Gandhi, the union movement and civil rights, and she also considers that such tactics enlisted public support, 'especially when government replied to them with police brutality, harsh prison terms (sic), and forced feeding for hunger strikers' (1977: 82). Again the evidence may point to this in the earlier period prior to 1911 (the public supported heckling, for instance, as a form of entertainment and were genuinely shocked at the harsh ejection of militants from meetings); but in the later period, militancy became a hindrance and there is much evidence of public hostility – even if it was fuelled by reports in the popular press.

Coverage of peaceful persuasion, with the exception of a few big events like the Coronation and the pilgrimage, was virtually obliterated by more dramatic but negative deeds of violence. From 1911 onwards bad news harmed the constitutional cause. Liberal papers did not go on the offensive for suffrage during 1910 to 1911 – a time when franchise supporters could have gained ground. Their inhibitions stemmed mainly from their loyalty to the Party and reluctance to criticize Asquith, which could have caused divisions in the ranks. Unity and the survival of the Party was a higher priority than women's suffrage, especially at a time when there was revolt and the party was under challenge not only on women's franchise but also by Ulster loyalists, Irish nationalists and syndicalists.

In contrast, the antis, and *The Times*, seemed to have no such inhibitions when it came to suggesting that all Tories were 'anti', even when this patently was not the case. Twice 'The Thunderer' (as *The Times* had been called during the nineteenth century) appears to have been a catalyst for the fortunes of the female suffrage movement: on the first occasion as a potential influence against the passing of the third Conciliation Bill, and on the second occasion as the potential creator of a bandwagon effect during 1916 and 1917 in favour of the vote. This behaviour supports the contention originally made by Seymour-Ure that the press 'by anticipating an event which would happen anyway, change its character' (1968: 288).

Any suffrage influence that was exerted on Fleet Street journalists often tended to result in the wrong sort of messages (from the pro-vote viewpoint) being projected, at the expense of other aspects of information that were ignored. The mainstream press emphasized tactics rather than ideas. Certainly suffrage supporters themselves were concerned with the nature of press representation: 'Deeds not words' representations of militants proudly projecting an image of orthodox femininity in dress and appearance, while performing distinctly unorthodox acts of violence did not always emerge in their favour. In some ways, the regular repetition of this kind of media representation became what Pickering (2001: 46) has described in the context of stereotyping as symbolically restricting. Militants were creating a new stereotype that was also symbolically confined.

The more suffragette supporters tried to accommodate media demands for unusual news angles, the more they became hostages to their own fortunes. Between 1911 and 1914 political issues were responsible for a context that was characterized by verbal and physical violence, thus it is feasible that readers became anaesthetized and that once battle lines were firmly drawn for and against, they actually ignored the opinion of their newspaper (Pugh, 2000: 229). This seemed to be the case from early 1912, according to the *Common Cause* (4 January 1912: 677), who conducted a survey of press attitudes. It found that 15 dailies and weeklies were pro-suffrage, 8 anti-suffrage and 10 were neutral, but the list did not include *The Daily Mail* that tended to be anti-suffrage.

The conversion of key national editors and proprietors to the cause was pivotal. In 1912, during the arson campaign, the *Westminster Gazette* had commented that the women's movement should take into account what it called 'the psychology of the male . . . the electorate and its representatives have been put in a position in which they feel they would look weak and ridiculous if they yielded to this agitation' (29 March). In other words, support was needed on male terms for compromise to happen. It is not possible to accurately assess how many MPs were influenced *against* supporting female franchise before World War I – in particular the Conciliation Bills – because of violence. C.P. Scott's diary entries for 1912 indicate that Churchill, for instance, was influenced adversely: 'He practically admitted that his present wrecking tactics are the outcome of resentment at the treatment he has received from the WSPU' (23 January; Wilson, 1970: 58).

The WSPU tactics of harassing prominent Liberal ministers such as Churchill, despite the fact that the majority of liberal MPs supported female enfranchisement, appear to some historians as promotionally perverse, but exacerbated by an immutable hostility to the female vote by many parliamentarians. This was always, in the pre-World War I period, 'a mixture of misogyny and chivalry. But the more stridently women advanced their claims and the closer they came to success, the greater the misogyny displayed by their male opponents and the more determined their will to resist' (Searle, 2004: 459–60). The public press acted as an outlet for such attitudes.

In contrast, during World War I, female supporters of the vote redeemed themselves by putting the war effort first and thereby compromising in their public attitude towards men. In other words, the female contribution to the war effort served to convert the men on masculine terms – something that militancy had not attempted previously. There is a certain irony connected to the fact that when women suspended suffrage activity, they were finally included in the bill for extension of the vote (over 30). The age bar was imposed because it was feared women would dominate the electorate; and their political allegiances were considered fickle and unstable. Had this attitude been exacerbated by the suffragettes themselves? Bolt points out that: 'The doctrines and practice that the suffragettes sought to propagate inclined their critics to see them as agents of emotion rather than the creators of democratic opinion' (Purvis and Holton, 2000: 49). Most 'public' newspapers reinforced, and often encouraged that view – even that great supporter of constitutional suffrage reform, the *Manchester Guardian*, with its views on suffragette 'madness'. The task of editors task in this respect was made easier by the fact that anti-suffrage opinions were well entrenched in the political establishment and a wide range of publications.

Contemporary scholarship on audience effects points to the fact that a successful political campaign is more likely when within an audience (or readership), 'the flow of personal communication and structure of relevant interpersonal status is supportive of the campaign' (McQuail, 1977: 79). In other words, readers need to be able to personally identify with the campaign, but newspaper representation of suffrage violence inhibited this from being achieved. Furthermore, 'the dispositions of the audience should at least be not antipathetic or resistant' (McQuail, 1977: 79). This was not the case from 1912 to 1914, when there were a number of examples of hostile public reaction to militancy, even anti-suffrage riots.

A differentiation between newspaper criticism of suffragette tactics and support for the principle of the vote for women needs to be made. By 1913, many journalists were arguing this very point: they believed in the principle of votes for women, but didn't like suffragette approaches for achieving this. Militant tactics were self-defeating and entailed 'a preoccupation with means which eventually became so overriding as to cause ends altogether to disappear from view' (Harrison, 1982: 290). Anti-suffrage leaders realized this when they pointed out in the *Anti Suffrage Review* (July 1913: 143) that they could win public allegiance simply by drawing attention to militant suffrage misconduct: their support was due to their 'scrupulous abstention from even a pale imitation of sensational methods'. In reality, this was not all the story: the anti-suffrage leaders also had elaborate arguments against the vote, and suffrage supporters felt they had to spend inordinate efforts refuting these, instead of propagating their own case.

Looking at the entire and long trajectory of the suffrage movement, there is a pattern. Most of the arguments were introduced early in the struggle, whereas at the critical last stage of the campaign, when they were really needed, they were drowned by the guerrilla militaristic, tactical rhetoric of extremist violence. Ultimately, the arguments of the suffrage movement as expressed in the press failed to win the vote, even though constitutional suffragists were not suggesting any radical challenge to the fabric of political society.

While it is clear that transnationally, interest in all things female was certainly evident during the end of the nineteenth and the beginning of the twentieth centuries, and was exemplified in the range, diversity and complexity of the debates, energies that went into this also exuded the tensions of the moment. This is also true within a colonial context, during a different period of history. The 1929 extension of women's voting rights in Britain proved to have resonances in India as colonial editors such as the liberal F.W. Wilson were inspired to write about what he referred to as 'The Awakening of Women'. Once more, the media spotlight centred on yet another popular manifestation of what, for want of a better phrase, could be called the Indian equivalent of late nineteenth century Europe's 'new women' – a discourse of awakening, channelled into the cause of independence. Once more, counter-hegemonic efforts at communication were challenging traditional expectations of how women should behave in public.

7
British India
Women and the Hegemonic Colonial Press

The representation of the establishment, in *The Pioneer* daily newspaper in British India, of women leading the local struggle for independence demonstrates that hegemonic version of 'conservative feminization' discussed in previous chapters provides only a partial understanding from the transnational standpoint. In fact, the representation of indigenous women protesters in *The Pioneer* acts as an example of how the hegemonic version of 'conservative feminization' discussed earlier can be challenged – in this case by multifaceted female-led tactics in a role of 'freedom fighters'.

Editors of colonial newspapers in India had to deal with a different kind of message to that of the suffragettes, to whom they had become accustomed back home. Some comparisons can be made between the impact of women's direct action protests on news values in mainland Britain and in colonial India with its phenomenon of female-led protests and economic boycotts. Kate Millett points out that some suffragette militant tactics inspired later campaigns such as those led by Gandhi, the union movement and civil rights (1977: 82).

The question that is addressed here is how in tough economic times, British-owned, English-language newspapers received and filtered news, especially gender-related and nationalist-related events and thinking. Using the North Indian English-language *The Pioneer* as the main archive, press articles on and about women's activism from 1928–34 will be examined in order to address a practical issue for counter-hegemonic expression in newspapers: how far it was possible for an establishment paper to entertain dissent within its pages, in particular the voice of indigenous, female supporters of the 'freedom movement'.

How does this kind of analysis add to the evolving picture of cultural citizenship? Women's Empire Studies is a growing field of study

(Kleinberg, 1988; Midgeley, 1998; Samson, 2001; Levine, 2004; Sangari and Vaid, 1989). Although the practice of Charkha and Khadi (home spun cloth) is well documented (Taneja, 2005; Mody, 2000; Jain, 1985; Jain and Mahan, 1996; Bakshi, 1994; Forbes, 1996; Kumar, 1993; Wieringa, 1995; Mohanty, 1996; Kaur, 1969; Woollacott, 2006; Nanda, 1976), there has been no systematic study of newspaper coverage of women's nationalist awakening as protesters. This chapter presents forms of active public dissent that helped to redefine female citizenship, as mediated and reflected on a daily basis in the pages of *The Pioneer*.

Based in the North Indian city of Allahabad (United Provinces), this venerable newspaper (founded 1865) was once the leading English language newspaper in British India, for all practical purposes a mouthpiece of the Government of India (Ahuja 1996: 106) famous for employing Rudyard Kipling as a reporter and assistant editor (Barns, 1940: 278), and carrying the despatches from the North West Frontier of the young Winston Churchill (*The Pioneer*, 9 September 1897). Despite the loss of its monopoly of official news with the establishment of the Associated Press of India in 1910, it remained 'the leading mouthpiece of those Anglo-Indians determined to preserve the political status quo in India' (Allen, 2007: 286). Yet by 1928 when a new, pro-independence and pro-female editor, F.W. Wilson[1] joined it, circulation was in decline and advertising revenue in need of a boost.

Why *The Pioneer*?

Although coverage of female protest can be found to a greater or lesser extent in most of the other English language press, *The Pioneer* is chosen here for analysis because as a newspaper business, it manifested *change* during a specific time frame. Newspapers such as *The Pioneer* had their own business dilemmas, and these made the paper part of the economic and ideological maelstrom that that it reported on. By 1928 the paper was produced by a handful of staff. Constitutional talks were reaching a crucial stage against a backdrop of the non-cooperation and civil disobedience movements, and the then British owners were prompted by the existing editorial staff themselves to beef up the managerial team by appointing F.W. Wilson, to improve the paper's fortunes. He did so by exhibiting liberal sympathies towards the nationalist movement, in the hope of increasing Indian readership. United Province, as one of the main centres of nationalist protest and the venue chosen by the Congress Party to launch the 'no rents' campaign, was a 'hard news' region. By 1928, the activities of the nationalist movement were wide ranging.

Wilson helped the freedom cause by offering coverage within an establishment organ during a period of censorship of indigenous newspapers. Within the context of the Raj, Wilson was a liberal who identified with Sir Tej Sapru and the Indian liberals. In the context of *The Pioneer*, this had wider implications: for instance, he gave a window to Indian women at a time when in Britain the franchise had just been extended (30 May 1929 elections), and three times as many women as men voted (*The Pioneer*, 1 June 1929: 3). The voting age in Britain was reduced from 30 years of age to 21, resulting in an increase of 5 million new female voters. This had an impact on public debate in India.

Wilson's progressive experiment lasted less than two years, and was followed by a move of headquarters to Lucknow in 1933, and the sale of the paper to a Cawnpore business group of Indian princes in 1934. The paper then reverted to a more conservative stance. Jawaharlal Nehru recognized this period of temporary flirtation with liberalism, selected as the time frame for analysis here, when he wrote: 'For a while it was a live paper, the most readable in India. It amused or pleased or irritated or angered, but it was not dull. And now that Mr. Wilson has left it, it has gone back to its old rut, and lest its hapless readers may be unable to find out what it is or what it stands for, it reminds them daily of "law and order"' (Wilson, 1929: vi–vii). Law and order notwithstanding, the episode raises bigger questions about gender issues and the dilemmas of hegemonic editorial expression during the transition from Empire to an independent India.

Wilson was close to both Motilal and Jawaharlal Nehru, who lived in Allahabad, and it was Jawaharlal Nehru who commented about protest during this period: 'Here were these women, women of the upper- or middle-classes, leading sheltered lives in their homes – peasant women, working-class women – pouring out in their tens of thousands in defiance of government order and police lathi. It was not only that display of courage and daring, but what was even more surprising was the organisational power they showed' (1946: 23). The Nehru family women were all brought up with encouragement to organize and inspire others: on his death bed, Motilal Nehru told his daughter Krishna to always be brave. That was what he had taught her and she was not to let him down. The young Indira Gandhi was also clearly influenced by leadership qualities that were encouraged within the family.

More generally, historians have acknowledged this new role for Indian women: 'Politics completely altered the goals and activities of organized women. Education, social reform and women's rights appealed to some progressive women, but the movement to rid the country of its foreign rulers attracted people from all classes, communities and ideological persuasions' (Forbes, 1996: 121). So did women, through their actions, speak in the pages of Wilson's paper? Nehru's statement about women's organizational ability refers to 1930 when nationalist men were in prison, but there is considerable evidence of female-led campaigning in advance of that date.

The Pioneer featured articles by Indian contributors and columnists (including prominent political women such as Annie Besant) with their own by-lines, according to the content analysis below. Most of the women mentioned here in relation to British India belonged to the highest castes and highest class of their region, and were often privileged, like the Nehrus, by Western education and in many cases by experiences abroad. They became the mouthpieces in *The Pioneer* of rural women and labourers who joined nationalist protests. This can be seen as an interesting counter-hegemonic interaction of class and gender in a colonial context. Indeed, the implications of class have prompted an important discourse, with scholars such as Howard Spodek (2010) suggesting that "all women" could be considered "subalterns", but members of the Subaltern Collective have defined women subalterns in terms of working class and lower caste (Guha and Spivak, 1988; O'Hanlon and Washbrook, 1991).

Thus, depending on the definition of 'subaltern' – a word popularized by Spivak's much quoted theorization 'Can the Subaltern Speak?' (1993), based mainly on nineteenth and early twentieth century India – the 'subaltern' could – and did – 'speak'. Yet, according to Jawaharlal Nehru (1936, 2004), the freedom movement was unable to communicate publically at this time – presenting activists with a big organizational problem. The *realpolitik* of the moment pointed to the fact that the 'freedom movement' needed to gain support for their tactics from the indigenous Indian civil service class if Gandhi's 'non-cooperation' campaign was to be really effective. This was precisely the readership that F.W. Wilson hoped that *The Pioneer* would also increasingly appeal to.

The need for the nationalist movement to win over a wide audience is articulated by Kamaladevi Chattopadhyaya who connected public awareness with the economic imperative and with a rationale for the political strategy of nationalist protest. She argued that: 'in order to mobilise and harness the mass energy to the anti-imperialist struggle there must be a political consciousness in the masses' (1939: 44). By this she meant to use the press as a platform when she included it in her ten point list for her anti-imperialism and, by association, women's emancipation (1939: 45). As seen in the case of French India, support for the nationalist cause had economic implications.

The Pioneer's style of reporting was unsensational, summing up the facts and presenting news in concise packages, augmented with direct speech. Sometimes court reports and accounts of women's conferences were covered verbatim. Significant technical improvements in the printing capability of the newspaper during Wilson's tenure facilitated the publication of a greater number of photographs, beyond the confines of the traditional pictures page. More photographs of Indians began to appear with a marked increase in the frequency that female activists' photographs appeared in the paper: for example, *The Pioneer* carried a photo of Annie Besant on 6 January 1930 and the front page for 10 September 1928 displayed a portrait of Sarojini Naidu, a female leader of the Congress and a noted poet, departing for a European tour.

The Pioneer was constructed of 24 pages, with the first four pages consisting of news, summary editorial and news in brief. Court reporting dominated pages five to six; pages seven to nine covered overseas news and some political comment; the occasional 'Women's Topics' column was located on pages ten to eleven – otherwise this space was reserved for book reviews. Although approximately 90 per cent of the paper reported news, political, judicial, sporting and economic affairs deemed to be of interest to the imperialist male, the rest of the paper focused on women, according to the empirical research conducted for this chapter. Pages 12 to 24 of *The Pioneer* consisted of editorial and letters, sporting events and results, local market and share reports, commentary on global markets and classified advertising. Given the fact that scholars of gender have regularly drawn attention to the exclusion or marginalization of women from the news (Tuchman et al. 1978; Krijnen, Alvares and Bauwel, 2011), even a small window of coverage merits further scrutiny, especially at a time when *The Pioneer's* editor was impressed by the social and political 'awakening of women' (*The Pioneer* 13 January, 1929: 12).

Editorial influence of F.W. Wilson

In the United Provinces, female indigenous protesters suffered from what Wilson described as the 'great police state' (Wilson, 1932) maintained by the British in India. Large amounts of court administrative paperwork – warrants for arrest, court statements with fingerprint records and translation notes, prosecution orders and other support documentation can be found in the regional archives in Allahabad, bearing witness to the burdensome nature of colonial surveillance. Typically, individual women would be arrested for 'preaching non-payment of rent' and sentenced to six months in prison, or a fine (that the Congress Party ordered them not to pay). Wilson was a foe of this 'great police state' (1932), its monumental waste and inefficiency. He was also a Labour sympathizer and was progressive on social issues. Of course, the Labour left, and more specifically the ILP, already supported Indian independence.

The Pioneer's new progressive stance was registered in the secret annual report on the press undertaken by the government reporter for the United Provinces civil secretariat. The 1929 report noted that '*The Pioneer* is one of the leading up-to-date papers in India and a most popular advertising medium . . . It sympathises with the constitutional efforts of Indians to advance and is opposed to revolutionary methods. Has grown wild of late and taken to criticizing the Government like any nationalist paper and expounding nationalist views in pursuance of the new editor Mr. Wilson's police' (British Library, 1929/30: 58–9). In fact Wilson was cautiously supportive of Dominion status. After he left, it was noted that *The Pioneer* 'has now reverted to a more responsible tone' (British Library, 1929/30: 58–9).

Journalistically, there was a choice in terms of editorial priorities for coverage, such as the positioning of a story within the paper, the size and nature of the headline and the number of column inches allocated to it. *The Pioneer* had its preferences, like any other paper. Wilson drew the line at supporting violence – although perceptions of what sells newspapers (professional new values) and professional journalistic 'objectivity' dictated that the paper would still cover it. Conversely, he favoured education and self-improvement for women and provided a platform for some Indian female writers. F.W. Wilson also recognized the importance of gender when he set out his opinion about women's struggle in a seminal editorial called 'the Awakening of Indian Women': 'Probably in no country in the world is it so necessary for women to take a prominent part in social and political life than in India' and that 'every encouragement should be given to the emancipation of the sex and to all attempts to give women their proper place in the body politic' (*The Pioneer*, 13 January 1929: 12). In 'The Awakening of Indian Women' Wilson also noted: 'recent conferences . . . dealing more particularly with subjects primarily affecting women . . . have shown that there is a new spirit abroad . . . and that, side by side with the wider political movement towards Swaraj, there will exist a parallel series of movements, without which any serious attempt at self-government will be doomed' (*The Pioneer*, 13 January 1929: 12, 1–2).

In the context of general interest in female citizenship, global campaigns were also reported in *The Pioneer*: Millicent Fawcett visited Ceylon, Lady Irwin campaigned on Indian women's behalf in London, Sarajini Naidu did a promotional tour of the United States. Similarly, in 'The Rights of Women – Plea for a Changed Outlook', Kamaladevi Chattopadhyaya[2] (who also travelled abroad as a representative of Indian women at international conferences) argued that the 'Women's Movement was one of the greatest forces in the world today and one of the factors shaping the life of humanity all over the world (*The Pioneer*, 14 January 1929: 4). Subsequent editors Thorniley then Young continued to report women's campaigns. For the first two weeks of October 1928 Wilson's campaign on conditions in the Indian army prompted a lively readers' postbag from officers' wives. During Wilson's short time as editor, there was an increase in reports of activities, campaigns and conflicts led by the nationalist movement: from November 1928 to February 1929 there was an increase of 30 per cent in the reporting of female conferences, similar events and speeches calling for reforms.

Wilson's support for the indigenous population also extended to sympathetic coverage of mass protests by the poor, often connecting past events with contemporary protest. In a three-part feature run over three days, 'Bardoli and the Future' (a land tax protest in Gujarat state in 1925[3]), a correspondent covered a pilot protest over raised land rent where on rent collection day, villagers simply deserted their dwellings and ran off into the forest. The rent collectors would not know which house was which since there were neither people nor written evidence to provide any sort of identification, so they went away empty handed. 'Determined men and women have seen the demonstration through' and the 'influence of the charka and looms for weaving khaddar' and Gandhi-ism allowed them to protest at unfair 'enhancement' of land rent (Part II, *The Pioneer*, 8 November 1928: 10). The protest caught on and those who continued the action elsewhere were said to have the 'Bardoli Spirit', as reported in *The Pioneer*, when 3,000 peasants gathered in Baglan and Bassein (near Bombay) to protest against the 'enhancement of land revenue' (*The Pioneer*, 10 January 1929: 3).

However, female *direct action* in the form of boycotts, pickets, burning of cloth and other forms of civil disobedience presented a dilemma. First, there was the question of appearing to condone violence; second the issue of giving publicity to illegal activities – for this could damage morale and British confidence; and third there was the question of economic damage to both *The Pioneer*'s revenue if advertisers withdrew support and the danger of the paper being accused of contributing to the damage that British business was already suffering.

Advertising

Reports of the nationalist and women's struggle for independence were embedded in a framework of advertising that supported the hegemonic status quo. Display advertisements were located on almost every page of *The Pioneer* – mostly for cars, alcohol, guns and machinery, with a few promoting toiletries and medication for women. Wilson was aware of the relationship between editorial and advertisement during a politically sensitive period, claiming that papers should be 'the watchdogs of freedom' while at the same time under pressure with a brief to improve the paper's economic position. He wrote twice at length on the subject, the first under the title 'Advertisement and Politics' in which he advocated sensitive juxtaposition of image, article and current politics.

Papers that did not entertain similar sensitivities were castigated: 'Indian newspapers which violently proclaim the boycott of foreign goods and declare that the purchase of such goods is a heinous sin and will delay the progress of the nation to the haven of Swaraj [self-government], do not hesitate to sell their advertising space to dealers in foreign goods' (*The Pioneer*, 28 April 1928: 12). During Wilson's tenure *The Pioneer* moved offices in London and procured new rotary printers for India – capable of producing 36,000 24-page editions per hour. F.W. Wilson wrote to encourage advertisers to take advantage of the broader demographic of this 'modern' paper. He highlighted the 'advertisers' opportunity' to utilize these machines to provide 'greatly enhanced value' for *The Pioneer* in order to reach its wider readership 'from the Viceroy to the humble inhabitants of the bazaar' who would have been able to afford the one anna paper (Wilson, *The Pioneer*, 1 October 1929: 1).

A sharp increase in advertising by the cotton mill companies occurred in March 1929 just after a fierce campaign of public foreign cloth burning on Swaraj Day, reported in *The Pioneer* 20 March 1929 on page three. Protests were also reported in Calcutta, Peshawar, Nagpur, Benares and New Delhi. One article described women's participation in a New Delhi Swaraj Day celebration on 10 March 1929:

India Celebrates Swaraj Day. Huge Processions and Foreign Cloth Bonfires. Women in Procession. The Demonstrators held National flags and placards and sang national songs along the route. A feature of the demonstration was the presence of about 60 women who formed a part of the procession. (*The Pioneer*, 13 March 1929: 3)

Extensive strike action severely affected production at the cotton mills. Jawaharlal Nehru urged the purchase of khadi (homespun cloth) only and not Swadeshi Mill cloth, as despite the name, this was a British owned mill. Mill owners placed a series of adverts in the paper at a time when they were in real trouble: a fierce campaign of public foreign cloth burning on Swaraj Day was followed in that same year by a sharp increase of advertising in *The Pioneer* by the cotton mill companies (*The Pioneer*, 10 March 1929: 1; 20 March 1929: 3). These appeared regularly from March 1929 and to January 1934, two or three appearing in each day's edition, generating an overall 1 per cent rise in advertisements in *The Pioneer*.

Assessing the influence of women as contributors to news

Using qualitative and quantitative methods to assess communications by and about pro-nationalist women, the challenge is to throw new light on how gendered identity, in what Chantelle Mouffe calls 'the multiplicity of relations of subordination' (1992: 372), is constituted.[4] To this end, coverage of female activities has been categorized into two groups: first educational, social and peaceful campaigns and second direct action such as strikes, burning of British cloth and business/land rent boycotts. In terms of research design, it is logical to differentiate between different sorts of coverage, with one data set for peaceful self-emancipation, such as education and conferences and one for direct action, sometimes but not always violent and/or illegal. The first category is important for the emerging citizenship of women, as well as in terms of social reform. The second reflects the interface of economics with ideology in the press, for it brought women into the public sphere with an organizational and collective consciousness reflected in trade union activities and politically motivated economic boycotts.

Content about women and protest has been analyzed in all 600 issues from January 1928 to January 1930. Peaceful democratic conferences and other meetings account for 78 per cent of political coverage on women and examples of direct action such as strikes, hartals, boycotts and cloth burning account for the remaining 22 per cent. Furthermore, records of amalgamated trade figures and tax revenues provide supporting evidence of severe economic difficulties faced by the Indian cotton trade due to strikes, boycotts and foreign cloth burnings.

It is important to differentiate between a newspaper speaking 'for' women, that is, on behalf of the colonial 'other' as framing and where a newspaper includes quotes from protagonists, or the protagonists themselves actually contribute articles to the newspaper. The data has been tabulated to show percentages of articles on women divided into framed reporting of their activities or use of direct quotes/writing from the women themselves (see Table 7.1). In terms of the latter, from November 1928 to February 1929 there was an increase of 30 per cent in the reporting of female conferences and similar events with direct speeches calling for social or political reforms. Women used the paper to announce events organized by Chattopadhyaya, the Nehrus, Dowager Maharani of Mandi and others; these were subsequently reported at length. Chattopadhyaya, Sarojini Naidu, Onila Chatterjee, Mandi, Maharani Sahiba of Lahore and Mrs. M. Nehru also wrote articles in the paper with by-lines, thus appealing directly to the readership. There were even debates in the paper between leading women: feminist Eleanor Rathbone, for instance, accused Miss Mayo of slandering 'Mother India' and not giving a true picture of national life – prompting an editorial in the same edition on her views (*The Pioneer*, January 18 1929: 10, 12).

On December 17 1928 (11, 1–2) the Maharani Sahiba of Lahore wrote a long article, 'Emancipate Indian Women', about the urgent need for social reforms and education. She proposed that 'there is nothing that will help the Indian woman to realise herself and make others realise her dignity, except the consciousness that she is free and independent'.[5] Probably the most controversial female contributor, best known for her gravitas but also her incisive and outspoken comments was Annie Besant. Initially she was sceptical about the chances of success for Gandhi's non-cooperation movement, calling his demand that the British government should accept Dominion status in its entirety, or else the Congress would not pay taxes, an 'insolent challenge' (30 December 1928: 1) and 'destructive' (11 January 1928: 9). However, by May that same year she

Table 7.1   Percentage proportion of framed reporting and women's direct quotes/writing in female-oriented articles

	Framed	Direct quotes
1928	67	33
1929	78	22
Jan 1930	83	17

had become convinced of the success of the tactic, stating in *The Pioneer* on 22 May that she was sure of India winning home rule (3).

Women and peaceful democratic self-emancipation

The Pioneer's most numerous accounts about women fall into the category of democratic meetings, conferences and lobbying for emancipatory parity in education, increases in marriageable age for child brides and changes to the status of widowed women so they could inherit and re-marry. The 1929 figures establish a 60 per cent increase from 1928 in reports supporting women's suffrage – in particular January to March that year, in anticipation of strong female voting in London (*The Pioneer*, 1 June 1929: 3).

In its early years the campaign to improve conditions for women that began with the United Provinces Social Conference (UPSC) in the 1880s, was largely dominated by a colonialist determination to assign only a partial mandate for women. Yet by the late 1920s a hardening of attitudes towards independence and the constitutional form it should take provided a parallel impetus for women to act and speak for their own emancipation – now the conferences and their mandates were run by women themselves. There had been a long trend of female activity and lobbying at national level, but now for the first time networks were extended to local level and reported in the press. This new trend in the movement of women from private into public spheres was underlined in 1929 by the UPSC's leader Uma Nehru, when in the presence of veteran campaigner Annie Besant[6] she expressed her regrets that over a 40-year period there had been a 'failure' to deal with women's issues at a communal level. However, she praised the All India Women's Conference (AIWC, established 1926) for its success at a national level (*The Pioneer*, 3 April 1929: 4). The deliberations of such organizations, consistently reported in *The Pioneer* along with other meetings and articles written by powerful women reflect a change in the way women organized, took part and voiced their concerns in Indian politics. *The Pioneer* also noted the increasing interest of Muslim women in social parity (June 18 1928: 17). A combination of attempts at self-emancipation and newspaper coverage amplified their voices.

This redefining of the notion of female citizenship and the associated rights and responsibilities was symbolized by the appointment in 1925 of activist Sarojini Naidu as the first female president of The Indian National Congress. By 1929 the women's movement had gathered momentum: alongside the AIWC, the Women's Indian Association was overseen by Dr. Muthulakshmi Reddi, the first Indian female to be elected as a deputy president of a legislative body. *The Pioneer* also reported on Allahabad Women's Meeting, Gonda Ladies Conference, Indian Women's Education Conference, Rajputana Conference, Delhi Women's Conference, Agra Province Education Conference, All India Women's Movement, Women's Franchise Union, All India Moslem Ladies Conference, World Conference for Women, Women's International Congress, Women's Institute Movement, All India Congress, and Women's Education Allahabad. In fact, 71 per cent of reported meetings were comprised of 18 separate organizations with 29 per cent of them AIWC.

Women and direct action

Gandhi's charisma attracted thousands of women to public life (Tomlinson 1993: 129; Forbes, 1996: 126; Jain, 1985: 37) and his return to politics in 1928 saw a change from 1920–21 Congress party non-cooperation, boycotting schools and law courts, to a more extensive form of civil disobedience. From February to August 1928 Vallabhbai Patel and Gandhi reignited the land rent dissent campaign and specifically sought women's support. *The Pioneer* reported on female led land 'satyagrahis', in an article called 'Path of India's Deliverance' (24 August). The article cited an

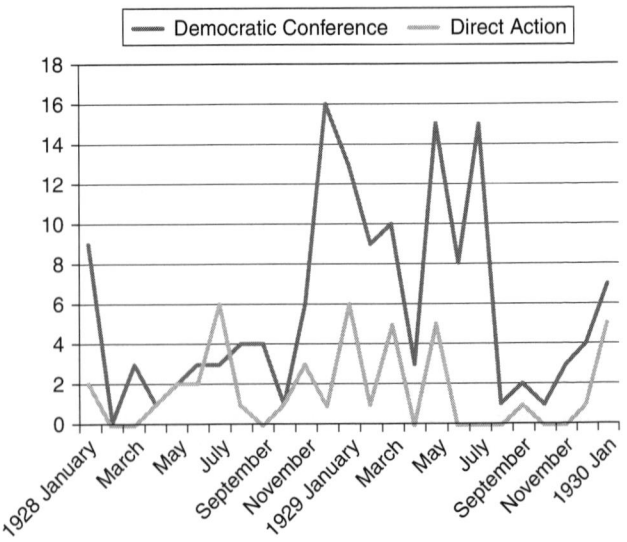

Figure 7.1   The Pioneer's coverage of women's protest 1928–1930

earlier incident in 1921 at Bardoli – the land tax protest in Gujarat state discussed earlier. In terms of the economic effects of such tactics, tax revenue figures for the period from 1921 to 1940 show a fall in land revenue from Rs27 million in 1921 to Rs23 million in 1930, decreasing further by 1940 to Rs19 million. Similarly, customs revenue fell from Rs36 million in 1930 to Rs28 million in 1940; and by 1946 salt tax had also declined to Rs2 million from Rs5 million in 1930 (Tomlinson, 1993, p.150).

The 42 (22 per cent of total) direct action articles during the period of this study are divided into 3 categories of women's participation: industrial strikes (50%); boycotts and hartals connected to the Simon Commission protests (17%), and open defiance linked to salt marches, land rent issues and foreign cloth burning (33%). The three most active peaks, June 1928, October 1928 and April 1929, are respectively linked to extensive coverage of women's involvement in mill strikes, Swaraj Day protests (*The Pioneer*, 10 March 1929) and the non-cooperation and civil disobedience movements (see Figure 7.1).

Simon Commission

Educated women spoke, led and participated in a series of protests against the Dominion Status proposed by the Simon Commission, arguing that it was an arrangement to ensure the continuation of British control. *The Pioneer* reported that the Dowager Maharani of Mandi had led a deputation before the Simon Commission claiming a reservation of seats for women in the legislatures. The paper also noted what was called 'The Feminine Touch': Lady Simon taking on board the appeals of women to have their concerns heard by the Commission (10 February 1929). Despite Lady Simon's categorical support for Indian women to take their part in (peaceful) public life (13 March: 13), Annie Besant was ready to do battle with the former's husband in the pages of *The Pioneer* for interfering in the Viceroy's business, as reported in *New India* (29 November 1929: 7). She even followed up with the blunt comment 'He (Simon) knows nothing about India and Indian feelings.' He refuted this as 'fantastic nonsense' (*The Pioneer*, 30 November 1929: 9). The disagreement made good copy.

Women and strikes

From 1928 to 1930 stories about textile strikes (where women formed a significant part of the workforce) were prominent – they account for 50 per cent of the 22 per cent 'direct action' category. While the paper deplored direct action and violence against the British political and economic infrastructure, it nevertheless reported accounts of women's attempts to improve their own wages upwards from Rs33 per month (*The Pioneer*, 9 December 1928: 20, 4) and subsequent arrests: 'Bombay Strikes. Determined to hold out. [At Kemp & Company] about 300 employees, consisting of compounders, clerks, hamals, and women labourers suddenly struck this morning' (*The Pioneer*, 21 April 1928: 1). The strike escalated and the paper reported that 150,000 workers were on strike (*The Pioneer*, 24 April 1928). 'The Sweepers Strike in Calcutta' (28 June 1928: 4) resulted in the arrest for alleged 'riotous conduct' of Miss Prabhati Gas Gupta, President of the union; while some carters were removing refuse, they were attacked by the strikers who pelted stones at them. She was sent before the magistrate but, as she was well educated and respectable, was bailed for Rs300.

Equally intimidation of strike-breakers was commented on: 'FEAR OF WOMEN PICKETS. [sic] Bombay. No attempt was made today to open the mills and the women pickets, who were posted at the mill gate to deal with the blacklegs, had an easy time. Clerks, oilmen, and other mechanics . . . hitherto abstained, fearing humiliating treatment at the hands of the pickets' (*The Pioneer*, 4 July 1928: 9).

'Women's excesses at Jamshedpur. Chastisement with brooms. Vigorous picketing continues. They have engaged women pickets with brooms and buckets of dirty water, and posted them at all important points. The women are indulging in excesses, male picketters, mostly Punjabis, always being at hand to encourage and incite' (*The Pioneer*, 16 July 1928: 9, 3). A few years later in French India the broom, along with the cauldron of oil, became the symbol of female pickets.

Reports of women's speech, protest and actions were set alongside contextual coverage of considerable trade difficulties especially in cotton mills, facing stiff competition from China, the United States and Japan by February 1929. The cumulative effect of sustained strikes exacted its toll: Anglo-Indian operations such as Elgin Mills, Currimbhoy and Cawnpore Cotton Mills had suffered during the Bombay Mill strikes in 1928 and their share prices were badly affected. Most mills recovered by March 1932 due in part to the import of new machinery, enabling production to increase exponentially (Tomlinson, 1993: 114; British Library, India Office), but five years later Currimbhoy Ebrahim & Sons Mill, the second largest Anglo-Indian mill in Bombay and one of *The Pioneer*'s most regular advertisers, was wound up. Its demise was reported on 18 January 1934 (4, 3).

Foreign cloth boycott and burning

Women also sought to disrupt mill production by making their own cloth. Although women were active in both nationalist and labour movements, that occurred at the same time, the women involved were not necessarily pursuing the same goals: whereas trade union led strikes and picketing were for wage increases and labour rights, Gandhi's Door-to-Door campaign encouraged women to participate in a foreign cloth boycott in every village and town, to 'collect foreign cloth and deliver or receive orders for khadi. Foreign cloth should be burnt whenever possible' and they were told to 'picket shops selling such goods' [Ahmedabad] (*The Pioneer*, 26 January 1929: 15). It was important to undermine British cotton production and its infrastructure: 'The help of patriotic ladies should be enlisted to prosecute this boycott campaign' (*The Pioneer*, 26 January 1929: 15). Gandhi also encouraged Muslim women to renounce foreign cloth to 'save Islam' (Forbes, 1996: 125).

Before Swaraj Day (10 March 1929) the paper covered an increasing number of stories involving the public destruction of foreign fabric in major cities including: 'India Celebrates Swaraj Day' (New Delhi March 10); 'Huge Processions and Foreign Cloth Bonfires' (*The Pioneer*, 13 March 1929: 3, 1–3; see earlier discussion). When women participated in bonfires of cloth, they would automatically be reported in black type pull quotes as if their presence were so unusual a concept as to be highlighted for special attention.

The bonfires spread far and wide across many cities including Calcutta, Peshawar, Nagpur, Benares and Allahabad. On 19 May 1929 Annie Besant called for a complete boycott of British produced cloth – an about turn that provoked the wrath of editor F.W. Wilson: on 29 June he penned an editorial headed 'Mrs. Besant's Foolish Speech'. It was a catch phrase that Wilson hoped would stick, for he followed it with a further article on 8 July referring again to: 'The Central Committee and its Dissentions. Mrs. Besant's foolish speech'.

Meanwhile the minutes of the United Provinces Chamber of Commerce recorded that British textile business had ground to a halt as a result of boycott (Mitra, 1930: 423). How could *The Pioneer*'s editor reconcile news values and liberalism with the obviously disastrous impact of direct action on the imperial economy? The effect of the strikes and cloth burnings on trade was also demonstrated by a correlation between the dates of highest protest activity and lowest production. As Gandhi encouraged workers to be independent and to spin their own cloth on charkas, and the impact of textile strikes was felt in the Britain, the paper rallied to boost interest in British goods.

As a newspaper business *The Pioneer* also experienced its own economic flux. When Young took over as editor in 1933, he sought funding from business interests based in Cawnpore and moved the paper to Lucknow. Refinancing started immediately after the princes (as the main regional landowning interest) had taken a lead – for the last time during British rule – at the Round Table constitutional negotiations, by accepting a federation to reduce their dependence upon London. Whereas under Wilson's editorship, *The Pioneer* reported on rent strikes, there was no coverage under this new regime.

Conclusions

Educated, progressive women who wanted reforms were able to take advantage of *The Pioneer's* short-lived liberalism at a time when almost anything female provided newspaper content – including book reviews, such as 'Mr. West's "The Life of Annie Besant"' (5 May 1929: 10). Events and activities provided news and this in turn enabled newspaper coverage that challenged existing assumptions about gender. On a daily basis *The Pioneer* showed a real sense of women's sorrows, aims, resolutions and triumphs.

During Wilson's period as editor, direct action provided 'bad news' coverage that simultaneously gave a small window for publicity. Less threatening peaceful campaigns provided a bigger window – enhanced by the novelty value of female activism. *The Pioneer's* coverage of women's boycotts exposed a weakness in the paper's imperialistic armour. Traditional Western journalistic values of objectivity and a preference for 'bad news' dictated that direct action be covered, but the ethical dilemma for *The Pioneer* was where to draw a line between support for the women's democratic cause, and women's unseemly behaviour in riots, boycotts, cloth-burning and strikes.

Although only receiving a small proportion of *The Pioneer's* political coverage, female conviction shines through their actions, intelligent use of the newspaper medium and in their language. Arguably even a short news report telling readers about an event where women were active, but without direct speech, nevertheless still gave those women a foothold (however tenuous) in the public sphere, by drawing their activities to the attention of readers and increasing their profile.

Historians need to look specifically at Indian newspapers during the struggle for independence for a counter-hegemonic discourse that reached a wide public.

The ongoing struggle by counter-hegemonic voices to achieve a public window in establishment communications challenged existing colonial assumptions about indigenous women, while simultaneously weakening the economic resolve of British business and administrative authority. In British India, when evidence of women's activism is paired with financial news, it becomes clear that women had a negative impact on colonial business. Findings underline female influence on both economics and ideology.

The window of opportunity during 1928–29 shows the dilemmas of owning and editing colonial newspapers in the transition from Empire to an independent India. Wilson was treading a precarious path as editor of *The Pioneer*. His own writings led the way on issues of female 'awakening' and social reform, but on economic boycotts and other forms of direct action, his paper was forced to follow events. It is clear that newspapers needed to obey the triple responsibility of embracing news values, reflecting ideological change and conveying political pressure and that as enterprises they are often not run primarily to maximize profits. Although newspaper fortunes do not always follow mainstream business cycles, in the process of conducting their everyday work, colonial organs such as *The Pioneer* became part of the economic and ideological maelstrom that they were reporting on. In-depth study of this process informs scholars about how easy, or difficult, it was to get ideas and information disseminated.

In this case the nationalist movement's limited counter-hegemonic window also demonstrated publically that the Congress Party, and their women, had organizational capabilities as a ruling party. The Congress Party's public activities led by women can be construed as a performance-influenced form of 'counter civil society' that provided grounding and experience for later mainstream leadership. By highlighting this process, the media were able to take a lead in public education, but the colonial press was forced to follow when faced with the dilemma of illegal direct action protest.

Whereas in both cases, newspapers clearly felt obliged to cover such acts of citizenship, the style of reporting was different. By and large, *The Pioneer*'s coverage was less sensational, more discursive and responsible. Female protesters were represented with more respect, even when the paper disagreed with their tactics, and day-to-day peaceful activities were reported with due prominence. In contrast, British suffragettes frequently complained that local and 'constitutional' lobbying was ignored by the press. Of course, by the 1930s women had the vote in India and in Britain, and cultural citizenship had become more sophisticated. Women had become more aware of the ways in which mainstream newspapers could be used to benefit their cause – thereby enabling their message to reach a bigger audience. Most significant for the developing scope of cultural citizenship is the fact that Indian women's engagement with the hegemonic public press had distinctly economic as well as political motivations.

Part V
Traces and Outcomes

8
Conclusion

Comparing and Contrasting Transnationally

Ongoing tensions in newspaper gender awareness

Across continents, periods, classes and political contexts newspapers held the potential as agents of communication to influence the emergence of a more fair and equal society, in which both sexes could participate more fully. This study has traced the development of forms of feminized cultural citizenship through specific organs of mass communication at different points in history between the 1860s and the 1930s, comparing and contrasting aspects of the phenomenon in France, Britain and India. The enquiry has revealed multifarious aspects of symbolism, connotations of cause and effect, influences of historical moment, contextual specificities and complexities in relationships between class and gender, colonizer and colonized.

What do such potentially diverse examples demonstrate about the nature of cultural citizenship framed by and through newspapers? The connection between media and public communications has manifested itself in dimensions of what is usually referred to as 'representational politics, embodied performativity and social constructions of reality' (Krijnen, Alvares and Bauwel, 2011: 222). In all the examples featured, aspects of gender awareness became lodged in national psyches through the agency of newspapers. Women from the periods of Second Empire and 'Belle Époque' France, Edwardian England and the twilight years of colonial India all influenced the agenda as participants in the public sphere and as readers. The study has also been concerned with how easy, or difficult, it was to get ideas and information disseminated, in that it begins and ends with examples taken from periods of press censorship.

Among the earlier examples here, France led the way in the newspaper world as a nineteenth century gender pioneer, even if this responsibility was often problematic, for the success of *Le Petit Journal* was built on risky and often illegal business dealings. These had the effect of over-prioritizing financial considerations, resulting in a cautious and socially conservative perception of women, both editorially and as consumers and/or readers. In 1863 the paper appeared to be a creature of its time – a reflection of Second Empire Bonapartism (Eveno, 2003: 22), a period when the government formally incentivized a 'non-political press', led by *Le Petit Journal*.

An obsession with circulation, dividends and profits underwrote a whole range of mainly traditional values towards women and how they should be both represented and catered for, influenced by the political support of *Le Petit Journal*'s various directors and proprietors for the Bonapartist centre and right.

By adopting a more socially cautious view of women's needs in order to gain mass appeal, mass circulation dailies offered the potential for distracting attention away from radical ideas and collective female protest at a time when there is ample evidence of these phenomena. It seems that conservative editorial content was motivated by the financial incentives of larger circulation, sensationalized morality tales became the vehicles whereby writers in *Le Petit Journal* could touch on issues such as divorce, childcare and education in editorials, and traditional upper-class and establishment values were encouraged through serialized novels and features.

The success or otherwise of newspaper developments depended first on contextual factors. From the 1880s onwards trends such as the influence of the 'new woman' in the Western world and of 'New Journalism' in Britain and the United States show that the battle to win the hearts and minds of consumers as citizens was now clearly on the agenda. Second, it depended on the willingness of readerships and advertisers to support new ideas. 'New women' demanded new civil rights that implied political engagement and social reorganization, not just by legislators but by society as a whole. The tensions are clearly evident in press communications of a gendered nature and emerge in quantitative and qualitative evidence.

In France the use of newspaper advertising carried a larger significance, as consumers were encouraged by a range of social organizations such as the 'Ligue Sociale d'Achêteurs' to use their material position for the furtherance of moral and public causes. Thus, a range of outlooks towards gender and newspapers as a consumer product were making their way into the mainstream agenda. They were aimed at a female readership within a broader framework of discourse and experiment, demonstrating both the availability of editorial choices during this formative period in representation of women and the inter-connectivity between economic consumerism and political citizenship.

Interpreting fragments

This study has searched for traces of gender, but what is the more general significance of fragmented evidence? That will certainly depend on what Ang calls 'a politics of interpretation . . . interpretations always inevitably involve the construction of certain representations of reality (and not others), they can never be "neutral" and merely "descriptive". After all, the "empirical" captured in either quantitative or qualitative form, does not yield self-evident meanings: it is only through the interpretative framework constructed by the researcher that understandings of the "empirical" come about . . . Here then the thoroughly political nature of any research manifests itself' (1989: 105).

'Conservative feminization' is one such interpretation. It emerged from a male monopoly on public communications and manifesting many of the characteristics of what has been more recently called 'tabloidization' in terms of simplistic, graphic and emotional writing styles. 'Conservative feminization' is not a twenty-first century revisionist invention but rather a phrase that is used to acknowledge the political nature of the conflict between more traditional and fairly new forms of female representation. This was still surfacing at the end of the nineteenth century: the interest in all things female was certainly evident, but so were the tensions of the moment. The examples of *Le Petit Journal* and the Harmsworth titles suggest that the contradictory nature of the performance of gender in the media origins of cultural consumerism is complex, multifaceted and closely linked to the male world of politics and business. The categories of 'victim, virtuous, victorious and vicious' that emerged clearly from content analysis of *Le Petit Journal*, were selected as a framework for the presentation of the findings in order to test Pickering's theorizations. They underline the concept of 'conservative feminization' during a period when other political choices were available to editors.

The significance of the growth in subaltern advocacy journalism with small but important traces of gender solidarity, as communicated in print publications, lies in the substantiation of economics and class as leading elements in cultural citizenship within colonial contexts. The differentiation in British India between women's lobbying for gradual, educational reforms on the one hand and the use of direct action on the other defines contemporary cultural citizenship in an economic as well as a political way. It helps us to appreciate the use of peaceful versus violent tactics – but the differentiation between the two aspects in research design involves a politics of construction as much as the reader's interpretation will involve a political judgement.

Transnational aspects of cultural citizenship

The first aspect of cultural citizenship identified in the Introduction as requiring further elaboration was how a range of roles for women were likely to emerge in press coverage in different countries under varying political circumstances. Diversity and contradictions in perceptions have been explored in India, France and Britain. *La Fronde*, for instance, provided a bridge between serious debates about and by women that were sometimes missing from the women's pages of mass circulation dailies and, conservative feminization of the popular dailies. The paper's initial impact shows that female readers were open to considering a variety of journalistic provision, including the discourses on 'new women'. In addition, Durand and Harmsworth both symbolized in different ways attitudes concerning the way female journalists should be employed. *La Fronde* was said to be *the* newspaper for school teachers, symbolized by a powerful visual record that encapsulates Durand's attitude towards education as a liberating force for working-class self-improvement. In a sponsored lithograph, a group of women overlook Paris from the heights of Monmartre, and the middle-class women show their working class sisters the socially uplifting benefits of education as they point towards the Sorbonne (Dufau, 1898). Harmsworth, on the other hand, did not favour well-educated professional women, suggesting instead that women should work their way up from being a secretary.

The comparison of *The Daily Mirror* in Britain and *La Fronde* in France is significant for an indication of the varying – and frequently conflicting – facets of cultural citizenship and its connection with consumer society that had emerged by the early twentieth century. Harmsworth's concept was to create the 'first daily newspaper for gentlewomen' and according to Kennedy Jones the idea was based on *La Fronde*. *The Daily Mirror* was to be staffed mainly by women journalists in a similar manner, but unlike *La Fronde*, not also by female production staff – and there turned out to be very different editorial philosophies. Whereas *La Fronde* provided a bridge between popular but socially cautious dailies and the specialist publications in which new ideas were discussed, the *Daily Mirror* continued the conservative feminization of *The Daily Mail*. One of the aims of *La Fronde* was to raise public consciousness of ways in which female identity was represented in French culture, and to widen its scope, giving women a greater visibility in representation.

Contemporary conflicts between emerging female citizenship – both consumer and political – and more traditional views of female domestic interests in the context of the continuing realities of economic, social and political disempowerment (despite reforms) were not always reflected by *Le Petit Journal*, *The Daily Mail* or the *Daily Mirror*. Even in *La Fronde* they were sometimes seen by contemporaries as editorial contradictions rather than as reflections of the diversity of discourse. This choice and variety that reflected women's changing relationship with the polity in Britain and France was recognized, for instance, by Britain's weekly *Illustrated London News* that carried regular discussions of suffragettes and citizenship issues in the women's page (British Library: MicB.51). Mass circulation dailies, however, frequently presented a narrower view.

Variations in framing according to progressive or conservative images of women have served to accurately reflect the emergence of options that education and independent income through work could provide. Some editors – especially Durand and Wilson – realized this potential only too well, but Wilson backed peaceful educational reforms as opposed to women's unconstitutional direct action in India – arguably the former approximates to a colonial 'reformist' version of conservative feminization, identified first in France, then in Britain. The transnational conflict between more traditional and fairly new forms of female influence also demonstrates that cultural citizenship was a multifaceted and political phenomenon.

If press was to be empowering, communications had to be manipulated and managed. As already stated, this was not achieved by the intermediary of public relations agencies as it is today, but by women (and men) themselves. Cultural citizenship could be both frustrating and empowering, especially in situations where women were involved in organizing around labour and political protest. The legacy for direct action came from the labour movement, where class took precedence over gender, demonstrating nevertheless the counter-hegemonic nature of the challenge posed by what has been referred to in the case of India as the 'discourse of awakening'.

The demands of the performative in direct action

In all countries the very act of mass spectacle in the streets and large public venues provided ongoing newspaper stories. The significance of gendered performance, however, is that it represented a form of female empowerment in the countries studied here. Public display of protest was one legacy from the trade unions, and by public display, women were manifesting their own cause. The iconology that banners provided had long been recognized by trade unionists for marches and other public events. Women developed their own visual motifs, slogans and symbols of protest that also became a focus for media illustrations and photographic representation. In India iconology also came to provide a symbol for identity and solidarity: from Bombay to Pondicherry women wielded brooms, and in French territories instability and violence was such that the cauldron of oil became a weapon of self-defence for supporters of independence.

The peaks of public communication coincided with the highest points of frequency for protests. This was equally true in Britain where early suffrage promotional efforts demonstrated to the public via newspapers that women were claiming for their sex a space that had become – especially since industrialization – a male-dominated domain. Pro-suffrage women opened up a new phase in the struggle. Cultural citizenship had achieved its first and most important breakthrough, but the tensions first identified in 1860s France, in relation to the potential clash between 'conservative feminization' and emerging female citizenship of a more political nature, were still present. The nature of performance started to become a central issue when public communications became dominated by discussions about protest tactics.

In terms of leading challenges to society, through the influence in newspapers of publicity, direct action was a more potent but controversial and risky weapon than peaceful, 'educational' events and organization. In Britain and France, success in gaining publicity was cumulative from the late 1860s onwards, but escalated after 1906. Promotion and news coverage helped to communicate ideas to a wider audience among the general public. There are parallels between the magnetic performative effect of female direct action on news values in mainland Britain with suffragette protests for the vote, and colonial India with female-led protests for independence. In both cases women were taking to the streets, but in Britain, unlike India, press coverage of peaceful persuasion was virtually obliterated in favour of newspaper interest in more dramatic but negative acts of violence. In Britain, unlike India, this harmed the constitutional cause and presented, via public communications, a certain illogicality, for violent tactics aimed to undermine the very constitutional system to which women were also campaigning for access.

The curiosity of the local and national press needed to be stimulated by the promise of a unique event, but the effectiveness, for instance, of suffrage tactics to court such publicity was controversial and has led to varying interpretations as to their effectiveness. In the case of the British suffrage movement's drive for the vote, initial publicity about protests had a positive influence in that it helped the cause to prosper. For instance, the public supported heckling at events, accepting it as a form of entertainment and embodied performance: they were genuinely shocked at the harsh ejection of female militants from meetings. Yet early publicity successes for militancy became a double-edged sword, for they created a precedent. As success led to further promotional efforts, necessitated by parliamentary intransigence, it then became more difficult to abandon such tactics.

Tabloidization

Presentation of the argument was crucial, but this was sensationalized by popular dailies in Britain and France. Is there a connection between performative suffrage tactics and the growth of tabloidization in British and French mass circulation newspapers? Contrary to the views of some scholars (see Glynn, 2000) that tabloidization is ultimately connected to post-modernism this study has found tabloid properties dating from the nineteenth century popular press onwards. Certainly the latter enhanced the importance of the visual – the *Daily Mirror* was initially called the first 'picture paper', based on halftone photography. Yet performance was also text related and not confined to tabloid values. Its significance lies in the interface with cultural citizenship.

The style of local reporting in India was different to that in mainland Britain. By and large, *The Pioneer's* reporting and comment was less sensational, more discursive and responsible than that of the British popular press both before and after World War I. Editor F.W. Wilson was sympathetic to the end goal of a constitutional settlement, while the Congress Party needed to persuade the paper's Indian middle-class readers, as well as colonial politicians, that it was a party of government not just at local level, but also nationally in the future. This was a serious issue that *The Pioneer* did not sensationalize. When the paper disagreed with female protest tactics, it did not adopt insulting language towards them, in the way that various British mainland papers (including 'serious' dailies such as the *Manchester Guardian*) had talked of suffragette 'insanity', for instance.

Whereas day-to-day peaceful activities were reported with due prominence in *The Pioneer*, British suffragettes frequently complained that local and 'constitutional' lobbying was ignored by the press. However, it is not possible to blame the press entirely for contributing to the long delay in obtaining the vote, although bad coverage could be damaging. How much did this matter? The main problem for the British suffrage campaign was that the mainstream press emphasized tactics rather than ideas. 'Deeds not words' representations of militants proudly projecting an image of orthodox femininity in dress and appearance, while performing distinctly unorthodox acts of violence, did not always emerge in their favour. This one-sided approach to coverage was potentially damaging, although historians are divided on the significance of this point. According to Pugh (2000: 229), it is feasible that readers actually ignored the opinion of their newspaper between 1911 and 1914. In Britain the Irish question had also raised the temperature, with the result that the political context was characterized by verbal and physical violence, between other interest groups, not merely the suffragettes and their opponents.

The outcomes and effectiveness of cultural citizenship

The outcomes of the interactions between media and women's activities were not always beneficial to campaigns for change. Chapter 6 indicates that in later periods, British militancy became a hindrance and there is much evidence of public hostility, fuelled by shocking reports of violence and vandalism in the press. Press intervention could be damaging, although it is possible that the British public became immune to constant reports of militant violence, as reactions to arson and other criminal acts certainly hardened. Kate Millett considers that such tactics enlisted public support, 'especially when government replied to them with police brutality, harsh prison terms, and forced feeding for hunger strikers' (1977: 82), but this was more the case at the early stages of direct action protest.

In Britain over 1,000 women were imprisoned for their support of female citizenship. The British suffrage movement, through its long, creative and vigorous campaigns put cultural citizenship on the map to an extent that no other country or activity hitherto can be said to have effected with the same intensity. Although the arguments of the suffrage movement as expressed in the press failed to win the vote, the campaign in Britain for the vote still represented a giant step forward for cultural citizenship. Despite problems in gaining national press interest in peaceful lobbying and the inadequacies of coverage, there were actually times when it dominated newspaper content.

By the 1930s women had the vote in India and in Britain, and the various manifestations of cultural citizenship had become more sophisticated, while women had become more aware of the ways in which mainstream newspapers could be used to benefit their cause. Editor F.W. Wilson, for example, was clearly influenced in the timing of his support for women by developments in women's suffrage that were taking place in mainland Britain. In both India and Britain women were newsworthy. As enterprises newspapers are often not run primarily to maximize profits. Although newspaper fortunes do not always follow mainstream business cycles, in the process of conducting their everyday work, colonial organs such as *The Pioneer* became part of the economic and ideological maelstrom on which they were reporting. Indian women's engagement with the hegemonic public press had distinctly economic as well as political motivations: reporting on their direct action protests had a negative impact on colonial business. Findings underline female influence on both economics and ideology. They also demonstrate that cultural citizenship can develop in a variety of different ways and change according to political circumstances.

The Indian experiences extend the scope of newspapers' role within the evolution of gendered citizenship both in the way that women operated within the public space and by the economic motivation for their strategy. In British India, female protest had a negative impact on colonial commerce. The connection between ideology and agency had evolved since the nineteenth century, but a third element was introduced into the equation by women's activism during the Indian campaign for independence – that of economics. Here the relationship with the public press was not only discursive and performance oriented, but was also aimed at communicating efforts to weaken British commercial resolve.

Newspapers enabled women's messages to reach a bigger audience, and editors clearly felt obliged to cover some (but not all) public activities. Contemporary scholarship on audience effects points to the fact that a successful political campaign is more likely when, within an audience (or readership), 'the flow of personal communication and structure of relevant interpersonal status is supportive' of the campaign (McQuail, 1977: 79). In other words, readers need to identify with the message. Newspaper history also demonstrates the importance of audience identification – indeed, alternative media and other specialist publications thrived on it. Supporters of the cause for which the newspaper existed (whether temperance, aspects of trade unionism or religion, the cooperative movement, or almost every political grouping) bought a paper with which, by and large, they agreed. There is therefore a certain perverse irony in the fact that when British women suspended suffrage activity (and hence newspaper communication about it), they were finally included in the bill for extension of the vote (over 30).

Stereotypes, vanguards or followers?

The question was raised in the Introduction as to whether newspapers led or followed public opinion in the discourses influenced by and about women. Twice 'The Thunderer' (*The Times*) appears to have been a catalyst for the fortunes of the female suffrage movement: on the first occasion as a potential influence against the passing of the third Conciliation Bill, and on the second occasion as the potential creator of a bandwagon effect during 1916 and 1917 in favour of the vote. This behaviour supports the contention originally made by Seymour-Ure that the press 'by anticipating an event which would happen anyway, change its character' (1968: 288). In their participation in the public sphere, women needed to reach the point of no return, when a cause or event began to look 'inevitable'. More than once the suffrage movement in Britain thought this had been achieved but was proved to be wrong, partly because parliamentarians did not prioritize franchise reform, partly because women activists tended to conflate notoriety and influence. High volumes of publicity did not necessarily persuade Fleet Street editors to argue for franchise reform nor did it persuade intransigent politicians to prioritize this particular legislative change for women over other issues requiring changes in the law. Nevertheless, the female sex worldwide has much to thank the suffragettes for.

Both the suffragettes and activist women in India challenged stereotypes, and analysis of this process as it was mediated by and in print communications is important, for as Pickering says: 'What is symbolically rejected defines the limits within which the centred, normative subject is located and naturalised' (2001: 200). He maintains that we need to pay close attention to marginalization, to what Foucault refers to as 'what has been rejected by our civilisation in terms of its systems of exclusion [and] refusal, in terms of what it does not want, its limits' (Foucault 1989: 65). Women had to transgress these limits, as Part IV demonstrates, for as Van Zoonen reminds us: 'The power to define situations and identities, to frame issues and problems, to legitimate interpretations and experiences is unequally distributed along lines of gender, ethnicity [and] class' (1994: 134). In all countries, both happened, often simultaneously.

In French India, indigenous leaders went to great lengths to explain their conduct in communications, in order counteract what they saw as unfair allegations; yet they also aimed to generate local support during the strikes. In Britain, the 1914–18 watershed cemented a conversion by key national editors and proprietors to the suffrage cause, exemplified by Northcliffe's change of heart on female enfranchisement. Similarly, during the 1920s, the example of F.W. Wilson's conversion to Dominion status for India and the consequential sympathy towards peaceful female protest proved pivotal. Contemporary observers had already talked before 1914 about women needing to appeal to the male ways of thinking. It was a question of how (if at all) to win men over.

When women did take the lead, and newspapers reacted to them, the effects were not always positive. In 1912, during the arson campaign, the *Westminster Gazette* commented that the women's movement should take into account what it called 'the psychology of the male'. Editor C.P. Scott's diary entries for 23 January 1912 indicate that Churchill, for instance, was influenced adversely by suffrage tactics. 'He practically admitted that his present wrecking tactics are the outcome of resentment at the treatment he has received from the WSPU' (Wilson, 1970: 58). In terms of the compromises needed in order to take into account the psychology of men, in contrast, during World War I, female supporters of the vote redeemed themselves by showing dedication to the war effort.

Bolt points out that: 'The doctrines and practice that the suffragettes sought to propagate inclined their critics to see them as agents of emotion rather than the creators of democratic opinion' (Bolt, 2000: 49). This is not true of India where women became agents of democracy. Yet women in both countries faced a common barrier: in empire India and in hegemonic Britain, influence was still located elsewhere in the all-male world of London's clubs and the Westminster establishment. Politics and newspapers coalesced into a number of networks.

British rulers as readers did not necessarily identify with congress protest campaigns as reported in the *Pioneer*, but F.W. Wilson was aiming to win over the Indian middle-class readership, and it is feasible that the Indian middle-class readership identified with the protests of Indian women. The Congress Party's public activities led by women can be construed as a form of 'counter civil society' that provided grounding and experience for later mainstream leadership. On the one hand, by highlighting this aspect, the colonial press were able to present themselves as taking a lead in propagating public education, but on the other hand editors were forced to follow events rather than to lead public opinion when faced with the dilemma of whether or not to report on illegal direct action protest.

Newspapers needed to obey the triple responsibility of embracing news values, reflecting ideological change and conveying political pressure, but who led and who followed? F.W. Wilson's own writings led the way on issues of female 'awakening' and social reform, but on economic boycotts and other forms of direct action, his paper was forced to follow events. In India many women were imprisoned for protest: the mass of local court records held in regional archives testify to the scale, even if a definitive number of women who were jailed is difficult to calculate.

Timing, significance and evolution of gendered traces

Timing is a crucial factor in the development of cultural citizenship. In French India, the timing was such that protest was fuelled by, and simultaneously gave rise to, nascent anti-colonial feeling, influenced by the situation in British India, and crucially by the instigation of France's Popular Front government. This event provided hope for social reformers through the introduction of positive legislation such as an eight-hour working day. Contextually, the combination of economic and political neglect led to class politics – escalating to such an extent that the French ruling elite faced a downward spiral: on 14 February 1923, Albert Londres had written in *L'Impartial de Saigon* that in Pondicherry life was 'idyllic', but by the 1930s, with increasing economic deprivation, trade unionism thrived.

In United Provinces, educated Indian women and their supporters were able to take advantage of *The Pioneer*'s short-lived liberalism. Events and activities provided news and this in turn facilitated newspaper coverage that challenged existing assumptions about gender. Peaceful campaigns appealed to liberal colonisers and therefore gained a bigger window in their local press, and this trend was enhanced by the novelty value of female activism. Conversely, *The Pioneer*'s coverage of women's boycotts exposed a weakness in the paper's imperialistic armour. Traditional Western journalistic values of objectivity and a preference for 'bad news' dictated that direct action had to be covered: it was, in the eyes of editors, an extension of the obsession of dailies with crime. Despite this limitation to framing, even a short news report telling readers about an event where women were active still gave those women a foothold (however tenuous) in the public sphere, by drawing their activities to the attention of readers and increasing their profile. Thus counter-hegemonic voices challenged existing colonial assumptions

about indigenous women, while simultaneously weakenir
nomic resolve of British business and administrative authoriy.

Content analysis findings underline that female influence on both
economics and ideology was framed by newspapers in which women
developed their own identity and manifested their own iconology.
Stevenson argues that part of the task, by definition, of cultural citizenship, is 'to pay attention to the material conditions and ideologies that
aim to exclude different voices from full participation' (2003: 145). In
the case of French 'comptoirs' in India, it was industrial conflict that
facilitated indigenous communications, contributing towards the origins of anti-colonialism as an empowering voice. Material conditions
for the indigenous Tamil population in Pondicherry had, over the years,
become so dire that excluded voices sought redress through widespread
but still illegal, industrial action.

In the case of the British suffrage movement, labour organizations
provided a space for communication and organizational experience for
women. Cultural citizenship became multifaceted, encapsulating both
a discursive, educational identity and more extreme, dramatic activities.
Again, timing was crucial. When women decided to take action it was
articulated in the media who found this newsworthy initially due to
its novelty value. From the suffragette perspective, such coverage could
potentially change public attitudes towards women and towards the
cause of franchise reform.

Interpretations of class, performance and collective action

Newspapers' early awareness of gender amounted primarily to an identification of female readership and purchasing power but conversely
women's involvement in collective actions as consumers, political and
trade union activists in the public sphere provided a reason to project
messages and an image to a wider public than would otherwise have
been reached. Collective action represented a form of political awareness, and the motivation to call for change entailed a choice of tactics
that could be adopted to achieve this. In French India women were
proactive in choosing the tactics – picketing and self-defence – but it
was in British India that women using such tactics, actively sought to
draw attention to their cause in newspapers.

If Spodek's (2010) suggestion that in a colonial situation, *all* indigenous women should considered 'subaltern', then this wider definition
of the term means that all their efforts, including those of educated
women as leaders, can be said to form part of a 'counter-civil' influence

on the public press that amounted to a redefinition of cultural citizenship. Class and caste definitions are problematic in a number of different instances, not least because of the evolution of women's activities in the polity. In Britain, for instance, the NUWSS experienced a revival during the years immediately preceding World War I. Many new, younger, recruits supported a suffrage–Labour alliance because they perceived sex and class barriers as combined problems emanating from monopoly and privilege. In 1913 the Trades Union Congress supported a clear suffrage motion, and the NUWSS now had a real industrial base that challenged its traditional sedate, middle-class image. There is evidence that between 1928 and 1930 in British India, and between 1936 and 1938 in French India, of a redefinition of female citizenship in relation to use and representation in the public press, again manifested in both hegemonic and counter-hegemonic communications. Class awareness became a precursor to gender considerations, and a contributory factor towards the evolution of cultural citizenship in its various manifestations.

The Introduction identified the existence of two different theoretical formations that this study has traced historically – the discourse of separate spheres (public and private) and the discourse of gender difference. The examples in the countries studied have illuminated an intersection between direct action with organizational origins in class, and newspapers as an agency for public communication of gender. The labour movement first pioneered confluence in Britain during the early history of suffrage. Radical suffragettes were not as attentive to the solicitation of publicity as suffrage militants later became but the precedent had been established. In India strikes and boycotts prompted communications that featured their actions in the public sphere.

A further evolution that caused redefinition of cultural citizenship took place in Britain when suffragette campaigns refined their impact and media image by establishing press sections, as media persuasion became the norm. What had started off as initiatives by newspaper proprietors and editors to decide how to cater for women ended up with women themselves trying to dictate the message – sometimes successfully, sometimes facing censorship, but sometimes being able to enter into a performative negotiation with the public press over the nature of mediation. In fact, suffragette tactics rather than content discourse dominated the British press from 1908 to 1914.

In the countries mentioned in this study, evolutions in forms of cultural citizenship involved a new performative way of 'doing' gender that sought to establish different behavioural norms in pursuance of equality. All classes, from 'untouchables' in India to middle- and upper-class suffragettes, claimed rights in ways that challenged accepted norms of feminine behaviour. This seems to concur with the spirit of Stevenson's contention that the pursuit of social inclusion as an aim means that cultural citizenship 'becomes defined through a site of struggle that is concerned with the marginalization of certain social practices' (2003: 24). Cultural citizenship has been characterized as comprising a range of tensions and interactions between economics, class and ideology, between consumerism and politics, between performance and social exclusion, between hegemonic domination of public communication and the articulations of counter hegemonic challenge.

Counter-hegemonic significations through repetitive challenges to stereotyping

Studies of present day gender serve to underline the ongoing task of identifying gendered considerations. In a recent anthology of present day gender studies, one contribution is entitled 'Silent witness: news sources, the local press and the disappeared woman', while another carries the heading 'Looking for gender equality in journalism' (Krijnen, Alvares and Van Bauwel, 2011). In other words, the binaries continue despite women's achievements in society over the years. The relationship between women's interests and demands and the way they were communicated is one of both success and failure: success in simultaneously gaining some influence and certainly in attracting attention, but failure to sustain adequate communication of ideas through mainstream papers.

However, militant suffragettes gained certain advantages through repetition of the act. In 1914 an American woman journalist staged a 'performance' of forced feeding in front of the cameras of New York's *World Magazine*. Her experience of how it felt to be force-fed is located at the interface of performative journalism and feminist activism, and 'blends the discursive strategies of the celebrity interview with those of the militant suffrage movement's polemical texts' (Green, 1997: 171). This example was only made possible because of the relentless and repetitive efforts of women to influence the public press on this, and other issues over the years. Without a regular build up of newspaper coverage, this particular media feature would have lacked public impact, and ultimately, reader recognition of the situation.

Groups of women could attract newspaper attention, some (but not many) could work as journalists (usually on domestic content), but in all the countries featured here, political decision making remained by and large in male hands and took place behind closed doors. As Stevenson says, 'The concept of hegemony has revealed that the domination of information flow is nearly always uneven. It certainly favours the voices and perspectives of the powerful, but it also provides space for critical reflections and other intersubjective relations' (2002: 219). In a colonial situation, this marginalization was endorsed by structural definitions of hegemony.

Regular stereotyping can be identified in all countries in every period, despite some fluidity in attitudes. For example, during the suffragette window of publicity between 1906 and 1914 newspaper attitudes fluctuated then changed as some editors were converted to the vote for women – a tendency that continued into World War I. Thus the counter-hegemonic space was not fixed, guaranteed or evenly distributed across periods of time and cultures. Nevertheless, findings support the Pickering view first mentioned in the Introduction: 'This is the dilemma which stereotyping faces: to resort to one-sided representations in the interests of order, security and dominance, or to allow for a more complex vision, a more open attitude, a more flexible way of thinking. Stereotyping functions precisely in order to forget this dilemma' (2001: 4). Yet the tensions created by this dilemma were a constant feature in all countries, where chinks in the hegemonic armour necessitated that women undergo a publicity treadmill that required an ongoing and constant effort.

Therefore newspapers continued to provide a forum for lively rhetoric and performance-influenced gendered discourses. The arguments were often recycled with varying angles, but the process of repetition constantly re-energized the polity, because the symbolic interaction of gender necessitated on a daily basis an obligation to re-stage the performance. Judith Butler's notion of a gendered subject being formed through repetition, through a 'practice of signification' points in this study to a process whereby women acted counter-hegemonically to first achieve that repetition in and through the public press.

However, repetition should not be confused with sameness, or simplicity, or even staleness. The adaptation of British suffrage supporters to the requirements of World War I exemplifies the adaptation of cultural citizenship. In World War II, nationalist supporters in French India supported the French Resistance, but gender came to the fore in 1947. The episodes and examples presented demonstrate that forms of citizenship developed through the agency of newspapers were multifaceted, complex, full of tensions and with no easy or quick route to equality. As Stevenson reminds us about feminism, 'There is no single story to tell about its relationship to citizenship, only many stories which bring out the internal and changing complexity of feminism in relation to the historical dynamics of democratic citizenship' (2001: 140).

Similarly, no single answer emerges from this study. Uses and meanings were contested politically in every era and in every country featured here, for the cultural knowledge that newspapers contributed to acts as a reflection of a means by which domination and subordination were constructed and co-existed as relationships of power. Influence, processes of communication and contradictions in press mediation should be part of that process of recuperation of women's achievements and experiences that contribute towards forms of gendered cultural citizenship. Ordinary voices need to be further teased out by researchers if the interactions between women and public communications are to be understood better. Just as campaigners in the past made this effort into an ongoing endeavour, so we today can take inspiration from their persistence.

Notes

1 Introduction

1. The literature on modernity is vast, but influential works for this study include Thompson (1995) and Berman (1983).
2. Thanks to the British Academy Small Research Grant scheme for funding *'Feminising Influences on Mass Circulation: A comparative study of* Le Petit Journal *and* The Daily Mail*'*, to the Economic and Social Science Research Council (ESRC) for funding *'Women, Press and Protest in British and French India, 1928–47'*, to Macquarie University Faculty of Arts where the author is an adjunct Professor, to Wolfson College and the Centre of South Asian Studies, University of Cambridge, where the author is a long term visiting fellow, to research assistant Kate Allison and to peer reviewers whose incisive comments have been so helpful.
3. *The Pioneer* has since survived four changes of ownership and is now owned and edited by a BJP politician, while *Swandanthiram* is now an organ of the Communist Party. Neither of these parties existed in the areas involved during the period studied. *Le Petit Journal* survived into the 1940s, the *Daily Mirror* and *The Daily Mail* are very much alive today, although the former was established with a very different brief (see Chapter 3).
4. In terms of usage, the word 'audience' is used in preference to 'readership', because newspapers were often read aloud to assembled groups, especially in French India (see Chapter 4). 'Readership' is used in the context of publishers.
5. See also: Wood (2007), McChesney and Nichols (2002), Williams (1969), Holzer (1993), Gillmor (2004), Boyce, Curran and Wingate (1978), Lee (1977), Altschull (1995).
6. Some of the journals that have been at the cutting edge of research have included: *Pénélope, Feminist Review, History Workshop, Documentation sur la Researche Féministe, Feminist Studies, Signs, Women's Studies Quarterly* and *Women and History*.
7. The journal *Media History*, for instance, was launched in 1998, and was formally known as *Studies in Newspaper and Periodical History* existing from 1993 to 1997.
8. Drawing on intellectual antecedents by T.H. Marshall and T. Bottomore (1992) and Raymond Williams (1961) Stevenson takes a broader sociological approach than, for instance, Kymlicka and Norman (2000) whose starting point derives more a narrower base in political theory.
9. See especially Foucault (1973, 1977, 1980).
10. Present day gender and media has a vast body of publication. See Kearney (2012) and Gill (2007) for an introduction.
11. She poses this question in the context of examining the usefulness of Stuart Hall's (1973) much discussed 'encoding/decoding' model.
12. For American attitudes, see Sneider (2008).

2   France

1. While the *Journal des Femmes* was long running, *La Voix des Femmes* only lasted a few months, with 46 editions, following the revolutionary (1789) feminist model of being printed by a female and with its own society for meetings and political activities. *La Politique des Femmes* lasted for 2 issues, while *L'Opinion des Femmes* survived for several months in 1849 (Rendall, 1985: 291–4).
2. For the French Revolution and women, see Goldberg Moses, 1984: 14–15; Zeldin, 1988: 509; Landes, 1988: 170; Reynolds 1986: 104, 113).
3. On British nineteenth century magazines, see Beetham (1996).
4. The phrase refers to the practice – opposite to the structure of a novel – of inserting all the key information at the beginning (when, where, what, who and how) then reducing the amount of facts so that the information flow narrows as the story reaches the end of the page. See Stensaas (2005).
5. Some of the sections of this chapter on business aspects were first published in Chapman (2011b).
6. Langer adopts this phrase in relation to tabloid television (1998: 5).
7. Before the liberalization of press controls in 1881, *Le Petit Journal* was prosecuted by the authorities for misrepresentation of facts in crime stories. Court reports from 1879 refer to an over-enthusiasm for blowing things out of proportion in coverage of a murder case, encouraged by the increase in sales during the Troppman affair (PP: BA1621).
8. Trimm's front page 'chroniques' became habit forming and he was headhunted for double his salary by *Le Petit Moniteur*, but he was not read. He moved papers several times before being given his own weekly – *La Semaine de Timothée Trimm*. All the initiatives failed ignominiously (Morienval, 1934: 228), demonstrating that it was the paper and not the individual that mattered. He was replaced at *Le Petit Journal* by a collective of five writers, including the editor Escoffier, and they collectively assumed the name of 'Thomas Grimm'. Readers did not realize, or even comment on the change.
9. For crime and 'faits divers' see Barthes (1964), Auclair (1970), Perrot (1983), Nye (1984), Berenson (1992: Ch. 6), Walker (1995), Shapiro (1996: Ch. 1) and Kalifa (1995).
10. On department stores more generally, see Crossick and Jaumain (1998).
11. The fact that the suffrage movement was less high profile in France has prompted some feminist historians to focus instead on the progressive influence of key individual late nineteenth century women in diverse fields. This emphasis is useful for a critical approach to 'conservative feminization', for it reinforces the argument that there were alternative contemporary role models available to the editors of *Le Petit Journal*. For mention of the influences of individual female journalists, see Chapter 3.
12. Quantitative research in this chapter was first published as work in progress in Chapman (2011c).
13. On advertising systems, see Chessel (1998), Williams (1982), Martin (1992) and Lagneau (1989).
14. Findings on the business orientation of *Le Petit Journal* were first published in Chapman (2011b).
15. On the forms of commodified spectatorship within Parisian Belle Époque society, see Schwartz (1998).

16. After the death of his first wife, Delphine Gay, in 1855, de Girardin married a German countess, divorced her in 1872 and denied paternity during a high profile court case (Préfecture de Police: Ba1096). Obituary writers commented that every business venture de Girardin launched had lost money (ANR: 65AQU257/2), despite his pioneer innovations in popular press (Chapman, 2005: 35, 46, 74). Editorially, he was interested in education and issues affecting women.
17. Marinoni bought *Le Figaro*, became the largest shareholder in *Le Jour*, and was awarded the Légion d'Honneur with the public support of *The Petit Journal*. By 1892 he was worth 25 million francs, and became general administrator of *The Petit Journal* after the death of de Girardin.
18. The novel *Une Vie* – first translated as 'A Woman's Life' – (Boulevard Novels, vol. viii, 1885) is a good example.

3 France and Britain

1. Harmsworth became a baronet in 1904 and a peer in 1905. He is referred to as Harmsworth up to 1905 and as Northcliffe thereafter.
2. For more on W.T. Stead, see Stead (1885), Whyte (1925), Walkowitz (1992), Chapman (2005a) and Chapman and Nuttall (2011).
3. The phrase 'conservative feminization' is used in Andrews and Talbot (2000) in relation to consumption and advertising for the Ideal Home Exhibition, but here it is applied for the first time to editorial content.
4. Papers connected with *La Fronde* are located at the Bibliothèque Marguerite Durand in Paris, categorized as 'ASF'.
5. For more examples see Onslow (2000).
6. For female readers more generally, see Flint (1993).
7. The author is grateful to Peter Putnis for drawing attention to these papers.
8. On achievements of other individual women see Clark (2008).
9. For an introduction to this text, together with an excerpt, see King and Chapman (2012).

4 French India

1. Some of the analysis in this chapter was first published in Chapman (2010) as work in progress.
2. Although the local economy was dependent on the British sector, French India's performance in volumes of trade compared favourably with many other empire territories. For comparative statistics on this aspect 1919–34, see Maestri (1993: 225–6, 232). Expenditure was always equal to income.
3. See Chapman (2011a) for a comparison with advocacy journalism as defined by Downing (2001).

5 Britain

1. For more on the radical suffragists, see Liddington and Norris (1978); Ramelson (1976: 130–1).
2. New halftone photographic capabilities were first developed by the *Daily Mirror* in 1904 and also popularized by the *Daily Sketch* in 1909.

6   Britain

1. See Bush (2007) for details on individuals who opposed female suffrage.
2. In terms of female enfranchisement in other countries, by 1914 it had been granted in 11 states in the United States; New Zealand granted the vote to all adult women in 1893 and Australia gave the federal vote in 1902; in Europe Finland had pioneered in 1906 and Norway in 1913. See Fletcher et al. (2000) for suffrage in the Empire and transnational suffragist ideas in the UK, including those of the Women's Freedom League (103–15).
3. In fact, Mrs. Fawcett only started to criticize WSPU tactics in public when the press reported that a member of the Women's Freedom league ('WFL', with 61 branches) threw acid in a Bermondsey polling booth during 1909. See Mayhall (2000: 365–6).
4. This realignment was all the more amazing when only a year or so previously, the WSPU had been vehemently proclaiming 'votes for women, chastity for men', a slogan based on the claim by Christabel Pankhurst (1913) that men should be avoided as 75–85 per cent of them had acquired gonorrhoea before marriage. See also Bland (1995). Previously the WSPU had a long standing anti-male strain within its ranks, the majority of whom were single.

7   British India

1. For more on Wilson, see Chapman and Tulloch (2013).
2. Chattopadhyaya used Wilson's headline 'The Awakening of Women' for inspiration for the title for her book (1939).
3. The Bardoli satyagraha was a protest against a 30 per cent tax rise on the Bombay Presidency's levy. After disastrous famines and floods affected farmers' crops and income that year, the Gujarat *taluka* (subdivision of a district) rebelled against Presidency's refusal to waive the extra payment on compassionate grounds.
4. Qualitative and quantitative findings for this chapter were first published in Chapman and Allison (2011) as work in progress.
5. The Maharani continues her article citing literacy statistics. 'In the whole of India, we see that where there are 139 literate men to a thousand, there are only 21 literate women to a thousand.'
6. On the pioneering influence of Annie Besant, see Cousins (1947).

Bibliography

AAN-S.O. (Archives de l'Assemblée Nationale, Statuts Ordinances) (1906) tome 1.

Acker, J. (1990) 'Hierarchies, Jobs, Bodies: A Theory of Gendered Organisations', *Gender and Society* 4, 139–58.

Adamowicz-Hariasz, M. (1999) 'The *Roman- Feuilleton* of the 19th Century French Press ', in D. De la Motte and J. Przyblyski (ed.) *Making the New: Modernity and the Mass Press in Nineteenth-Century France* (Amherst: University of Massachusetts Press), pp. 160–84.

Adler, L. (1979) *A l'Aube du féminisme: les premières journalistes, 1830–1850* (Paris: Payot).

Adorno, T. (1970) *Aesthetic Theory*, trans. R. Hullot-Kentor (London: Continuum).

Ahuja, B.N. (1996) *History of the Indian Press* (Delhi: Surjeet).

AITUC (2009) *75 Years of Swandanthiram 1934–2009* (Pondicherry: Liberty Press)

Allen, C. (2007) *Kipling Sahib: India and the Making of Rudyard Kipling* (London: Little, Brown).

Allen, M. V. (1979) *The Achievement of Margaret Fuller* (University Park and London: Pennsylvania State University Press).

Allport, G. W. (1954) *The Nature of Prejudice* (Cambridge, MA: Addison Wesley).

Althusser, L. (1969) *For Marx*, trans. Ben Brewster (London: Penguin Books).

Altschull, J.H. (1995) *Agents of Power*, 2nd edn (New York: Longman).

AN (Archives Nationales) F18 /294/295/296; F18/401; F18/2365; 45AP6.

Anderson, B. (1991) *Imagined Communities: Reflections on the Origins and Spread of Nationalism*, 2nd edn. (London: Verso).

Andrews, M. and Talbot, M.M. (eds) (2000) *All the World and Her Husband* (London and New York: Cassell).

ANFOM (Archives Nationales de la France d'Outre Mer): Inde E15; E16/1934; FM:1AFFOL/709; FM:1AFFOL2888.

Ang, I. (1989) 'Wanted Audiences. On the Politics of Empirical Audience Research', in E. Seiter, et al. (eds) *Remote Control: Television, Audiences and Cultural Power* (London: Routledge) pp. 96–115.

Annasse, A. (1975) *Les Comptoirs français de l'Inde (1664–1954)* (Paris: La Pensée Universelle).

ANR (Archives Nationales de Roubaix) 65AQA211; 65AQU257/1; 65AQ U257/2.

Arnold, M. (1887) 'Up to Easter', *Nineteenth Century*, XX1 (May), 629–43.

Arnold, M. (1987) *Selected Prose*, P.J. Keating (ed.) (London: Penguin).

Auclair, G. (1970) *Le Mana quotidien: Structures et fonctions de la chronique des faits divers* (Paris: Éditions Anthropos).

Bakshi, S.R. (ed.) (1994) *Aruna Asaf Ali* (New Delhi: Anmol).

Bakshi, S.R. (2000) *Kamala Nehru: Participation in Non-Violent Satyagraha* (New Delhi: Om Publications).

Baldasty, G. (1992) *The Commercialization of News in the Nineteenth Century* (Madison and London: University of Wisconsin Press).

213

Bard, C. (1995) *Les Filles de Marianne: histoire des féminismes 1914–1940* (Paris: Fayard).

Bard, C. (2010) *Une Histoire politique du pantalon* (Paris: Editions de Seuil).

Barns, M. (1940) *The Indian Press. A History of the Growth of Public Opinion in India* (London: George Allen and Unwin).

Barrier, N.G. (1974) *Banned: Controversial Literature and Political Control in British India, 1907–1947* (Columbia, MO: University of Missouri Press).

Barthes, R. (1964) 'Structures du fait divers' in *Essais critiques* (Paris: Éditions du Seuil).

Bellanger, C. et al. (1969) *Histoire générale de la presse française*, vol. 3 (Paris: Presses universitaires de France).

Beetham, M. (1996) *A Magazine of Her Own? Domesticity and Desire in the Woman's Magazine 1800–1914* (London: Routledge).

Bell, A. (1994) *Language in the News* (Oxford: Blackwell).

Berenson, E. (1992) *The Trial of Madame Caillaux* (Berkeley: University of California Press).

Berman, M. (1983) *All That is Solid Melts into Air* (London: Verso).

Bhabha, H. (1983) 'The Other Question', *Screen*, 24, 18–36.

Bingham, A. (2004) *Gender, Modernity, and the Popular Press in Interwar Britain* (Oxford: Clarendon Press).

Bird, S.E. (1992) *For Enquiring Minds: A Cultural Study of Supermarket Tabloids.* (Knoxville: University of Tennessee Press).

Blanchard, P. and Lemaire, S. (2003) *Culture Colonial: La France conquise par son empire, 1871–1931* (Paris: Autrement).

Bland, L. (1995) *Banishing the Beast; English Feminism and Sexual Morality, 1885–1914* (London: Harmondsworth).

Blom, I., Hagemann, K. and Hall, C. (2000) (ed.) *Gendered Nations: Nationalisms and Gendered Order in the Long 19th century* (Oxford: Berg).

BN (Bibliotheque Nationale de France) (1863) *Le Petit Journal* LC2 3011 February–June; Micr-13; Micr-M-309.

Bolt, C. (2000) 'The Ideas of British Suffragism', in J. Purvis and S. Holton (ed.) *Votes for Women* (London: Routledge).

Bonvoisin, S.-M. and Maignian, M. (1986) *La Presse féminine* (Paris: Presses universitaires de France).

Bostick, T. (1980) 'The Press and the Launching of the Women's Suffrage Movement, 1866–1867', *Victorian Periodicals Review*, 13(4) (winter), 125–31.

Bourne, R. (1990) *Lords of Fleet Street: The Harmsworth Dynasty* (London: Unwin Hyman).

Boyce, G., Curran, J. and Wingate, P. (1978) *Newspaper History from the 17th Century to the Present Day* (London: Constable).

Brendon, P. (1982) *The Life and Death of the Press Barons* (London: Secker & Warburg).

Brewer, J. and Trentmann, F. (2006) *Consuming Cultures, Global Perspectives* (Oxford: Berg).

Bricknell, C. (2005) 'Masculinities, Performativity, and Subversion: A Sociological Reappraisal', *Men and Maculinities*, 8(1), 24–43.

British Library (1897) *La Fronde* BL: MF19 NPL.

British Library (1926) *Northcliffe Collection* (Ottawa: Government of Canada).

British Library (nd) Indian Office V/14/284.

British Library (1929/30) Indian Office V/8-27.

British Library: Northcliffe papers: BL 62234, 62382, 62225, 62922A, 62153; *The Daily Mail* LON LD6NPL.

British Museum (1908) *Maud Arncliffe-Sennett Papers*, vol.3, p. 79.

British Museum (1921, 1936) *The Times of India:* BL: 013894677.

Brown, L. (1985) *Victorian News and Newspapers* (Oxford: Clarendon Press).

Burton, A. (1994) *Burdens of History: British Feminists, Indian Women and Imperial Culture, 1865–1915* (London and Chapel Hill: University of North Carolina Press).

Bush, J. (2007) *Women Against the Vote: Female Anti-suffragism in Britain* (Oxford: Oxford University Press).

Butler, J. (1987) 'Variations on Sex and Gender: Beauvoir, Wittig and Foucault', in S. Benhabib and D. Cornell (eds) *Feminism as Critique* (Minneapolis: University of Minneapolis Press) pp. 128–42.

Butler, J. (1990) *Gender Trouble: Feminism and the Subversion of Identity* (Routledge, London and New York).

Butler, J. (1993) *Bodies that Matter: On the Discursive Limits of Sex* (London and New York: Routledge).

Caine, B. (1997) *English Feminism 1780–1980* (Oxford: University Press).

Caird, M. (1892) 'A Defence of the so-called "Wild Women"', *Nineteenth Century* XXXI, 829.

Carey, J.W. (1989) *Communication as Culture: Essays on Media and Society* (Boston, MA: Hyman Publishers).

Catterall, P. et al. (2000) (ed.) *Northcliffe's Legacy* (Basingstoke: Macmillan).

Chaffard, G. (1965) *Les Carnets secrets de la décolonisation* (Paris: Calmann-Lévy).

Chafur, T. and Sackur, A. (eds) (1999) *French Colonial Empire and the Popular Front: Hope and Disillusion* (Basingstoke: Macmillan).

Chafur, T. and Sackur, A. (eds) (2002) *Promoting the Colonial Idea: Propaganda and Visions of Empire in France* (Basingstoke: Palgrave).

Chalaby, J.K. (1996) 'Journalism as an Anglo-American Invention: A Comparison of the Development of French and Anglo-American Journalism, 1830s–1920s', *European Journal of Communication*, 11(3), 306–26.

Chambers, D., Steiner, L. and Fleming, C. (2004) *Women and Journalism* (London: Routledge).

Chapman, J.L. (2005a) *Comparative Media History* (Cambridge: Polity Press).

Chapman, J.L. (2005b) 'Republican Citizenship, Ethics and the French Revolutionary Press', *Ethical Space*, 2(1), 7–12.

Chapman, J.L. (2007) 'George Sand: Thwarted Newspaper Publisher or Pioneer Literary Journalist?', *Modern and Contemporary France*, 15(4), 479–95.

Chapman, J.L. (2010) 'The Origins of a Public Voice for Marginalized Workers and Anti-colonialism in French India, 1935–37', *Web Journal of French Media Studies* (WJFMS), no.8, http://wjfms.ncl.ac.uk/splash.htm, accessed 27 October 2012.

Chapman, J.L. (2011a) 'Counter Hegemony, Newspapers and the Origins of Anti-colonialism in French India', *International Journal of Social Economics* 38(2), 128–39.

Chapman, J.L. (2011b) 'A Business Trajectory: Assessing Female Influence and Representation in *Le Petit Journal*, Europe's First Mass Circulation Daily', in M. Allison and A. Kershaw (eds) *Parcours de femmes – Twenty years of Women in French* (Oxford & Bern: Peter Lang).

Chapman, J.L. (2011c) 'Female Representation, Readership and Early Tabloid Properties', *Australian Journal of Communication*, 38(2), 53–70.

Chapman, J.L. and Allison, K. (2011) 'Women and the Press in British India 1928–34, a window for protest?', *International Journal of Social Economics* 38(9), 676–92.

Chapman, J.L. and Nuttall, N. (2011) *Journalism Today: A Themed History* (Malden: Wiley-Blackwell).

Chapman, J.L. and Tulloch, J. (2013) 'F.W. Wilson: Renegade Colonial Newspaper Editor or Indian Nationalist Hero?', *Media History*, 38, August.

Chattopadhyaya, K. (1939) *The Awakening of Indian Women* (Madras: Everymans Press).

Chaudhuri, N. and Strobel, M. (eds) (1992) *Western Women and Imperialism: Complicity and Resistance* (Bloomington: Indiana University Press).

Chessel, M.-E. (1998) *La Publicité: Naissance d'une profession 1900–1940* (Paris: CNRS Editions).

Clark, L. (2008) *Women and Achievement in Nineteenth-Century Europe* (Cambridge: Cambridge University Press).

Clarke, T. (1950) *Northcliffe in History: An Intimate Study of Power* (London: Hutchinson & Co Ltd.).

Cobbe, F.P. (1888) 'Journalism as a Profession for Women', *Women's Penny Paper*, 3 November.

Confer, V. (1969) 'The Depot in Aix and Archival Sources for France Outre-Mer', *French Historical Studies* 6(1), 120–6.

Cooper, F. and Stoler, A.L. (1997) (ed.) *Tensions of Empire: Colonial Cultures in a Bourgeois World* (Berkeley and London: University of California Press).

Corner, J. (1991) 'Meaning, Genre and Context: The Problematics of "Public Knowledge" in the New Audience Studies', in J. Curran and M. Gurevitch (eds) *Mass Media and Society* (London: Edward Arnold) pp. 267–306.

Cottle, S. (2000) 'Rethinking news access', *Journalism Studies* 3(3), 427–48.

Cousins, J.H. (1947) (ed.) *The Annie Besant Centenary Book* (Adyar: The Besant Centenary Celebrations Committee).

Crawford, E. (1999) *The Women's Suffrage Movement: A Reference Guide, 1866–1928* (London: UCL Press).

Crossick, G. and Jaumain, S. (eds) (1999) *Cathedrals of Consumption: The European Department Store, 1850–1939* (London: Scolar Press).

Crubellier, M. (1974) *Histoire culturelle de la France XIX–XX siècles* (Paris: A. Colin).

Crubellier, M. (1991) *La Mémoire des Français: recherches d'histoire culturelle* (Paris: Henri Veyrier).

Cudlipp, H. (1953) *Publish and be Damned: The Astonishing Story of* The Daily Mirror (London: Andrew Dakers).

Dangerfield, G. (1971) *The Strange Death of Liberal England* (Geneva: Edito-Service).

Datta, S.C. (1997) *Five Eminent Women: Annie Besant, Sarojini Naidu, Vijay Pandit, Indira Gandhi, and Mother Teresa* (New Delhi: Anmol Publications).

de Comarmond, J.M. (1985) 'La Communauté française de Pondichéry – l'oubli ou l'espérance', *L'Afrique et L'Asie* 146, 3–20.

De Grazia, V. (1996) 'Introduction', in E. Furlough (ed.) *The Sex of Things* (Berkeley: University of California Press), pp. 151–62.

De la Motte, D. and M. Przyblyski (ed.) (1999) *Making the News: Modernity and the Mass Press in Nineteenth-century France* (Amherst: University of Massachusetts Press).

Decraene, P. (1994) *Trois siècles du presence française en Inde: Actes du Colloque du 21 septembre 1994* (Paris: Centre des Hautes Etudes sur l'Afrique et l'Asie Modernes).

Delporte, C. (1998) 'Presse et culture de masse en France (1880–1914), *Revue historique* 605(1), 93–121.

Derrida, J. (1992) *The Other Heading: Reflections on Today's Europe*, trans. P.-A. Brault and M.B. Naas (Indianapolis: Indian University Press).

Desvaux, U. (1868) *Les Lecteurs du journal à un sou à MM les deputés des départements* (Paris: Imprimerie centrale des chemins de fer, A. Chaix et Cie.).

DiCenzo, M. (2000) 'Militant Distribution: Votes for Women and the Public Sphere', *Media History* 6(2), 115–28.

DiCenzo, M. with Delap, L. and Ryan, L. (2011) *Feminist Media History: Suffrage, Periodicals and the Public Sphere* (Basingstoke: Palgrave Macmillan).

Dowling, L. (1978) 'The Decadent and the New Woman in the 1890s', *Nineteenth Century Fiction*, 33, 434–53.

Downing, J. (1984) *Radical Media: The Political Organization of Alternative Communication* (Boston: South End Press).

Downing, J. (2001) *Radical Media: Rebellious Communication and Social Movements* (London: Sage).

Downs, L.L. (2010) *Writing Gender History*, 2nd edn (London: Bloomsbury Academic).

Dufau, C.-H. (1898) 'La Fronde' Lithograph (Canberra: National Gallery of Australia).

Eveno, P. (2003) *L'Argent de la presse française des années 1820 à nos jours* (Paris: Editions du CTHS).

Ezra, E. (2000) *The Colonial Unconsicious: Race and Culture in Interwar France* (Ithaca and London: Cornell University Press).

Fawcett Archives (1912) box 52, *Minutes of the NUWSS* 1st February.

Fawcett Archives (1912–13) box 320 *Report of Press Work*, October 1912–January 1913.

Fawcett Archives (1916) *Autograph Collection*, 22 December, Northcliffe to Lady Balfour.

Fenwick Miller, F. (1884) *Harriet Martineau* (London: J.H. Ingram).

Ferenczi,T. (1993) *L'Invention du journalisme en France* (Paris: Plon).

Fletcher, I., Christopher, N., Mayhall, L.E. and Levine, P. (2000) *Women's Suffrage in the British Empire: Citizenship, Nation and Race* (London: Routledge).

Flint, K. (1993) *The Woman Reader, 1837–1914* (Oxford: Clarendon Press).

Flory (1897) Annexe au rapport, Chambre des députés, session de 1893, réimpression de 1897 (Paris: Impr.de la Chambre des députés).

Forbes, G. (1996) *Women in Modern India,* New Cambridge History of India, IV.2, (Cambridge: Cambridge University Press).

Forrester, W. (1980) *Great-Grandmama's Weekly* (London: Lutterworth Press).

Foucault, M. (1973) *The Order of Things: An Archaeology of the Human Sciences* (New York: Vintage).

Foucault, M. (1977) *Language, Counter-Memory, Practice* (Ithaca: Cornell University Press).

Foucault, M. (1980) *The History of Sexuality*, Vol.1 (New York: Vintage).

Foucault, M. (1989) *Madness and Civilisation: A History of Insanity in the Age of Reason* (London: Routledge).

Franklin, B. (1997) *Newzak and News Media* (London: Arnold).

Fraser, N. (1991) *Revaluing French Feminism: Critical Essays on Difference, Agency and Culture* (Bloomington: Indiana University Press).

Fraser, N. (1992) 'Rethinking the Public Sphere: A Contribution to the Critique of Actually Existing Democracy', in C. Calhoun (ed.) *Habermas and the Public Sphere* (Cambridge: MIT Press).

Furlough, E. (1991) *Consumer Cooperation in France: The Politics of Consumption, 1834–1930* (Ithaca: Cornell University Press).

Fyfe, H. (1930) *Northcliffe: An Intimate Biography* (London: George Allen and Unwin).

Fyfe, H. (1949) *Sixty Years of Fleet Street* (London: W.H. Allen).

Geertz, C. (1983) 'Blurred Genres: The Refiguration of Social Thought', in *Local Knowledge: Further Essays in Interpretive Anthropology* (New York: Basic Books).

Gill, R. (2007) *Gender and the Media* (Cambridge: Polity Press).

Gillmor, D. (2004) *We the Media: Grass Roots Journalism by the People, for the People* (Cambridge, MA: O'Reilly).

Gleadle, K. (1995) *The Early Feminists: Radical Unitarians and the emergence of the women's rights movement, 1831–51* (Houndmills: St. Martin's Press).

Gleadle, K. (2002) *Radical Writing on Women 1800–1850: An Anthology* (Houndmills: Palgrave Macmillan).

Glynn, K. (2000) *Tabloid Culture: Trash Taste, Popular Power, and the Transformation of American Television* (Durham NC: Duke University Press).

Goffman, E. (1974) *Frame Analysis* (New York: Harper and Row).

Goffman, E. (1979) *Gender Advertisements* (New York: Harper Colophon).

Goldberg Moses, C. (1984) *French Feminism in the 19th Century* (Albany: State University of New York Press).

Goodman, J.R. (2001) 'The Women's Suffragist Movement Through the Eyes of *Life* Magazine Cartoons', in M.P. McAllister, E.H. Sewell Jr. and I. Gordon (ed.) *Comics & Ideology* (New York: Peter Lang).

Grabe, M.E., Zhou, S., and Barnett, B. (1999) 'Sourcing and Reporting in News Magazine Programs: *60 Minutes* versus *Hard Copy*', *Journalism and Mass Communication Quarterly*, 76(2), 293–311.

Green, B. (1997) *Spectacular Confessions: Autobiography, Performative Activism, and Sites of Suffrage 1905–1938* (London: St. Martin's Press).

Greenberg, G.S. (1996) *Tabloid Journalism: An Annotated Bibliography of English-language Sources* (Westport, CT: Greenwood Press).

Gripsrud, J. (2000) 'Tabloidization, popular journalism and democracy', in C. Sparks and J. Tulloch (eds) *Tabloid Tales – Global Debates over Media Standards* (Lanham, MD: Roman & Littlefield), pp. 285–300.

Guha, R. and Spivak, G.C. (1988) (ed.) *Selected Subaltern Studies* (Oxford: Oxford University Press).

Gullace, N.F. (2002) *'The Blood of Our Sons': Men, Women, and the Renegotiation of British Citizenship during the Great War* (London: Palgrave).

Habermas, J. (1989) *The Structural Transformation of the Public Sphere* (Cambridge: Polity Press).

Harmsworth, A. (1903) 'The Making of a Newspaper', in A. Lawrence *Journalism as a Profession* (London: Hodder & Stoughton).

Hall, C. (2000) (ed.) *Cultures of Empire: A Reader* (Manchester: Manchester University Press).

Hall, C. and McClelland, K. (eds) (2010) *Race, Nation & Empire* (Manchester: Manchester University Press).

Hall, S. (1973) 'Encoding/decoding', reprinted in S. Hall et al. (eds) (1980) *Culture, Media, Language* (Hutchinson: London).

Hall, S. (1993) 'Metaphors of Transformation', in A. White (ed.) *Carnival, Hysteria, and Writing* (Oxford: Clarendon Press), pp. 1–25.

Hampton, M. (2004) *Visions of the Press in Britain, 1850–1950* (Champaign: University of Illinois Press).

Hardman, T.H. (1909) (ed.) *A Parliament of the Press: The First Imperial Press Conference* (London: Horace Marshall & Son).

Harmsworth, A. (1903) 'The Making of a Newspaper', in A. Lawrence (ed.) *Journalism as a Profession* (London: Hodder & Stoughton).

Harrison, B. (1978) *Separate Spheres: The Opposition to Women's Suffrage in Britain* (London: Croom Helm).

Harrison, B. (1982) 'Press and Pressure Group in Modern Britain', in J. Shattock and M. Wolff (eds) *The Victorian Periodical Press: Samplings and Soundings* (Leicester: Leicester University Press).

Hause, S. with Kenny, A.R. (1984) *Women's Suffrage and Social Politics in the French Third Republic* (Princeton: Princeton University Press).

Hobsbawm, E.R. (2005) *The Making of the Modern World*, Vol. 3 (London: The Folio Society).

Holland, P. (1998) 'The Politics of the Smile: "Soft News" and the Sexualisation of the Popular Press', in C. Carter, G. Branston and S. Allan (eds) *News, Gender and Power* (London: Routledge) pp. 17–32.

Holzer, H. (ed.) (1993) *The Lincoln-Douglas Debates: The First Complete, Unexpurgated Text* (New York: Harper Collins Publishers).

Honneth, A. (1995) *The Struggle for Recognition: The Moral Grammar of Social Conflicts* (Cambridge: Polity Press).

Hopkin, D. (1978) 'The Socialist Press in Britain, 1890–1910', in G. Boyce, J. Curran and P. Wingate (eds) *Newspaper History from the Seventeenth Century to the Present Day* (London: Constable).

Hunt, L. (1989) (ed.) *The New Cultural History* (Berkeley: University of California Press).

Hunt, L. (1992) *The Family Romance of the French Revolution* (London: Routledge).

Huyssen, A. (1986) 'Mass Culture as Women', *After the Great Divide* (London: Macmillan).

Israel, M. (1994) *Communications and Power: Propaganda and the Press in the Indian Nationalist Struggle* (New York: Cambridge University Press).

Jackson, H. (1988) *The Eighteen Nineties* (London: The Cresset Library).

Jacoby, R.M. (1976) 'Feminism and Class Consciousness in the British and American Women's Trade Union Leagues, 1890–1925', in B.A. Carroll (ed.) *Liberating Women's History: Theoretical and Critical Essays* (Urbana: University of Illinois Press).

Jones, K. (1919) *Fleet St. and Downing St.* (London: Hutchinson & Co.).

Jain, P. (1985) *Gandhian Ideas, Social Movements and Creativity* (Jaipur: Rawat Publications).

Jain, P. and Mahan, R. (1996) *Women Images* (Jaipur and New Delhi: Rawat Publications).

Jami, I. (1981) La Fronde *(1897–1903) et son rôle dans la défense des femmes salariées* (Université de Paris 1: Mémoire de maitrise).

Jensen, C. (2002) *Stories That Changed America: Muckrakers of the Twentieth Century* (New York: Seven Stories Press).

Joll, J. (1977) *Gramsci* (London: Fontana).

Jones, W.B. (1983) *Politics of Indian Freedom Movement and Thought* (New Delhi: Sterling Publishers).

Kalifa, D. (1995) *L'Encre et le sang: Récit de crimes et soci*été *à la belle époque* (Paris: Fayard).

Kaplan, J. (1975) *Lincoln Steffens: A Biography* (London: Jonathan Cape).

Kaplan, J.H. and Stowell, S. (1994) *Theatre and Fashion: Oscar Wilde to the Suffragettes* (Cambridge: Cambridge University Press).

Kaul, C. (1999) *Press and Empire: The London Press, Government News Management and India, Circa 1900–1922* (Oxford: University of Oxford Press).

Kaul, C. (2003) *Reporting the Raj: The British Press and India, c. 1880–1922* (Manchester: Manchester University Press).

Kaul, C. (ed.) (2006) *Media and the British Empire* (Basingstoke: Palgrave Macmillan).

Kaur, M. (1969) *Great Women of India* (New Delhi & Jullundur City: Sterling Publishers).

Kearney, M.C. (2012) *The Gender and Media Reader* (London and New York: Routledge).

King, E. and Chapman, J. (2012) *Key Readings in Journalism* (New York and London: Routledge).

Kleinberg, S.J. (ed.) (1988) Retrieving Women's History (Oxford: Berg).

Koss, S. (1981) *The Rise and Fall of the Political Press in Britain*, vols 1 & 2 (London: Hamish Hamilton).

Krijnen, T., Alvares C. and Van Bauwel, S. (eds) (2011) *Gendered Transformations: Theory and Practices on Gender and Media* (Bristol: Intellect).

Kroeger, B. (1994) *Nellie Bly: Daredevil, Reporter, Feminist* (New York: Random House).

Kumar, R. (1993) *The History of Doing: An Illustrated Account of Movements for Women's Rights and Feminism in India, 1800–1990* (London: Verso).

Kymlicka, W. and Norman, W. (eds) (2000) *Citizenship in Diverse Societies* (Oxford: Oxford University Press).

Lagneau, G. (1989) 'La Société générale des annonces, 1845–1865', *Le Mouvement social*, 146, 5–24.

Landes, J.B. (1988) *Women and the Public Sphere in the Age of the French Revolution* (Ithaca and London: Cornell University Press).

Landry, D. and MacLean, G. (1993) *Material Feminisms* (Cambridge, MA and Oxford: Blackwell).

Langer, J. (1998) *Tabloid Television: Popular Journalism and the 'Other News'* (New York: Routledge).

Lawrence, D.H. (1977) *Sons and Lovers* (London: Penguin).

Lee, A.J. (1977) *Origins of the Popular Press in England* (London: Croom Helm).

Leonard, T.C. (1996) *News for All: America's Coming-of-age with the Press* (New York: Oxford University Press).

Lermina, J. (1884–5) *Dictionnaire universelle illustrée biographique et bibliographique de la France contemporaine ... Par une société de gens de lettres et de savants sous la direction de J. Lermina* (Paris: no named publisher).

Levine, P. (2004) (ed.) *Gender and Empire* (Oxford: Oxford University Press).

Lewis, J. (1984) *Women in England, 1870–1950: Sexual Divisions and Social Change* (Brighton: Wheatsheaf).

Liddington, J. and Norris, J. (1978) *One Hand Tied Behind Us: The Rise of the Women's Suffrage Movement* (Virago: London).

Lieten, G.K. (1982) 'Strikers and Strike Breakers: Bombay Textile Mills Strike, 1929', *Economic and Political Weekly* 17, 697–704.

Livois, R. (1965) *Histoire de la presse française*, vol. 2 (Paris: Les Temps de la Presse).

MacKenzie, J.M. (1984) *Propaganda and Empire: the Manipulation of British Public Opinion 1880–1960* (Manchester: Manchester University Press).

MacKenzie, J.M. (1986) *Imperialism and Popular Culture* (Manchester and New York: Manchester University Press).

Maestri, E. (1993) 'Les Etablissements français dans l'Inde et leurs chemins de fer, 1858–1934', in M. Pousse (ed.) *L'Inde, Etudes et Images* (Paris: Saint-Denis), pp. 211–45.

Marks, P. (1990) *Bicycles, Bangs, and Bloomers: The New Woman in the Popular Press* (Lexington: University Press of Kentucky).

Marsh, K (2007) *Fictions of 1947: Representations of Indian Decolonization 1919–62* (Oxford: Peter Lang).

Marshall, T.H. and Bottomore, T. (1992) *Citizenship and Social Class* (London, Pluto Perspectives).

Martin, M. (1992) *Trois Siècles de publicité en France* (Paris: Odile Jacob).

Marx, K (1867/1947) *Das Kapital I* (Berlin: Dietz).

Matignon, R. (1992) 'Ponson du Terrail: le Napoléon du roman-feuilleton', in *Le Figaro Littéraire*, 6 April, 5.

Maxwell, W. (1914) 'Old Lamps for New: Some Reflections on Recent Changes in Journalism', *Nineteenth Century and After* 75, 1085–96.

Mayhall, L.E.N. (2000) 'Defining Militancy: Radical Protest, the Constitutional Idiom, and Women's Suffrage in Britain, 1908–1909', *Journal of British Studies*, 39, 365–6.

Mazumdar, A. (1993) *Indian Journalism: Origin, Growth and Development from Asoka to Nehru* (Mysore: Prasaranga).

McChesney, R.W. and Nichols, M. (2002) *Our Media, Not Theirs: The Democratic Struggle against Corporate Media* (New York: Seven Stories).

McClintock, A. (1992) 'The Angel of Progress: Pitfalls of the Term "Post-colonial"', *Social Texts* 31/32, 84–98.

McClintock, A. (1995) *Imperial Leather: Race, Gender and Sexuality in the Colonial Conquest* (New York and London: Routledge).

McKenzie, F.A. (1921) *The Mystery of the Daily Mail 1896–1921* (London: Associated Newspapers Ltd).

McMillan, J.F. (1981) *Housewife or Harlot: The Place of Women in French Society, 1870–1940* (Brighton: Harvester Press).

McQuail, D. (1977) 'The Influence and Effects of Mass Media' in J. Curran, M. Gurevitch and J. Woollacott (eds) *Mass Communication and Society* (London: Arnold).

Meijer, I.C. (2001) 'The Public Quality of Popular Journalism: Developing a Normative Framework', *Journalism Studies* 2(2), 189–205.

Michalon, P. (1993) 'Des Indes françaises aux indiens français', in Michel Pousse (ed.) *L'Inde, Etudes et Images* (Paris: Editions l'Harmattan/Université de la Réunion), 245–78.

Midgeley, C. (1998) (ed.) *Gender and Imperialism* (Manchester: Manchester University Press).

Miles, W.F.S. (1995) *Imperial Burdens: Counter colonialism in Former French India* (Boulder and London: Lynne Rienner Publishers).

Miller, M.B. (1981) *The Bon Marché: Bourgeois Culture and the Department Store, 1869–1920* (London, George Allen & Unwin).

Millett, K. (1977) *Sexual Politics* (London: Virago).

Mills, K. (1988) *A Place in the News* (New York: Dodd Mead).

Milton, I. (1994) *Communication and Power* (Cambridge: Cambridge University Press).

Mitra, N.N. (ed.) (1930) *The Indian Annual Register*, Vol.1, Jan.–June, Vol.2, July–September (Calcutta: the Annual Register Office).

Mitterand, H. (1962) *Zola journaliste: de l'Affaire Manet à l'affaire Dreyfus*. (Paris: Kiosque).

Mody, N.B. (2000) (ed.) *Women in India's Freedom Struggle* (Mumbai: Allied Publishers).

Mohanty, J. (1996) *Glimpses of India Women in the Freedom Struggle* (New Delhi: Discovery Publishing House).

Mollier, J.-Y. (1991) *Le Scandale de Panama* (Paris: Fayard).

Morienval, J. (1934) *Les Créateurs de la grande presse en France: Emile de Girardin, H.de Villemessant, Moïse Millaud* (Paris: Editions Spés).

Mouffe, C. (1992) 'Feminism, citizenship, and radical democratic politics' in J. Butler and J.W. Scott (eds) *Feminists Theorize the Political* (London: Routledge) pp. 369–85.

Mulvey R.M. and Mizuta, T. (1995) (ed.) *Controversies in the History of British Feminism*, Vol.5 (London: Routledge/Thoemmes).

Murdock, G. (2000) 'Reconstructing the Ruined Tower: Contemporary Communications and Questions of Class', in J. Curran and M. Gurevitch (eds) *Mass Media and Society* (London: Arnold), pp. 7–26.

Murthy, N.K. (1966) *Indian Journalism: Origin, Growth and Development of Indian Journalism from Asoka to Nehru* (Mysore: Prasaranga).

Museum of London (1908) *(N)WSPU* report, 29 February.

Museum of London (n.d.) *Women's National Anti Suffrage League* leaflet, no 3.

Nanda, B.R. (1976) (ed.) *Indian Women: From Purdah to Modernity* (New Delhi: Vikas Publishing House).

Navarane, V.S. (1997) *Sarojini Naidu Her Life, Work and Poetry* (New Delhi: Orient Longman).

Nehru, J. (1936) *An Autobiography* (New Delhi: Penguin).

Nehru, J. (1946) *The Discovery of India* (London: Meridian Books).

Nehru, J. (2004) *Before Freedom, 1909–1947: Nehru's Letters to his Sister*, Nayantara Sahgal (ed.) (New Delhi: Roli Books).

Neogy, A.K. (1997) *Decolonization of French India: Liberation Movement and Indo-French Relations 1947–1954* (Pondicherry: Institut Français de Pondichéry).

Nessheim, R. (1991) *British Political Newspapers and Women's Suffrage, 1910–1918* (University of Oslo: unpublished thesis).

Northcliffe, Lord (1921–22) 'Correspondence, Keith Murdoch papers' (Canberra: National Library of Australia, MS 2823/3/7).

Nye, R.A. (1984) *Crime, Madness, and Politics in Modern France: The Medical Concept of National Decline* (Princeton: Princeton University Press).

Offen, K. (1994) 'Women, Citizenship & Suffrage with a French Twist, 1789–1993', in C. Daley and M. Nolan (eds) *Suffrage and Beyond: International Feminist Perspectives* (Auckland: Auckland University Press).

O'Hanlon, R. and Washbrook, D. (1991) 'Histories in Transition: Approaches to the Study of Colonialism and Culture in India', *History Workshop* 32, 110–27.

O'Malley, T. (2002) 'Media History and Media Studies: Aspects of the Development of the Study of Media History in the UK 1945–2000', *Media History* 8(2), 155–73.

Onslow, B. (2000) *Women of the Press in Nineteenth-Century Britain* (Basingstoke: Macmillan Press).

Pakulski, J. (1997) 'Cultural Citizenship', *Citizenship Studies,* 1(1), 73–86.

Palmer, M.B. (1972) 'Some Aspects of the French Press during the Rise of the Popular Daily', DPhil dissertation (Oxford: Oxford University).

Palmer, M.B. (1983) *Des Petits Journaux aux grandes agences: naissance du journalisme moderne* (Paris: Aubier, collection historique).

Pankhurst, C. (1911) *Autograph Letter Collection: to Mrs Badley,* April 3rd (London: Women's Library).

Pankhurst, C. (1913) *The Great Scourge and How to End It* (London: Women's Library).

Pankhurst, S. (1977) *The Suffragette Movement: An Intimate Account of Persons and Ideals,* first published 1931(London: Virago).

Perrot, M. (1983) 'Faits divers et histoire du XIXe siècle', *Annales: E.S.C.* 38, 911–19.

Perrot, M. (1986) 'Women, Power and History: The Case of 19th century France', in S. Reynolds (ed.) *Women, State & Revolution: Essays in Power & Gender in Europe since 1789* (Brighton: Wheatsheaf Books), pp. 44–59.

Pethwick-Lawrence, F.W. and Edwards, J. (eds) (1907) *The Reformers' Year Books* 1901–1909 (Brighton: Harvester Press).

Pickering, M. (2001) *Stereotyping: The Politics of Representation* (Basingstoke, Palgrave).

Pioneer, The (1928, 1929) (London: British Library bound volumes uncatalogued).

Pitoeff, P. (1991) 'L'Inde Française en Sursis 1947–1954', *Revue française d'histoire d'outre-mer,* t.LXXV111 (290), 105–31.

Potter, S.J. (2003) *News and the British World* (Oxford: Oxford University Press).

Pound, R. and Harmsworth, G. (1959) *Northcliffe* (London: Cassell).

Power Cobbe, F. (1888) 'Journalism as a Profession for Women', *Women's Penny Paper* 3 November, 5.

Prakash, G. (1994) (ed.) *After Colonialism: Imperial Histories and Post Colonial Displacements* (Princeton: Princeton University Press).

Préfecture de Police (PP) BA1621, correspondence générale de presse, 1852–1881; Ea109 Ponson du Terrail; Ba1096 Emile de Girardin; Ba10094 Eugene Gibiat;

Ba1066 Aimable Marie Escoffier; BA1125 Charles Jenty, Ba 1228 Frederic Prévet; Ba1173 Hippolyte Marinoni, Ba105 daily reports for1896, BA678 elections 1896.

Pugh, M.D. (1974) 'Politicians and the Women's Vote 1914–18', *History*, 59(197) 358–74.

Pugh, M.D. (1980) *Women's Suffrage in Britain 1867–1928* (London: Historical Association).

Pugh, M.D. (2000) *The March of Women: A Revisionist Analysis of the Campaign for Women's Suffrage* (Oxford: Oxford University Press).

Purvis, J. and Holton, S. (eds) (1999) *Votes for Women* (London: Routledge).

Queffélec, L. (1989) *Le Roman-Feuilleton français au XIXe siècle* (Paris: Que sais-je? Presses universitaires de France).

Ramamurphy, A. (2003) *Imperial Persuaders: Images of Africa and Asia in British Advertising* (Manchester: Manchester University Press).

Ramasamy, A. (1987) *History of Pondicherry* (Madras: Sterling Publishers Private Ltd.).

Ramelson, M. (1976) *The Petticoat Rebellion: A Century of Struggle for Women's Rights*, 3rd edn (London: Lawrence and Wishart).

Rendall, J. (1985) *The Origins of Modern Feminism: Women in Britain, France and the United States, 1780–1860* (Basingstoke: Macmillan).

Reynolds, S. (ed.) (1986) *Women, State and Revolution: Essays in Power and Gender in Europe since 1789* (Brighton: Wheatsheaf Books).

Rhondda, Lady (1920) 'Report to Members of the Board', *Time and Tide*, Robins Papers, Fales Library, New York University.

Rioux, J.-P. and Sirinelli, J.-F. (2002) *La Culture de masse en France: de la Belle Époque à aujourd'hui* (Paris: Fayard).

Roberts, M.A. (1999) 'Subversive Copy: *La Fronde*, in D. De la Motte and M. Przyblyski (eds) *Making the News: Modernity and the Mass Press in Nineteenth-century France* (Amherst: University of Massachusetts Press), pp. 302–50.

Roberts, M.L. (2002) *Disruptive Acts: The New Woman in fin de siècle France* (Chicago: University of Chicago Press).

Rogers, H. (2000) *Women and the People: Authority, Authorship and the Radical Tradition in Nineteenth-century England* (Aldershot: Ashgate).

Rosaldo, R. (1999) 'Cultural Citizenship, Inequality and Multiculturalism', in R.D. Torres, L.F. Mirón and J.X. Inda (eds) *Race, Identity and Citizenship* (Oxford: Blackwell).

Rosen, A. (1974) *Rise Up, Women!* (London: Routledge, Kegan Paul), pp. 253–61.

Rousseau, J.-J. (1906) *L'Emile or A Treatise on Education*, W.H. Payne (ed.) (New York and London: Appleton).

Ryan, M.P. (1992) 'Gender and Public Access: Women's Politics in Nineteenth Century America', in Craig Calhoun (ed.) *Habermas and the Public Sphere* (Cambridge: MIT Press), pp. 259–88.

Said, E. (1978) *Orientalism* (London: Routledge, Kegan Paul).

Samson, J. (ed.) (2001) *The British Empire* (Oxford University Press).

Sangari, K. and Vaid, S. (eds) (1989) *Recasting Women* (New Delhi: Kali for Women).

Schudson, M. (1982) 'The Politics of Narrative Form: The Emergence of News Conventions in Print and Television', *Daedelus* 111, 97–112.

Schwartz, V. (1998) *Spectacular Realities: Early Mass Culture in fin de siècle Paris* (Berkeley: University of California Press).

Scott, J.W. (1999) *Gender and the Politics of History* (New York: Columbia University Press).

Searle, G.R. (2004) *A New England? Peace and War, 1886–1918* (Oxford, Clarendon Press).

Sebba, A. (1994) *Battling for News: The Rise of the Woman Reporter* (London: Hodder and Stoughton).

Seneca, T. (2009) 'The History of Women's Magazines: Magazines as Virtual Communities': http//besser.tsoa.nyu.edu/impact/f93/students/tracy/tracy_hist.html, accessed 27 October 2012.

Seymour-Ure, C. (1968) *Press, Politics and the Public* (London: Methuen).

Shapiro, A.-L. (1996) *Breaking the Codes: Female Criminality in fin de siècle Paris* (Stanford: Stanford University Press).

Shaya, G. (2004) 'The Flâneur, the Badaud, and the Making of a Mass Public in France', *America Historical Review* 109(1), 41–77.

Shorter, E. (1976) *The Making of the Modern Family* (London, Collins).

Showalter, E. (1992) *Sexual Anarchy: Gender and Culture at the fin de siècle* (London: Virago).

Smith, A. (1979) *The Newspaper – An International History* (London: Thames and Hudson).

Sneider, A.L. (2008) *Suffragists in an Imperial Age: U.S. Expansionism and the Woman Question 1870–1929* (Oxford: Oxford University Press).

Sparks, C. (2000) 'Introduction: The Panic over Tabloid News', in C. Sparks and J. Tulloch (eds) *Tabloid Tales: Global Debates over Media Standards* (Oxford: Roman & Littlefield Publishers), pp. 1–40.

Spivak, G.C. (1988) 'Can the Subaltern Speak?', in C. Nelson and L. Grossberg (eds) *Marxism and the Interpretation of Culture* (Basingstoke: Macmillan Education), pp. 271–313. Republished in *Colonial Discourse and Post Colonial Theory*, ed. P. Williams & L. Chrisman (Hemel Hempstead: Harvester Wheatsheaf).

Spodek, H. (2010) *The World's History* 4th edn (London and New Jersey: Prentice Hall).

Spurr, D. (1993) *The Rhetoric of Empire: Colonial Discourse in Journalism, Travel Writing, and Imperial Administration* (Durham and London: Duke University Press).

Stead, W.T. (1885) 'Maiden Tribute of Modern Babylon', *Pall Mall Gazette*, July 7, p. 3 www.attackingthedevil.co.uk/pmg/tribute/, accessed 27 October 2012.

Steiner, L. (1992) 'Construction of Gender inNewsreporting Textbooks: 1890–1990', *Journalism Monographs* 135(October), 1–48.

Stensaas, H.S. (2005) 'The Rise of the News Paradigm', in S. Høyer and H. Pöttker, *Diffusion of the News Paradigm 1850–2000* (Goteburg, Nordicom), pp. 37–49.

Stevenson, N. (2001) (ed.) *Culture and Citizenship* (London: Sage).

Stevenson, N. (2002) *Understanding Media Cultures*, 2nd edn (London: Sage).

Stevenson, N. (2003) *Cultural Citizenship: Cosmopolitan Questions* (Maidenhead: Open University Press).

Subbiah, V.S. (1971) 'Oral History Interview by Dr Hari Dev Sharma' (New Delhi: Nehru Memorial Museum and Library).

Subbiah, V.S. (1991) *Saga of Freedom of French India: Testament of My Life* (Madras: New Century Book House).

Suleri, S. (1992) *The Rhetoric of English India* (Chicago: University of Chicago Press).

Sullerot, E. (1966) *Histoire de la presse féminine en France des origines à 1848* (Paris: Colin).

Sussman, C. (2000) *Consuming Anxieties: Consumer Protest, Gender and British Slavery, 1713–1833* (Stanford: Stanford University Press).

Swanwick, H. (1935) *I Have Been Young* (London: Victor Gollancz).

Taneja, A. (2005) *Gandhi, Women, and the National Movement* (Delhi: Har Anand Publications).

Taylor, B. (1983) *Eve and the New Jerusalem* (London: Virago).

Taylor, S.J. (1998) *The Great Outsiders: Northcliffe, Rothermere and* The Daily Mail (London: Phoenix Orion Books).

Terdiman, R. (1985) *Discourse/Counter Discourse: The Theory and Practice of Symbolic Resistance in Nineteenth Century France* (Ithaca and London: Cornell University Press).

Thompson, J.B. (1990) *Ideology and Modern Culture* (Cambridge: Polity Press).

Thompson, J.B. (1995) *The Media and Modernity: A Social Theory of the Media* (Cambridge: Polity Press).

Thompson, J.L. (2000) *Northcliffe: Press Baron in Politics, 1865–1922* (London: John Murray).

Tickner, L. (1987) *The Spectacle of Women* (London: Chatto and Windus).

Tidrick, K. (2009) *Empire and the English Character: The Illusion of Authority* (London: Taurus Park Paperbacks).

Tiersten, L. (2001) *Marianne in the Market: Envisioning Consumer Society in fin de siècle France* (Berkeley: University of California Press).

Tomlinson, B. R. (1993) *The Economy of Modern India*, New Cambridge History of India, III.3 (Cambridge: Cambridge University Press).

Tuchman, G., Daniels, A.K. and Benet, J. (eds) (1978) *Hearth and Home: Images of Women in the Mass Media* (New York: Oxford University Press).

Turner, G. (1999) *Film as Social Practice*, 3rd edn (London, and New York: Routledge)

Turner, G. (2004) *Understanding Celebrity* (London: Sage).

Tusan, M. (2005) *Women Making News: Gender and Journalism in Modern Britain* (Urbana and Chicago: University of Illinois Press).

van Zoonen, L. (1994) *Feminist Media Studies* (London: Sage).

Veblen, T. (1899) *The Theory of the Leisure Class: An Economic Study of Institutions* (New York: Macmillan).

Walker, D.H. (1995) *Outrage and Insight: Modern French Writers and the 'faits divers'* (Oxford, Berg Publishers).

Walkowitz, J.R. (1992) *City of Dreadful Delight: Narratives of Sexual Danger in Late Victorian London* (London: Virago).

Walton, W. (2000) *Eve's Proud Descendants: Four Women Writers and Republican Politics in Nineteenth Century France* (Stanford: Stanford University Press).

Ward, K. (1989) *Mass Communication and the Modern World* (London: Macmillan).

Weber, J. (1996) *Pondichéry et les comptoirs de l'Inde après Dupleix* (Paris: Denoel).

Weber, J. (2002) *Les relations entre la France et l'Inde de 1673 à nos jours* (Les Indes Savantes: Pondicherry).

Weitbrecht, M. (2009) *The Women of India and Christian Work in the Zenana* (Charleston: BiblioBazaar).

Welfele, O. (1982) *La Fronde: histoire d'une entreprise de presse* (Ecole de Chartres: thèse du doctorat).

Whyte, F. (1925) *The Life of W.T. Stead*, 2 vols (London: Jonathan Cape).

Wieringa, S. (1995) *Subversive Women* (New Delhi: Kali for Women).

Williams, F. (1969) *The Right to Know* (London & Harlow: Longmans).

Williams, R. (1961) *The Long Revolution* (London: Chatto and Windus).

Williams, R.H. (1982) *Dream Worlds: Mass Consumption in late Nineteenth Century France* (Berkeley: University of California Press).

Wilson, F.W. (1929) *Some Indian Problems. Being Some Essays Addressed to Patriots with the 'Congress Mentality'* (Allahabad: Lala Ram Mohan Lal).

Wilson, F.W. (1932) *The Indian Chaos* (London: Eyre and Spottiswoode).

Wilson, T. (1970) (ed.) *The Political Diaries of C.P. Scott 1911–1928* (Ithaca: Cornell University Press).

Wood, J.R. (2007) *The Struggle for Free Speech in the United States, 1872–1915: Edward Bliss Foote, Edward Bond Foote, and Anti-Comstock Operations* (New York: Routledge).

Woollacott, A. (2006) *Gender and Empire* (Palgrave: Basingstoke).

Wright, A. (1913) *The Unexpurgated Case Against Woman Suffrage* (London: Constable).

WSPU (1910) *Fifth Annual Report* (London: Women's Library, Universal Decimal Classification Pamphlets).

Yeatman, A. (2001) 'Feminism and Citizenship', in N. Stevenson (ed.) *Culture and Citizenship* (London: Sage) pp. 138–52.

Zeldin, T. (1977) *France 1848–1945*, Vol. 2 (Oxford: Oxford University Press).

Zeldin, T. (1988) *The French* (London: Collins Harvill).

Index

Note: A page number in *italics* refers to a table or illustration.